W9-AGI-176

Center for Basque Studies
Current Research Series, No. 7

Behavior and Organizational Change

Edited by

Sabino Ayestarán and Jon Barrutia Goenana

Current Research Series No. 7

Center for Basque Studies
University of Nevada, Reno

Published in conjunction with the University of the Basque Country
UPV/EHU

Universidad   Euskal Herriko
del País Vasco Unibertsitatea

Current Research
Selections of the ongoing work done by the faculty of the University of
the Basque Country (UPV/EHU), www.ehu.es

Editorial Committee
Amaia Maseda (Chair, UPV/EHU), Arantza Azpiroz (UPV/EHU), Javier
Echeverría (Ikerbasque), Jon Landeta (UPV/EHU), Sandra Ott (UNR), Joseba
Zulaika (UNR), Santos Zunzunegui (UPV/EHU)

Current Research Series No. 7
Center for Basque Studies
University of Nevada, Reno
Reno, Nevada 89557
http://basque.unr.edu

Copyright © 2011 by the Center for Basque Studies.
All rights reserved. Printed in the United States of America.
Cover and series design © 2011 by Jose Luis Agote.
Cover design based on engravings by Eduardo Chillida and Jorge Oteiza.

Library of Congress Cataloging-in-Publication Data

Behavior and organizational change / edited by Sabino Ayestarán and Jon
Barrutia Guenaga.
    p. cm. -- (Current research series ; no. 7)
Includes index.
 Summary: "Collection of articles on behavior and organizational change
from researchers at the University of the Basque Country"--Provided by
publisher.
 ISBN 978-1-935709-18-3 (pbk.)
1. Organizational behavior--Spain--País Vasco. 2. Organizational
change--Spain--País Vasco. I. Ayestarán Etxeberria, Sabino. II. Guenaga,
Jon Barrutia.

HD58.7.B4194 2011
302.3'809466--dc23

                        2011048123

Contents

Introduction: SABINO AYESTARÁN and JON BARRUTIA GUENAGA   7

1. Human Resources and Innovation: A Study of Practices
   Developed by Innovative Companies in the Basque Country   25
   IBON ZAMANILLO ELGUEZABAL and EVA VELASCO BALMASEDA

2. Vectors of Organizational Change in European Union
   Company Law.   47
   JUAN PABLO LANDA and IGONE ALTZELAI

3. Company Stakeholder Responsibility (CSR)   79
   JOSE LUIS RETOLAZA, LEIRE SAN-JOSE, and ANDRÉS ARAUJO
   DE LA MATA

4. Origins and Development of Industrial Clusters in the Basque
   Country: Path-Dependency and Economic Evolution   99
   JESÚS MARÍA VALDALISO, AITZIBER ELOLA,
   MARÍA JOSE ARANGUREN, and SANTIAGO LÓPEZ

5. A Systemic and Multilevel Approach to Organizational Analysis . .   123
   NEKANE BALLUERKA

6. How Do Cultural Changes Influence the Psychological Contract
   between Worker and Organization?   153
   JOSÉ VALENCIA GÁRATE

7. Leadership Conduct and Its Consequences for Organizations
   in the Basque Country   167
   JUAN JOSE ARROSPIDE, DANIEL HERMOSILLA, FÉLIX YENES,
   and IÑIGO CALVO

8. Emotional Intelligence and Innovation: An Exploratory Study
   in Organizational Settings   183
   AITOR ARITZETA

Index 203

List of Contributors 211

Introduction

Sabino Ayestarán Etxeberria and Jon Barrutia Guenaga
Translated by Julie Waddington

Advanced societies produce open and internationalized economies where competitiveness is a necessary requirement, although this in itself is not enough to guarantee sustained success. Social, political, and cultural complexities, along with increasingly greater social and collective needs, are another feature of the environment in question. This means that the social mechanisms of regulation and governance require resources with which to finance these needs. Competitiveness is once again a highly significant factor, this time as an important basis of these resources. Given this environment, companies and organizations in general have to maintain a high level of strategic tension and a significant capacity to adapt and be flexible when faced with different contingent situations.

The strategy of innovation, a basic factor for competitiveness, means that organizations must be driven by people who are committed to its goals, who actively participate in the management of labor processes, who have creative skills, and who are capable of getting on well with others and working as part of a team. In accordance with the characteristics developed in workers, the leadership of the organization must lean toward transformational leadership, which is to say toward a shared leadership in which both the management and workers assume responsibility for the growth of its people, for the achievement of the organizations goals, and for the quality of the product or services offered to clients. Cooperation between workers and managers is based on the experience that insofar as the company's goals are achieved, so will those of each individual person. To appreciate the change, it is important to understand organizational behavior, as there can be no sustainable organizational change without a change in people's behavior.

To analyze corporate evolution, it helps to consider the modern company as a triangle made up of a coherent *organization* with a *strategy* that has been elaborated to respond to the needs of the *environment* (Roberts 2004). The company has to build a coherent organization with either exploitative or exploratory strategies, which the company develops in response to the change in the needs of the environment.

From this perspective, the work that this involves can be divided into two groups. In one group is the work that represents the most structural core of the technological, economic, sociological, and legal systems and that establishes the structure of the organization. All these structures generate vectors of organizational change. In the other group is the work that relates to the "people" axis and that underpins human behavior in the organization. These elements have been selected in line with the methodological requirements of the scholarly journals that are considered to have a notable impact in the field of social sciences and for the social and corporate interest that they generate. Taken together, we believe that they help to demonstrate in a succinct way the phenomenology of change and current organizational behavior.

Structural Axis of the Organization

In their chapter "Human Resources and Innovation: A Study of Practices Developed by Innovative Companies in the Basque Country," Ibon Zamanillo Elguezabal and Eva Velasco Balmaseda study the relation between human resource management and its role in innovation by considering a list of innovative companies in the regional context of the Comunidad Autónoma del País Vasco/Euskal Autonomia Erkidegoa (CAPV/EAE, Autonomous Community of the Basque Country). Innovation is an essential part of the basic strategies that constitute competitiveness. In advanced economies, the importance of differentiation is vital in terms of innovation in order to be able to survive in an economy that is increasingly more internationalized and in which cost strategies have more and more active supporters—supporters that traditionally developed countries cannot challenge given their socioeconomic position.

In this context, it would seem reasonable to ask the companies and organizations of these countries to develop innovation processes that are also sustainable in the long term. These processes have direct implications for the organization, both in terms of its structure and size, as well as in the field of decision-making and management in general. To take on innovation as a strategy also means taking on its management, and this question becomes complex in both theory and in practice. In fact, innovation is difficult to pin down conceptually, and its determination remains vague. The result is that a wide array of models is available for representing and implementing innovation management (Velasco 2010; OECD 2005).

According to Joe Tidd, John Bessant, and Keith Pavitt (1997), innovation management (IM) is a global and multifactorial process with significant components of uncertainty, given which it would also appear advisable to approach the subject from a multidisciplinary perspective. Among the different factors that have a decisive influence on IM, the question of human resources is particularly noteworthy. The way HR is managed and directed has a direct impact on innovation, and both HR and innovation reciprocally influence each other in a circular causality that generates important changes for both of them. According to Keld Laursen and Nicolai J. Foss (2003), as well as Marianne Gloet and Milé Terziovski (2004), this is indeed the case, as long as the organizational variable is considered to be moderate (Lorenz and Valeyre 2005; Arundel et al. 2007).

The European Union (EU) is an indispensable institutional framework for the organizations that fall within its geographical sphere. For those outside it, it can also be of interest insofar as it represents a different model of socioeconomic and political organization on the international stage. In fact, it functions as a leading model for the rest of the world, combining competitiveness, social cohesion, and environmental sustainability. In this context, it is important to consider the impact of the activities carried out in terms of legal and policy frameworks in organizational change, in particular, those related to corporate governance that affect the "small" business and flexicurity in the labor market and that function as vectors of organizational change.

Since the Lisbon Summit of 2000, the EU has had one highly significant strategic goal: "The Union has today set itself a new strategic goal for the next decade: to become the most competitive and dynamic knowledge-based economy in the world, capable of sustainable economic growth with more and better jobs and greater social cohesion" (European Council 2000, n.5; Dion 2005). This goal remains intact today in the strategic framework for Europe 2020, and in order to maintain this competitiveness small and medium enterprises (SMEs) are considered to be essential, as is the effective planning of the labor force. In quantitative terms, most employment opportunities are provided by small businesses, and to ignore them is to ignore the chance to foster some of the goals of social progress that can be achieved by the widening of employment or through low levels of unemployment. On the other hand, global competitiveness forces the European labor market to support SMEs in terms of high levels of flexibility as a necessary condition for increasing their productivity. The combination of this flexibility with the social focus on security underpins the concept of flexicurity.

The EU has created a political framework for developing and promoting SMEs that generates a favorable environment for them—the "Small Business Act"—together with the development of a new kind of company, the European Private Company, as a new option for corporate construction and organization. These are active approaches that have the potential to transform the structural configuration of organizations and that attempt to give companies as much independence as possible in terms of their organization, thereby helping to make them more flexible.

In the same sense, flexicurity offers a way of organizing the workforce based on the speed of external changes, minimizing or avoiding their negative impact on the well-being of the worker, and focusing more on locating any problems within their social context and finding potential solutions than on the specific organization. Although it is certain that there are various models to follow in this respect, it is not so clear which of them is the best one to opt for. Both ways of proceeding attempt to promote maximum adaptability and a competitive response to the environment, which is considered to be global, by combining external and internal flexibility.

This requires an organizational response based on designs that are consistent with the opportunity offered by the system, as well as the adoption of cultural changes concerning how to understand work and its organization at a macro and micro level. In their chapter "Vectors of Organizational Change in European Union Company Law," Juan Pablo Landa and Igone Altzelai contend that it is important to recognize that the path toward realizing these legal-political measures is conditioned by the relation between the governmental bodies of the EU and its different member states. Landa and Altzelai advocate a cross-sectoral approach to the problem and base its solution on new approaches to governance together with the now almost taken for granted World Trade Organization (WTO) (European Commission 2001; Scharpf 2001, 2002, 2003; Trubek and Trubek 2005), which, despite difficulties and complications, has been the best method for taking EU decisions up to now.

In "Company Stakeholder Responsibility (CSR)," Jose Luis Retolaza, Leire San-Jose, and Andrés Araujo de la Mata argue that equal participation (in terms of nonsubordination) affects the traditional notion of agents, in the sense that it now has a complex and diverse role and therefore has to satisfy the interests of all. They also argue that for this model of participation, it is important to establish an ethical form of leadership, whose main strength lies in its credibility in the eyes of different people, and the fact that it defends the interests of everyone without preferential asymmetries or hierarchies. The analysis is presented within the area of stakeholder theory and its impact on corporate social responsibility (CSR) and identifies a development between the different strategic considerations of the company and the different ways of considering participation that helps to understand and locate the central stakeholder theory.

The "ideal" level of participation (who, how many, how, to what extent) in corporate organization is one of the key questions faced by both business practice and organizational theory. Also related to this is the concurrent problem of the different participation mechanisms and their relation or lack of relation to different "ideologies of participation."

The initial point of enquiry lies in responding to the question of who establishes the goals in an organization (in a wide sense, including aims and philosophies) and who is responsible for "ensuring" that these are achieved. Until recently, the most common answer to this, from an economic perspective, was the owner (Barber 1967).

This approach is formalized even further with the kind of "employment" outlined in agency theory, which associates the role of principal with ownership and that of the agent with management, and whose mandate is quite clearly one of satisfying that responsibility (Jensen and Meckling 1976; Jensen 1986; Williamson 1986; Coase 1937; Fama 1980; Ross 1973).

Within this context, a debate emerges about the role of other factors as well their augmentation—in other words, the consideration of clients, suppliers, the state, and society in general, as factors linked to the organization.

One of the basic arguments for considering these factors as participating subjects is that they help to achieve the goals established by the ownership in a more effective way. This is the utilitarian approach, which not only holds fast to the initial approach, but supplements it further by simultaneously including other factors in the field of participation, albeit in a subordinate fashion.

In a more extreme way, the regulatory approach considers different factors or subjects to be of equal stature and without hierarchies in terms of their participation in the organization. The basis of this participation is established within the framework of the necessary equality of said participants' contributions and therefore does not consider capital as the leading factor (Freeman 1984; Donaldson 2008).

In a competitive society, where the very essence of success is knowledge, it would be reasonable to assume that its place within the organization depends upon all the agents who have a role within it. This implies a challenge from an organizational viewpoint and represents a significant vector of organizational change.

The chapter "Origins and Development of Industrial Clusters in the Basque Country: Path-Dependency and Economic Evolution" by Jesús María Valdaliso, Aitziber Elola, María Jose Aranguren, and Santiago López, explores the origins and evolution of industrial clusters in the Basque Country since the nineteenth century. The region is one of the flag-bearers of industrial activity and entrepreneurship in Europe, with its high industrial composition being noteworthy even up to today, especially in relation to the Spanish and European economy. Furthermore, it suffered a severe crisis during the 1970s and 1980s, which meant it had to reposition itself in an extremely competitive way, not only in economic-business terms, but also in social terms, and in a way that was framed within a political transformation that resulted in a new institutional landscape.

Environmental conditions, understood in the widest sense, are fundamental for explaining the structural characteristics of the economic activity of a region or country, which also gives an idea of the structural characteristics of the sectors, business groups (clusters), and so on, that it contains. At the same time, these also determine the structural characteristics of the organizations that establish them (Porter 2000). These characteristics can be understood as a response to the requirements and possibilities that are demanded of them both at macro- and meso-economic levels (Hommen and Doloreux 2005). The opposite path could also be taken, starting with the characteristics of the business organizations and ascending toward meso- and macro-economic levels. In short, the economic system and the rules of play in force for agents and operators of the system are made up by mutual dependency.

A study of the system throws up relevant explanations of the choices made by different agents and users of the system. More precisely, the analysis of business clusters in an area or region, which are framed within the system, epitomize this system from an economic perspective.

If one seeks to reveal the same from a more dynamic viewpoint, looking ahead to the future, it is worth introducing the evolutionary perspective (Cooke, Gomez Uranga, and Etxebarria 1997)—in other words, to understand that the clusters and systems that harbor them adopt ways and contents that are specific but which change over time (Gomez Uranga, Etxebarria, and Barrutia 2009). This enables an understanding of the vectors of organizational change that impact on businesses and "force" them to take a particular organizational shape or another (Wright and Snell 1998; Zhang, Vonderembse, and Lim 2002). To do this, an historical analysis can be introduced in order to see how, over the course of time, the origin and evolution of a cluster is or is not determining its current situation and that of its future (path-dependency, Coombs and Hull 1998).

The Axes of Human Behavior

In her chapter "A Systemic and Multilevel Approach to Organizational Analysis," Nekane Balluerka presents a theoretical framework for analyzing organizations that takes in the principles of isomorphism, organization into hierarchies, and relative autonomy, and compares general systems theory (von Bertanlanffy 1968) with the multilevel organizational theory (Klein and Kozlowski 2000), proposing a multilevel framework of analysis that would facilitate the operationalization of the principles of isomorphism, organization into hierarchies, and relative autonomy.

Over the last twenty years, organizational psychology has adopted a multilevel model as a way interpreting human behavior in organizations. The Department of Social Psychology and Methodology at the Universidad del País Vasco/Euskal Herriko Unibertsitatea (UPV/EHU, University of the Basque Country) is also using multilevel analysis of organizations in the research carried out in collaboration with Innobasque, the Basque Innovation Agency.

We have been working on shared projects with Innobasque for two years. In December 2010, we established a new Project "Universidad-

Empresa" ("University-Business"), in collaboration with Innobasque, which is headed by Nekane Balluerka. The aim of this research is three-fold: (1) To show how a working team, *as long as the people in the team perform well and show a high capacity to innovate,* becomes an agent for change in the organizational environment that immediately surrounds them. The competencies acquired when people work as a team are passed on to their overall behavior in the organization. (2) To show that the degree of influence that these teams have on the organizational environment depends not *only* upon the characteristics of the innovation team (high performance and high capacity to innovate), but also depends on the *strategies developed by the people in the team to extend group learning at an organizational level.* (3) To show that the level of influence that these teams have on the organizational environment does not depend *solely* on (a) the characteristics of the innovation team (high performance and high capacity to innovate) and (b) the strategies that the people in the team develop to involve people in the organization in the team's work, but rather that it *also* depends on (c) the strategies of the organization: "exploitative" or "exploratory" strategies being indicators of the strategies that define the organizational environment and the work that the team is entrusted with.

On the basis of studies that associate the participation of people in the management of organizations with the kind of leadership exercised by the organizations (Quinn et al. 2007), and accepting that innovation teams have a different function from those of the classic "Improvement teams" (Ayestarán 2010), our research attempts to confirm the general hypothesis that innovation teams will encourage the creation of a more participative culture and of a more shared style of leadership (focused on people, on the goals of the organization, on the quality of the project, and on ethical behavior), as long as the following three conditions are met: (1) that the teams have been built to function as efficient teams oriented toward innovation; (2) that the teams function openly, which is to say that each member of the team should work in collaboration with two or three people who do not belong to the innovation team but who do belong to the organizational team that the team is a part of; and (3) that the dominant strategy of the organizations in which the innovation teams are situated be an "exploratory" one.

The influence of innovation teams is not limited to the people who participate directly in their work; instead, their influence extends to other people who are members of the organization but do not participate directly in the teams.

Edgar H. Shein (2005) describes how and why the methods used in organizational development increasingly concentrated on the changes made by individuals, forgetting that organizational development is a task that involves teams and organizations. Frequently, especially in the United States, organizational development has been associated with the formation of leaders, with leadership being considered a feature pertaining to individuals when, in actual fact, leadership is a characteristic that defines the way that teams and organizations operate. An intervention oriented toward organizational development will always end up changing how the teams and the organizations function, regardless of what technique is used. In Europe, the tradition of the Tavistock Institute in London maintained the idea that teams are socio-technical systems, meaning that we should consider both the technology upon which the working system is based and the social system in which the work is carried out. A working team needs a working methodology with technology befitting the task with which it has been entrusted. At the same time, the social system of the team must ensure that the work is carried out efficiently. The quantity and quality of the work carried out will depend as much on the technology that makes the work possible as on the people who carry it out. For these people to form a team, a whole series of "emerging intermediaries" and a shared leadership need to be developed (Ilgen et al. 2005; Mathieu et al. 2008; Ayestarán 2010). The "emerging intermediaries" are feelings, actions, and thoughts that are built by all members of the group. These are shared psychological states that make the efficiency of the group possible. In the first place, it is necessary to build the group in such a way that it becomes viable. When building the team, three emerging intermediaries need to be taken into account: *feeling confident in the group* ("this group is powerful and gives me security; it will help me to develop my individual capacities"); a succession of actions based on a *working methodology and a technique* that enables the team to be efficient; and a *cognitive structuring of the group* based on two elements: *shared representation* of the goals, the working method and the way of managing differences among the members of the group and a *shared memory* of what each of the members of the team knows how to do best. In second place, once a viable and synergetic team has been built, the need arises to ensure the efficiency of the team by way of three new "emerging intermediaries": the constructive use of differences for the creative negotiation of conflicts of interest; quick adaptation to changes in working and organizational environments and changes in the working group's tasks; and the appreciation of the contributions of all members of the group, meaning the sharing of leadership and responsibility for the team's results.

Jeana Wirtenberg, Lilian Abrams, and Carolyn Ott (2004) carried out a survey on the "strengths" and "weaknesses" of organizational development, sending 6,000 questionnaires to members of the Organization Development Network, the International Organization Development Association, and the Organization Development Institute. Among the "strengths" of organizational development, "teamwork" is one of the two most frequently cited techniques, the other one being the formation of leaders. Once again, "teamwork" appears as a technique that is seen as separate from the "formation of leaders." This separation reveals the observers' conceptions of both leadership and teamwork. Working as part of a team depends, to a large extent, on how the group is led (Ayestarán 2010).

The correct functioning of teams also depends on organizations' strategies. There are "exploitative" strategies that exploit a patent and "exploratory" strategies that encourage innovation (Roberts 2004). Organizations that develop exploratory strategies usually encourage teams to work innovatively.

Innovation teams have been defined elsewhere (Ayestarán 2010). In that definition, four characteristics are highlighted that make them different from improvement teams: (1) to emerging behavioral intermediaries can be added affective and cognitive intermediaries; (2) emerging cognitive intermediaries, especially "transactive memory," encourage the group's synergy; (3) reflexivity enables the innovation teams to constantly think about the working methodology and the functioning of the group as a social system; and (4) reflexivity and the consequent creativity of the teams demands shared leadership. The greater complexity of the innovation team means that its formation as a group requires more time than in the case of improvement teams.

In his chapter "How Do Cultural Changes Influence the Psychological Contract between Worker and Organization?" José Francisco Valencia Gárate takes up one of the key issues for organizational psychologists: the *psychological contract*. The *psychological contract* has been described as "an individual's belief in mutual obligations between that person and another party such as an employer" (Rousseau and Tijoriwala 1998, 679).

Continuing with the idea of the exchange and with that of a contract between two parties, David E. Guest offers the following definition of the psychological contract: "The perception of both parties to the employment relationship, organization and individual, of the reciprocal promises and obligations implied in that relationship" (2004, 545). Perceptions of *promises* and *obligations* vary depending on how such promises and obligations are transmitted. In collectivist cultures, whether this be a vertical (stratified and hierarchized collectivism) or horizontal collectivism (egalitarian collectivism), the psychological contract is based on the declared values of the organization. When an organization writes its *mission, vision, and values*, the promises and obligations are defined in an *implicit way* by the organization and by the collective of workers. The awareness of any failure to comply with the psychological contract has an objective basis in the lack of agreement between declared values and practiced values in a given organization. The explanatory basis for the psychological contract lies in the culture of the organization and, in particular, in the organization's declared values in its mission statement (Topa 2005, 42).

The working environment is changing: We are moving from a mechanistic environment to work based on knowledge creation. Workers are expected to be more personally involved: as well as being asked to do the job well, they are also required to think about clients' or users' needs and to try to find new ways of responding to these needs, because innovation consists in finding new responses to society's needs. The demand for innovation changes the mutual expectations between the worker and the management of a company. Workers contribute effort, time, skills, and creativity, while companies contribute resources and recognition of workers' autonomy in their work.

This change in the working environment leads to working relations that are more individualized and less collective (Guest 2004, 542). Direct communication between management and workers favors the individualization of promises and obligations, which makes the contents of the psychological content more explicit. The process of communication implied by new working relations is possibly equivalent to the process of communication in the psychological contract (Guest and Conway 2002, 23).

The progressive individualization and flexibility of working relations means that people more than collectives are the final reference point of the promises and obligations and that these become increasingly more explicit. The values of horizontal individualism (responsibility, entrepreneurship, commitment, and personal efficiency), together with the values of horizontal collectivism (co-responsibility, synergy, and teamwork), change the conceptual framework that is commonly used when researching the psychological contract (Guest 2004, 544).

Changes to the conceptual framework affect the following three elements. First, it affects the collective versus individual character of the reciprocal promises and obligations in the psychological contract—as individualization and flexibility in working relations increases, so does the individualization of the psychological contract and, to the same extent, promises and obligations become increasingly more explicit. Second, the conceptual frame affects the content of the psychological contract—the psychological contract focuses more on relational contents, reserving aspects that are more transactional for the legal contract: (a) transactional content, which relates to specific aspects of a monetary nature, for example the salary amount, incentives for achieving goals, job stability, and so on (Zhao et al. 2007) and (b) relational content, which refers to more personal and more prolonged exchanges, such as personal support, the significance of the job, the kind of supervision, career development, training, promotion, and so on. Third, the conceptual framework affects the status of the psychological contract. Thus, according to David E. Guest and Neil Conway (2002), as well as Francisco Javier Gracia, Inmaculada Silla, José María Peiró, and Lina Fortes-Ferreira (2005), three basic elements have been introduced into the status of the psychological contract: (1) the fulfillment of promises; (2) confidence in the organization; and (3) distributive, procedural, and interactive justice.

Juanjo Arrospide, Daniel Hermosilla, Félix Yenes, and Iñigo Calvo author the chapter "Leadership Conduct and Its Consequences for Organizations in the Basque Country." The subject of leadership has been another of the classic themes studied in organizational psychology. Leadership is a person's capacity to influence the ideas, feelings, and behavior of others. Within a Taylorist conception of work, leadership was associated with the management and direction of an organization. The assumption was that only managers were capable of influencing people. For many years, it was difficult to distinguish between the concept of "manager" and that of "leader." The managers or directors of organizations carry out the job of organizing the work and motivating the personnel with salaries in line with each worker's performance. This is called "transactional leadership." The term "transformational leadership" was coined by James MacGregor Burns (1978) and Bernard M. Bass (1985). This kind of leadership introduced a concern for workers' personal growth into the concept of transactional leadership, reinforcing the intrinsic motivation of the worker. By moving from a Taylorist working environment to one based on the creation of shared knowledge and, therefore, more egalitarian, transactional leadership came to be seen as insufficient, and "transformational leadership" started to be discussed instead. Transformational leadership evolved toward shared leadership because managers and workers share the responsibility for people and the company's objectives, and therefore they should also share in its leadership.

In summary, we can distinguish between two types of leadership: (1) *external leadership*, exercised in an top-down manner, which is the traditional paradigm of the leader who is responsible for the results of a team and endowed with the authority to direct the team's activities; and (2) *shared leadership*, which has appeared recently in literature on the subject and is becoming increasingly accepted among authors under different headings such as emerging leadership, distributed leadership, and shared leadership—the central idea is that this kind of leadership emerges out of the team itself and has not been imposed by any external authority (Mathieu et al. 2008, 449–51). Ultimately, the best kind of leadership is that which best fits the characteristics of the task at hand and the people of the team.

In recent years, there has been an evolution from organizational models focused on technical/rational competencies toward the greater relevance of models that incorporate emotions in the workplace (Barsade and Gibson 2007). A significant line of thought is developing that recognizes the central role of emotional management in the processes of individual creativity and organizational innovation.

In his chapter, "Emotional Intelligence and Innovation: An Exploratory Study in Organizational Settings," Aitor Aritzeta discusses the relation between four types of variables—*emotional intelligence* (EI), *emotional creativity, innovative cognitive style, and organizational innovation*—on the basis of an empirical study carried out with 221 workers at twenty-five industrial companies and services in the Basque Country. The results obtained do not support the link between EI measured as a skill (Mayer and Salovey 1997) and creativity as examined through Kirton's cognitive style of innovation (1977). Previous research (Ivcevic, Brackett, and Mayer 2007), in which the relation between EI, emotional creativity, and the capacity of each of these constructs to predict creative behavior, had already concluded that it is emotional creativity more than EI that anticipates creative behavior. While EI requires analytical ability along with the correct way of responding to emotional problems, emotional creativity relates to the ability to differentiate oneself from what is common (normative) and to generate new emotional reactions and, with these, original ideas.

It is also important to distinguish innovation in personal behavior from innovation in organizations. It is widely recognized that innovation in organizational contexts is not one-dimensional; it is a complex concept with wide fields of application, such as strategic, financial, technological, or organizational innovation or innovation in marketing or processes, and so on. All these are necessary in order to achieve a culture of innovation or to guarantee the systematic management of innovation in all areas of the company.

References

Arundel, Anthony, Edward Lorenz, Bengt-Åke Lundvall, and Antoine Valeyre. 2007. "How Europe's Economies Learn: A Comparison of Work Organization and Innovation Mode for the EU-15." *Industrial and Corporate Change* 16, no. 6: 1175–210.

Ayestarán, Sabino. 2010. "De los equipos de mejora a los equipos innovadores." *Dyna* 85, no. 2: 131–38.

Barber, William J. 1967. *A History of Economic Thought*. Harmondsworth: Penguin.

Barsade, Sigal G., and Donald E. Gibson. 2007. "Why Does Affect Matter in Organizations?" *Academy of Management Perspectives* (February): 36–59.

Bass, Bernard M. 1985. *Leadership and Performance Beyond Expectations*. New York: Free Press.

Burns, James MacGregor. 1978. *Leadership*. New York: Harper & Row.

Coase, Ronald H. 1937. "The Nature of the Firm." *Economica* 4, no. 16 (November): 386–405.

Commission. 2001. *European Governance—A White Paper* COM (2001) 428 final, 25.07.01.

Cooke, Philip, Mikel Gomez Uranga, and Goio Etxebarria. 1997. "Regional Systems of Innovation: Institutional and Organisational Dimensions." *Research Policy* 26: 475–91.

Coombs, Rod, and Richard Hull. 1998. "Knowledge Management Practices and Path-dependency in Innovation." *Research Policy* 27, no. 3: 237–53.

Dion, David-Pascal. 2005. "The Lisbon Process: A European Odyssey." *European Journal of Education* 40, no. 3: 295–313.

Donaldson, Thomas. 2008. "Two Stories." In Bradley R. Agle, Thomas Donaldson, R. Edward Freeman, Michael C. Jensen, Ronald K. Mitchell, and Donna J. Wood. 2008. "Dialogue: Toward Superior Stakeholder Theory." *Business Ethics Quarterly* 18, no. 12: 172–76 (153–90).

European Council. 2000. *Presidency Conclusions.* Lisbon, March 23–24.

Fama, Eugene F. 1980. "Agency Problems and the Theory of the Firm." *Journal of Political Economy* 88, no. 2 (April): 280–307.

Freeman R. Edward. 1984. *Strategic Management: A Stakeholder Approach.* Boston: Pitman Publishing.

Gloet, Marianne, and Milé Terziovski. 2004. "Exploring the Relationship Between Knowledge Management Practices and Innovation Performance." *Journal of Manufacturing Technology Management* 15, no. 5: 402–9.

Gomez Uranga, Mikel, Goio Etxebarria, and Jon Barrutia. 2009. "Estudios de los cambios en los sistemas regionales de innovación a través de la evolución y diversificación de los sectores más representativos de la industria vasca." *Ekonomiaz* 70, 1er cuatrimestre: 106–31.

Gracia, Francisco Javier, Inmaculada Silla, José María Peiró, and Lina Fortes-Ferreira. 2006. "El estado del contrato psicológico y su relación con la salud psicológica de los empleados." *Psicothema* 18, no. 2: 256–62.

Guest, David E. 2004. "The Psychology of the Employment Relationship: An Analysis Based on the Psychological Contract." *Applied Psychology: An International Review* 53, no. 4: 541–55.

Guest, David E., and Neil Conway. 2002. "Communicating the Psychological Contract: An Employer Perspective." *Human Resource Management Journal* 12, no. 2: 22–38.

Hommen, Leif, and David Doloreux. 2005. "Bringing Labour Back In: A 'New' Point of Departure for the Regional Innovation Systems Approach?" In *Knowledge Spillovers and Knowledge Management*, edited by Charlie Karlsson, Per Flensburg, and Sven-Ake Hörte. London: Edward Elgar Publishing.

Ilgen, Daniel R., John R. Hollenbeck, Michael Johnson, and Dustin Jundt. 2005. "Teams in Organizations: From Input-Process-Output Models to IMOI Models." *Annual Review of Psychology* 56: 517–43.

Ivcevic, Zorana, Marc A. Brackett, and John D. Mayer. 2007. "Emotional Intelligence and Emotional Creativity." *Journal of Personality* 75, no. 2: 199–235.

Jensen, Michael C. 1986. "Agency Costs of Free Cash Flow, Corporate Finance and Takeovers." *American Economic Review* 76, no. 2 (May): 323–29.

Jensen, Michael C., and William H. Meckling. 1976. "Theory of the Firm, Managerial Behavior, Agency Costs and Ownership Structure." *Journal of Financial Economics* 3, no. 4 (October): 305–60.

Kirton, Michael J. 1977. *Manual of the Kirton Adaption-Innovation Inventory*. London: National Foundation for Educational Research.

Klein, Katherine J., and Steve W.J. Kozlowski, eds. 2000. *Multilevel Theory, Research and Methods in Organizations: Foundations, Extensions and New Directions*. San Francisco: Jossey-Bass.

Laursen, Keld, and Nicolai J. Foss. 2003. "New Human Resources Management Practices, Complementarities, and the Impact on Innovation Performance." *Cambridge Journal of Economics* 27, no. 2: 243–63

Lorenz, Edward, and Antoine Valeyre. 2005. "Organisation Innovation, Human Resource Management and Labour Market Structure: A Comparison of the EU-15." *Journal of Industrial Relations* 47, no. 4 (December): 424–42.

Mathieu, John, M. Travis Maynard, Tammy Rapp, and Lucy Gilson. 2008. "Team Effectiveness 1997–2007: A Review of Recent Advancements and a Glimpse into the Future." *Journal of Management* 34, no. 3: 410–76.

Mayer, John D., and Peter Salovey. 1997. "What is Emotional Intelligence?" In *Emotional Development and Emotional Intelligence: Implications for Educators*, edited by Peter Salovey and David J. Sluyter. New York: Basic Books.

OECD (Organisation for Economic Co-operation and Development). 2005. *Oslo Manual: Guidelines for Collecting and Interpreting Innovation Data*. 3rd ed. Paris: OECD and Eurostat.

Porter, Michael E. 2000. "Location, Competition, and Economic Development: Local Clusters in a Global Economy." *Economic Development Quarterly* 14, no. 1 (February): 15–34.

Quinn, Robert E., Sue R. Faerman, Michael P. Thompson, Michael McGrath, and Lynda S. St. Clair. 2007. *Becoming a Master Manager: A Competing Values Approach.* John Wiley and Sons.

Roberts, John. 2004. *The Modern Firm: Organizational Design for Performance and Growth.* Oxford: Oxford University Press.

Ross, Stephen A. 1973. "The Economic Theory of Agency: The Principal's Problem." *American Economic Review* 63, no. 2: 134–39.

Rousseau, Denise M., and Snehal A. Tijoriwala. 1998. "Assessing Psychological Contracts: Issues, Alternatives and Measures." *Journal of Organizational Behavior* 19, no. S1: 679–95.

Scharpf, Fritz W. 2001. *European Governance: Common Concerns vs. The Challenge of Diversity.* MPIfG (Max Planck Institut für Gesellschaftsforschung) Working Paper 01/6, September 2001. At www. mpifg.de/pu/workpap/wp01-6/wp01-6.html.

———. 2002. "The European Social Model: Coping with the Challenge of Diversity." *MPIfG Working Paper* 02/8, July.

———. 2003. "Problem Solving Effectiveness and Democratic Accountability in the EU." *MPIfG Working Paper* 03/1, February.

Schein, Edgar H. 2005. "Organization Development: A Wedding of Anthropology and Organizational Therapy." In *Reinventing Organization Development: New Approaches to Change in Organizations,* edited by David L. Bradford and W. Warner Burke. San Francisco: Pfeiffer.

Tidd, Joe, John Bessant, and Keith Pavitt. 1997. *Managing Innovation: Integrating Technological, Market and Organizational Change.* Chichester: Wiley and Sons.

Topa, Gabriela. 2005. "Introducción: Perspectivas de futuro para el contrato psicológico." *Revista de Psicología Social* 20: 41–43.

Trubek, David M., and Louise G. Trubek. 2005. "Hard and Soft Law in the Construction of Social Europe: The Role of the Open Method of Coordination." *European Law Journal* 11, no. 3: 343–64.

Velasco, Eva. 2010. *La gestión de la innovación, elementos integrantes y su aplicación en empresas innovadoras del País Vasco.* Bilbao: Servicio Editorial, UPV/EHU.

Von Bertalanffy, Ludwig. 1968. *General System Theory: Formulations, Developments and Applications.* London: Brazilier.

Williamson, Oliver E. 1986. *Economic Organization, Firms, Markets and Policy Control*. New York: New York University Press.

Wirtenberg, Jeana, Lilian Abrams, and Carolyn Ott. 2004. "Assessing the Field of Organization Development." *The Journal of Applied Behavioral Science* 40, no. 4: 465–79.

Wright, Patrick M., and Scott A. Snell. 1998. "Toward a Unifying Framework for Exploring Fit and Flexibility in Strategic Human Resource Management." *Academy of Management Review* 23, no. 4: 756–72.

Zhang, Qingyu, M.A. Vonderembse, and Jeen-Su Lim. 2002. "Value Chain Flexibility: A Dichotomy of Competence and Capabilities." *International Journal of Production Research* 40, no. 3: 561–83.

Zhao, Hao, Sandy J. Wayne, Brian C. Glibkowski, and Jesus Bravo. 2007. "The Impact of Psychological Contract Breach on Work Related Outcomes: A Meta-analysis." *Personnel Psychology* 60, no. 3: 647–80.

1

Human Resources and Innovation: A Study of Practices Developed by Innovative Companies in the Basque Country

Ibon Zamanillo Elguezabal and Eva Velasco Balmaseda

Translated by Jennifer Martin

At a meeting in Lisbon in March 2000, the European Council established a goal for the European Union (EU) of becoming the most competitive and dynamic knowledge-based economy in the world, capable of sustainable economic growth, with more and better jobs and with greater social cohesion. One of the bases of this ambitious goal was to considerably increase the EU's innovative capacity, not only for purely economic purposes, but also as a way to generate productivity growth and through it, to establish the conditions for a more cohesive society.

Based on the Lisbon Strategy, as well as on the guidelines launched by the European Commission in January 2005 on its new growth and employment strategy for the EU, the Basque government presented a discussion paper in 2005 entitled "Business Competitiveness and Social Innovation: Strategy Bases and Guidelines" (Gobierno Vasco 2005) that set out the three aspects of the Basque Country's future competitive strategy: the new values and the people ready for the second great transformation,[1] the scope

---

1. The *second great transformation* suggests that the societies that had reached the level of development that Basque society now possesses could not continue to build for the future by adopting foreign technologies and cost advantages, but should instead decisively face the challenge of innovation, of quality, and of knowledge creation (Gobierno Vasco 2005).

envisaged and the necessary groups to compete in a global economy, and innovations in companies and in society (Gobierno Vasco 2005). This last aspect became the main path toward better productivity and as a result, toward greater competitiveness and quality of life.

In this approach, innovation seemed to be the most immediate answer to the intense international competition that companies in more developed economies faced. Presently, the key factor in the competitive success of companies is the ability to constantly develop new products, processes, and services, providing clients with greater functionality, performance, and ultimately, added value.

Theoretical Framework

Human resource (HR) management and innovation are closely related aspects, as most of the literature on innovation and its management—which dedicates a lot of attention to HR policy-related topics—points out (Laursen 2002; Laursen and Foss 2003; Pérez López, Montes Peón, and Vázquez Ordas 2005; Leede and Looise 2005; Shipton et al. 2006). Moreover, the experiences of innovative organizations have shown that a multitude of practices exist in the field of HR that are vital to creating organizations in which innovation becomes part of the DNA of the people who integrate these practices. For example, well-known organizations like 3M or Google have demonstrated that one of the keys to innovative success is having motivated people in the right atmosphere. Indeed, the HR policies that both companies deploy have been decisive in reaching this objective. Ultimately, the theory, as well as the practice, in these companies indicates that HR management and innovation are strongly connected.

Capital Objectives

Bearing this phenomenon in mind, the aim of this chapter is to analyze to what extent a set of innovative companies in the Basque Country have employed HR practices that support innovation in their organizations. As this is a select group of companies known for their advanced management practices and innovative character, it was expected that they would not only consider HR policies favorable to innovation as essential, but that they would also stress carrying out a widespread implementation of such policies.

Gaps in the Literature

One of the main difficulties in offering a definition of *innovation management* (IM) has resided in the absence of a standard terminology and in the diverse assumptions adopted by different authors on the topic. In many cases, the term *innovation management* has been used as a synonym for *technology management, technological resource management*, or *technology asset management*. Consequently,

> *technology management,* which tries to maintain and improve a company's competitive position through the use of technology, coincides on many points with *innovation management*, and many times both forms are used interchangeably since their boundaries are not clearly defined. It is also often referred to as *innovation and technology management*, attempting to gather all matters related to the optimization of technology use in business under just one name. (Escorsa and Valls 2003, 47)

IM is a broad concept that covers, among other things, technology management. Technology is clearly a very important component of innovation, but as will be seen, innovation does not have to be based in technology. Innovation relates to the world of ideas and creativity, whether linked or not to technological development.

Thus, according to professors of the IESE Business School at the University of Navarre, José Antonio Muñoz-Nájar and Joaquim Vilà (2000, 4):

> innovation management implies running a system that combines *knowledge, resources* and *abilities*. Underlying knowledge (specialized know-how abilities or scientific-technological developments), complementary resources to bring a concept to market, and management and commercialization capacities would vary according to the type of innovation concerned. To innovate means to direct people and manage resources, tangible as well as intangible. Good innovation system governance requires combining leadership styles, managing people, the strategy and the processes related to innovation.

Joseph Tidd, John Bessant, and Keith Pavitt make similar observations. For them, IM is an inherently difficult and risky activity, where the majority of new technologies have failed to be incorporated into new products and services, and where many of the new products and services have not been commercially successful. Therefore, while innovation has increased competitiveness, it has required a comprehensive set of knowledge and management abilities that differ from those of day-to-day administrative management (2005, xiii).

Thus, one of the most significant managerial challenges involves equipping an organization with an innovative capacity, because this entails moving into areas in which the organization has no previous experience. This challenge is greater still due to the fact that innovation has had its own managerial method that is not the result of mere extensions of traditional managerial ways (Muñoz-Nájar and Vilà 2000, 18).

Even though IM has become an extremely attractive and interesting area of research within the administration field, there is still no consensual theoretical basis or solid conceptual framework for its study that combines all the scholarly contributions on the topic. "The only thing that exists are guidelines, a few aspects, that set a course and guide researchers in their work" (Morcillo Ortega 1997, 33).

In addition to lacking a consensual methodological framework, another problem that this managerial area has encountered is that, owing to the complexity of the technological innovation process, this field of study must be multidisciplinary in nature (Nieto 2003, 136). For Tidd, Bessant, and Pavitt (2005, xiii) "the management of innovation is inherently interdisciplinary and multifunctional, but most management texts tend to emphasize a single dimension, such as the management of research and development, production and operations management, marketing management, production and operations management, marketing management, product development, or organizational development." These are valuable references, but they do not provide a consistent framework for understanding the different problems associated with this topic.

Chapter Structure

In addition to the introductory section above concerning theoretical issues, our objectives, and the gaps in the academic literature that justify our approach, the chapter is structured simply to facilitate its understanding. Below, in the second section, we present the results obtained from our comparative analysis of the selected IM models for this research, providing a list of the selected models as well as the justification for their choice. In the third section, we examine the methodological aspects of this work, placing special emphasis on the fieldwork aimed at analyzing the importance attached to and the degree of applying IM components in a sample of companies. We then list and classify the results of this work, and highlight the differences between the theoretical importance that the respondents granted the components and their practical application, thereby introducing the "gap" concept. The final section recaps these results and describes the most relevant findings.

Results from the Study on Innovation Management Models

Although there were no single or simple answers to the challenge of IM, the distinct research and experiences of organizations that tried to manage innovation contributed certain ideas on how to face this challenge. As a result, we have a set of knowledge and models on what and how we can better manage innovation.

We sampled twenty IM models to form the object of this study. They date from a ten-year period and were derived from diverse areas. In each case, the application of some or all of the following criteria was used in the selection of the models: its relevance and dissemination,[2] the excellence of the submitting organizations (academic, institutions, and prestigious consulting firms in the field of innovation) and following an in-depth analysis of the literature, those whose inclusion involved incorporating new elements, or alternatively, a different design or approach in their presentation.

After analyzing these models, we believe that it is essential to adopt an all-encompassing approach to IM that considers, in addition to the *innovation process* itself,[3] another series of elements: strategy, leadership, innovative culture, organizational development, people, financial resources, innovation management methodologies and tools, information and communication technologies, knowledge management, customer orientation, networking, keeping a close eye on the business environment, measurement and monitoring of goals, and continual learning.

---

2. The most referenced and cited models in the relevant literature on innovation were selected, using the Impact Factor (Science Citation Index) and journal impact factors (obtained from the *Journal Citation Reports*). Moreover, some of the models were published on web pages, either by public bodies or by the authors themselves, hence they had a large dissemination among the companies.

3. The *innovation process* is an element that consists of two aspects. On the one hand, if the innovation process forms part of the company's critical processes, it is identified and managed systematically (objectives have been established and indicators defined); and on the other, if the innovation process is reviewed regularly (annually, for example), this ensures that it does not become static and might periodically be improved.

As most of the proposals studied indicate, it is essential to design an innovation *strategy,* with objectives that have been widely communicated, that guides the efforts of the organization's members in the right direction, and that focuses on using limited resources (Club Excelencia en Gestión 2006; Tidd, Bessant, and Pavitt 2005; Goffin and Mitchell 2005).

The organization's senior management or *leaders* should show their commitment to innovation, comprehensively steering innovation and encouraging initiative and the generation of new ideas among their members. The executives who take innovation seriously meditate on it, demonstrate the importance that they give it by their actions, and monitor innovation. The commitment to innovation must go beyond the top executive, but should have started with him or her (Loewe and Dominiquini 2006; Hidalgo Nuchera, Vizán Idoipe and Torres 2008; Von Stamm 2003).

As many authors point out (Dobni 2008; Von Stamm 2003; Loewe and Dominiquini 2006), establishing an *innovative culture*, whose bases are the ability to face the uncertain, accept risk, promote creativity, and exchange knowledge, is fundamental. When an innovation-prone culture exists, all employees are encouraged to propose new ideas, there is autonomy and decision-making ability, the value of a creative and entrepreneurial attitude is recognized at all levels of the organization, and failure and error are fully accepted as an inherent element of innovation.

The company should be equipped with adequate *organization,* which allows it to achieve its established innovation goals. The organizational structure must favor the flow of information and teamwork, as well as communication and cooperation between the members and among these members and outside agents. Moreover, innovation should be the main operational responsibility of a company member (Andrew and Sirkin 2008), so that one or more departments hold specific innovative responsibilities and their leaders report directly to the chief executive (Vilà and Muñoz-Nájar 2002).

People are the source of innovation and nothing takes place without them. Almost all the models coincide in affirming that it is not the company that innovates, but the people who work for it. It is therefore necessary to establish favorable conditions so that the staff is motivated and voices its ideas, knowledge, and creativity. HR management and innovation are closely related aspects (Laursen and Foss 2003; Pérez López, Montes Peón, and Váquez Ordas 2005; Leede and Looise 2005; Shipton,

West, Dawson, Birdi, and Patterson 2006; Scarbrough 2003); because of this, selection, development, evaluation, and employee recognition and reward policies should be designed according to the innovation needs of the company.

Although they usually appear implicitly in the models studied, *financial resources* make up another fundamental element that allows people to launch their ideas and permits the development of innovation projects in the organization. Companies must allocate funds for the proper development of long-term innovation plans, so that the innovation activities have stable financing. Furthermore, they must stay informed of subsidies and other existing public finance sources, making full use of them to sustain their innovation strategy.

In order to achieve innovative success, companies must provide their employees with the innovation management methodologies and tools (IMTs) that they require and the training necessary for their utilization (Hidalgo and Albors 2008). Innovation does not always involve the use of sophisticated technology, but is in fact more a question of thinking and looking for creative solutions within the company. In this context, IMTs should be understood as a set of instruments, techniques, and methodologies that help companies adapt to the circumstances and deal systematically with the challenges of the market (European Commission 2004).

Information and communication technologies (ICTs), although indirectly present in the IM models studied, are an important IM element since they accelerate the exchange of information between company members and the fluid communication with integral partners of an alliance for innovation development.

The innovation process requires the support of *technology management,* which involves formulating a technological strategy as well as selecting, creating, and providing technology (deciding what technologies will be developed internally and which will be procured externally), and managing intellectual property assets (patents, authors' rights, trademarks, trade secrets, brand names, and so on.

Knowledge is the key to innovation, therefore *knowledge management*—which guarantees that people have access to it at the right time—is a fundamental element of IM. Knowledge management (its structure in the company, whether it is classified and can be accessed and used simply; its efficient distribution within the company; and the sharing of it among members of the company) is essential in order to innovate and becomes an important part of the innovation process (OECD 2005; Scarbrough 2003).

Furthermore, the innovation process must be *customer oriented*. In other words, the customer must be central to innovation, for which it is necessary to understand, listen to, and respond to his or her requirements (Marco de Referencia de Innovación 2006). This element usually appears implicitly in most of the IM models as a *sine qua non* condition of success in the *innovation process*.

Various external agents and innovation funding resources promote innovation. Most of the IM models analyzed emphasize the phenomenon of open innovation (Chesbrough 2006; Gassman 2006), highlighting the role of *networking* (or *collaboration and third-party alliances*), which means building and maintaining effective external links in such a way that the knowledge, resources, and intelligence of the whole set of agents outside the limits of the organization are exploited.

Surveillance of the environment, which means analyzing and looking for environmental signs of potential innovations, threats, and opportunities for change, is also important. Thus, surveillance is understood as the "set of coordinated actions directed toward the search, treatment (filtrating, classification, and analysis), and distribution of useful information (internal as well as external) for the decision-making process" (Marco de Referencia de Innovación 2006). This collection of information must be undertaken in a systematic and organized way.

The company must turn any improvements that it achieves into a competitive advantage. Just as many IM models stress, *measurement* and *monitoring* are imperative for continuous improvement. Extremely innovative companies believe that innovation and its results can be assessed and they devote considerable time and attention to the development of their own systems and to other systems of innovation measurement (Andrew and Sirkin 2008).

Organizational *learning* involves reviewing successes and failures with the aim of learning to improve IM and acquiring relevant knowledge that can be drawn from experience (Tidd, Bessant, and Pavitt 2005). Innovation system audits allow improvements and corrections to be made in those systems.

Finally, the *process of innovation* in general does not occur sequentially, but as an interactive and flexible process, with information constantly coming from the market and technology (Ortt and Smits 2006) and in stages that are related to and overlap one another, that are multifaceted and multilevel, based on many forms of knowledge, that depend on the internal as well as the external environment of the organization, and that cannot be analyzed separately from companies' sets of systems and processes. The innovation process must be specifically designed according to the companies' specific nature and cannot be regarded as an isolated activity (Velasco and Zamanillo 2008).

Thus, on the one hand, companies must ensure that the innovation process forms part of their critical processes, that it is identified and managed systematically; and on the other, that it is reviewed regularly in order to assure that it does not become static and so as to periodically improve it. Although not all, some of the IM models analyzed, such as those of the London Business School (1996), IESE (2000), and Tecno-Lógica (2002), detail sub-processes, such as

- *Concept generation*, which implies adopting a systematic approach to generating ideas and concepts for new products and services; using tools for generating new ideas; establishing a systematic approach to filter and select ideas; and periodically reviewing rejected ideas.
- *Product development,* which entails several areas of the company participating in product development work from the beginning; which assigns a leader with total responsibility and authority to each project and a team of people from diverse areas; in which customers and suppliers participate from the beginning in product development; and in which proper tools are employed (CAD/CAM/CAE, QFD, value engineering, virtual prototype, and so on).
- *Production process innovation*, in which there is a planned allocation of resources for its development; in which there is a leader with a budget and a team of internal and external collaborators whose task is to redefine and improve it; in which manufacturing technologies and organizational models are monitored and production process management takes place; and in which advanced tools are used to redefine and control it (Failure Mode and Effects Analysis, statistical process control, process simulation, total plant maintenance, and so on).
- *Innovation in marketing processes*, which entails establishing mechanisms to understand and measure the best practices of

competitors as well as of reference sectors in this area; which implies that a precise definition of the distribution channel as well as sales and post-sale service methods are present in the product development process; and which involves constantly coming up with new marketing forms and strategies to increase the value of products.

Ultimately, a company might establish extremely sophisticated and refined *innovation processes*, but if these were not accompanied and strengthened by all these elements analyzed above, it would undermine the results of the process (Velasco and Zamanillo 2008). A systemic approach must be adopted in IM, in the sense that companies must understand these elements as a cohesive set of measures.

A second important conclusion derived from studying these models is that experts in innovation coincide in *highlighting the role of HR in IM*. HR is one of the most often cited elements in the specialized literature on innovation, right behind the *innovation process*.

Thus, almost all of the analyzed models coincide in affirming that a company's success resides in having knowledgeable, skilled workers who develop their potential and work toward achieving the company's vision. It is not the company that innovates, but the people who work for it, so it is necessary to establish favorable conditions so that employees are motivated and voice their ideas, knowledge, and creativity.

Thus, people and the networks they belong to are able to create, transfer, and institutionalize knowledge (Shipton et al. 2005, 118). One should bear in mind that innovation is increasingly based on many forms of knowledge. In fact, innovation occurs though knowledge application (Padmore, Schuetze, and Gibson 1998, 613), which is disseminated within as well as outside of the organization, and which people who work in companies access.

Presently, it is widely recognized that people who develop their professional activities in a company are its most valuable employees and the basis of its creativity (Hidalgo Nuchera, Vizán Idoipe, and Torres 2008, 10). Therefore the ideas and the knowledge needed to create new products and services, or to add value to the old, reside in the minds of individuals (Johannessen, Olaisen, and Olsen 1999, 123). Some factors of HR management (the selection methods for working groups, taking account of people's qualities and attitudes; the compensation strategies that give precedence to those who share knowledge; or designing careers that encourage acquiring and exchanging knowledge), are essential to promoting behavior that favors sharing knowledge; and this flow of knowledge is indispensable for innovation development (Scarbrough 2003, 502–4). Ultimately, HR management practices influence innovation from the moment in which they promote or hinder knowledge from being shared, and they shape the skills and attitudes of the individual (Scarbrough 2003, 504).

Thus, a deliberate and specific HR management strategy could help a company that aspires to create an innovative organization. In IM, HR management should be seen as a strategic and integrated field that contributes to the organization as a whole, and not only as a set of fragmented practices that supports certain activities, areas, types, or phases of innovation (Leede and Looise 2005). Likewise, some studies indicate that adopting a set of HR management practices that are complementary has a greater impact on innovation results than adopting individual practices (Laursen and Foss 2003; Laursen 2002).

In conclusion, traditional HR management practices have had to be updated in accordance with the organization's innovation strategy. Now, it is not only necessary to have a systematically managed innovation process, but HR policies must also be designed according to the innovation needs of the company. Moreover, some organizations go even further and try to promote innovation in the HR policies themselves, in such a way that they evaluate and positively reward personnel that propose a certain amount of creative ideas on this matter every year (Pollitt 2006, 6).

Human Resources in the Innovation Management of Innovative Companies in the Basque Country

The concept of innovation concept employed here seeks to escape from a more restrictive notion that limits it to the field of technology alone. Therefore, we adopt the definition of the Organisation for Economic Co-operation and Development (OECD) in its third edition of the *Oslo Manual*, which considers innovation "the implementation of a new or significantly improved product (good or service), or process, a new marketing method, or a new organisational method in business practices, workplace organisation or external relations" (OECD 2005, 46).

Methodological Aspects of the Study

The aim of this work was to obtain a sample from renowned companies in the field of innovation so that we could closely analyze the IM practices in this group of innovative organizations.[4] To do this, we first examined the relationship of the 150 companies that were awarded the most funding in the last Intek grant announcement by the Basque government(2006). The Strategic Unit for Technology and Innovation (Unidad Estratégica de Tecnología e Innovación—UETI), part of SPRI (the Basque Development Agency), supplied the list, which included companies that had developed some type of innovation technology project during the previous year.

Next, we looked at these companies to determine which ones were also found among the eighty-three selected by the Basque Country Knowledge Cluster[5] as "Advanced Management Companies." Since 1998, this Knowledge Cluster has developed a series of publications titled *Advanced Management Cases*, which analyze the management fundamentals of some of the most outstanding and innovative companies in the Basque Country. This listing was also used in other research projects,[6] because it provided a directory of companies that were selected by virtue of their excellent business results, financial income, growth, international expansion, as well as possessing a distinct and innovative characteristic in their management method, the key to a competitive advantage.

Thus, twenty-two companies were obtained for analysis that were part of the Basque Country's most cost-intensive sectors in innovation and among the most representative of the industrial fabric. They were leaders in the auxiliary automotive sector, aeronautics, home appliances, electrical

---

4. We did not attempt in this empirical work to achieve a widespread sample of every indus-trial sector in the Basque Country according to the individual provinces that make up the region or company size. Instead, following Cotec (2001) in its Benitec project that analyzes twenty Spanish companies, our idea was to select a sample of companies that would allow us to analyze IM in different sectoral and business contexts.

5. The Basque Country Knowledge Cluster, created in 1996 and integrated into Innobasque (the Basque Innovation Agency), encompasses all things related to the field of business manage-ment, on the one hand, incorporating the demand for services and knowledge in management (primarily companies), and on the other, offering those services (universities, centers dedicated to training managers, consulting agencies, engineering firms, and so on), in addition to public administration. Its goal is to create a space that stimulates and facilitates the creation of new concepts, ideas, and practices with which to tackle the challenges faced by the cluster's partners stemming from the globalized economy and a network society.

6. This reference has been used, among others, by a team of researchers from the University of the Basque Country, for procuring a sample of advanced management companies in which to compare the absorptive capacity of R&D results and the factors that they favor (Rodriguez Castellanos et al. 2006).

equipment, machine tools, and electronic equipment, among others, that had an average research and development (R&D) expenditure of close to 3.5 percent of turnover. The selected companies encompassed all business sizes,[7] achieved an average turnover of 332 million euros in 2006, and had an average of seventy people dedicated to R&D activities in the company. Specifically, four of the selected companies were included among the one thousand EU companies with highest R&D spending, according to the "EU Industrial R&D Investment Scoreboard" published in 2009.[8]

Finally, the questionnaire incorporated a total of eighty-five questions that allowed a personal evaluation to be made of the organization's senior leadership, in which two aspects were of concern: on one hand, the *importance* that a set of practices, processes, and routines held in the context of the organization; and on the other, the *application* level of these in the company.[9] When the interviewee evaluated the importance of the company's processes and routines, zero expressed *not relevant*; one *a little important*; two *indifferent*; three *important*; and four *essential*. When considering the level in which they were put into practice in the organization, zero indicated *never*; one *hardly never*; two *sometimes*, three *regularly*; and four *always*.

Study Results

In the opinion of the twenty-two companies questioned, the integral IM elements were ordered according to their importance, as shown in the first columns of table 1.1.[10] As can be seen, none of the items, not even the last two, were thought of as irrelevant to IM. Furthermore, with regard to

---

7. Specifically, 2.7 percent of the companies analyzed were SMEs, 9.1 percent had between 250 and 499 employees, another 27.3 percent had between 500 and 999 employees, and 36.4 percent had more than 1,000 employees.

8. These were Fagor Appliances, which held position number 247; The ITP Group (Industria de Turbo Propulsores) that occupied number 267; Gamesa, 345; and CIE Automotive, which reached position 637.

9. Of the eighty-five questions, nineteen were on the *innovation process* (innovation process, concept generation, product development, production process innovation, and marketing process innovation); six dealt with *leadership*, the *culture* of innovation, *human resources*, and *finances*, and five were on *strategy, organization, technology management*, and *networking*. Four questions were on the use of *ICTs* and *monitoring* the environment, three concerning the employment of *IMT*, *knowledge management*, *client orientation*, and organizational *learning*, and two questions were about *measurement and monitoring*.

10. The values reflect the average score from the different questions asked about each one of the elements. For example, the importance attributed to *human resources* was obtained by calculating the average from the answers to the six questions regarding that item on the questionnaire.

the formal and systematic application of the IM elements, the companies studied followed the order of implementation shown in the final columns. Just as observed, some elements were put into practice regularly, while others were only applied on some occasions.

Table 1.1. Importance and application of IM elements in the opinion of the innovative companies analyzed (averages)

Element	Importance		Element	Application	
Customer orientation	1st	3.64	Organization	1st	3.14
Product development	2nd	3.47	Financial resources	2nd	3.09
Innovation process	3rd	3.43	Customer orientation	3rd	3.03
Strategy	4th	3.42	Product development	4th	2.96
Organization	5th	3.40	Production process innovation	5th	2.85
Financial resources	6th	3.39	Leadership	6th	2.82
Leadership	7th	3.38	Technology management	7th	2.81
Measurement and monitoring	8th	3.36	Networking	8th	2.77
Human resources	9th	3.30	Strategy	9th	2.77
Technology management	10th	3.29	Innovation process	10th	2.73
Networking	11th	3.29	ICTs	11th	2.67
Knowledge management	12th	3.29	Measurement and monitoring	12th	2.59
Innovation culture	13th	3.24	Domain awareness	13th	2.59
Production process innovation	14th	3.20	Innovation culture	14th	2.54
Domain awareness	15th	3.19	IMT	15th	2.52
ICTs	16th	3.17	Knowledge management	16th	2.48
Concept generation	17th	3.08	Human resources	17th	2.45
IMT	18th	3.03	Concept generation	18th	2.22
Commercialization Process Innovat.	19th	3.02	Commercialization Process Innovat.	19th	2.16
Learning	20th	2.92	Learning	20th	1.83
	Mean	3.28		Mean	2.65
	First quartile	3.39		First quartile	2.83
	Third quartile	3.19		Third quartile	2.51

If the opinion of the innovative Basque companies is contrasted with the presence of the elements in the analyzed models (the first column of table 1.1), it follows that the Basque companies seemed to have fully assumed the importance of some of the dominant elements among the IM models. This was true of the *innovation process*, *leadership*, and *strategy*. For their part, the companies granted relatively minor importance to the elements that were less emphasized by the models, like the *use of ICTs* and *IMTs*.[11]

However, one of the main divergences found between the elements' presence, according to the models studied and the opinion of the companies, was centered on the *people*. The companies seemed to be out of step with the literature that values the importance of people in IM, which was the second most dominant element among the models analyzed, but not considered so relevant by the Basque companies (it was not in the top 25 percent or first quartile).

Furthermore, the results showed that application of the elements was always lower than its importance, so a series of gaps was identified with each one of the elements. The gaps were nothing more than the difference between the average importance and the average application of each element.

The smallest gaps were found in *organization, financial resources, production process innovation*, and *technology management*. For its part, the largest gaps were in *learning, concept generation, innovation in marketing processes, human resources, knowledge management*, and *measurement and monitoring*.

The gap in the area of *human resources* was among the greatest since it was the fourth highest of all those analyzed. This shows that innovative Basque companies are not consistent in implementing this element. Although they place considerable importance on it, the effort made at the time of implementation is less than desirable.[12]

In the companies' opinion, the importance of HR components was near the average given to IM elements as a whole. The Basque companies studied particularly valued their *ability to hold onto the most valuable and experienced employees*. This was followed in importance by *personnel development policies that enabled the staff to acquire innovation capabilities*, as well as *recognition and reward policies*. Nevertheless, having a *per-*

---

11. The fact that these two elements, along with *knowledge management*, were among those with the lowest presence in the models, may be due to their late incorporation into the IM proposals. In its benchmark innovation and technology management study of 2001, Cotec predicts the growing role of *knowledge management* and the *impact of the Internet* on IM (Cotec 2001).

12. In the case of the SMEs studied, the gaps in the area of human resources increased even more. Thus, this group of companies greatly valued this element (3.33), but when it came time to put it into practice in the organizations, the intensity with which it was done was less than the average (2.25) (in this group the gap in the human resources sector widened at 1.08).

sonnel selection policy that supported innovation was not as important to the companies.

However, when it was time to applying these HR management elements, the Basque companies generally did not make a systematic effort to develop them. One thing that they did apply was the *retention of talented personnel* (the only component whose implementation stayed above average), which 54.5 percent practiced with some degree of regularity yet just 13.6 percent always accomplished (see figure 1.1). It was followed by *personnel development policies*, which, again, 54.5 percent of the companies practiced with some degree of regularity, and *personnel selection policies* that supported innovation were found in third place, which 50 percent regularly applied (precisely one of the components that was valued less by the companies).

For its part, in contrast to the importance allocated by the companies to *personnel reward policies*, when it was time to put those into practice, the organizations were less committed to doing so (just two companies developed them and only five with some regularity, while 45.5 percent did once and 22.7 percent hardly ever). It was the same case with the *appropriation of time and resources for the development of ideas*. Although the Basque companies granted considerable importance to this, when it came time to implement them, they were more restrictive (54.5 percent did it once and 13.6 percent hardly ever). Both IM practices were among the lesser used of the eighty-five that the companies were questioned on.

Thus, the Basque companies had considerable room for improvement in the area of HR policies. Although more than half of the companies reg-

Figure 1.1. Frequency with which the human resources components are applied

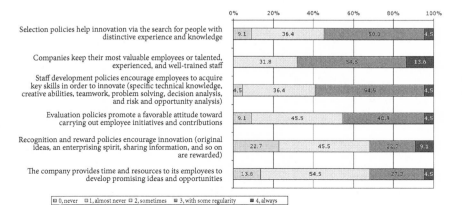

ularly used *personnel development policies* that promoted the acquisition of abilities key to innovation, the difference between the application and the importance of this component was very significant. Likewise, most companies *barely recognized and rewarded the innovator*, so that gap was the third highest of all those studied.

Finally, the companies *did not usually grant personnel the time and the resources needed in order to innovate and develop ideas*. In fact, like the previous item, this one was among the elements that the companies applied less and where more inconsistency was detected in its performance.

Another relevant aspect of the study was the interesting association between *innovation culture* and *HR policies* (correlation coefficient = 0.718). Innovative culture is founded on a series of values that shape the performance of the organization's members and make them more likely to undertake innovative activities. If the members incorporate the values of freedom, initiative, curiosity, passion, intuition, teamwork, exchange of ideas, and error tolerance, the company will have greater innovative potential.

Just as certain experiences of companies known for their innovative capacity demonstrate (Brand 1998), in addition to counting on personnel that have internalized innovation values, the companies have a wide array of practices in the area of HR policies. In fact, according our conclusions, both elements would be mutually reinforcing.

Thus, in the group of the twenty-two innovative companies that were analyzed, insofar as the companies regularly used innovation-promoting HR policies, it was found that these companies tended to have a more developed innovation culture.[13] The Basque companies that formally and systematically promoted personnel policies conducive to innovation were those that had a more solid innovative culture.

---

13. Specifically regarding the innovation culture element, the respondent had to value the importance and application of the following practices and routines in his or her company: (1) A wide appreciation of the value of a creative and entrepreneurial attitude exists at all levels of the organization. (2) The company culture is inclined toward change and capitalizes on new ideas and opportunities. (3) The company culture is encouraging to all employees so that they can propose new ideas. Employee suggestions are listened to, because small improvements and even great innovations can emerge from these. (4) Acceptance of the risk that is attached to innovation exists in the company culture. Failure and error are fully accepted as an inherent element of innovation. (5) The organization supports open communication in all respects with the aim of exchanging information that promotes identifying innovation opportunities (it could be the existence of forums, an intranet, and so on). (6) The physical layout of the workspace facilitates and promotes collaboration and communication (creative interaction).

Most important in this respect was the fact that those companies in which a wide *appreciation of the value of a creative and entrepreneurial attitude existed on all levels of the organization* were more able to retain *their most valuable and experienced employees* (correlation coefficient = 0.600). Furthermore, in companies where the evaluation policies were designed to promote a favorable attitude toward carrying out employee initiatives and contributions, a culture that encouraged all employees to propose new ideas prevailed (correlation coefficient = 0.589).

Conclusions

Innovation and HR are two closely related areas. As is the case with quality, where the objective is to attain quality people, in the field of innovation, innovation rests in the people. As this work demonstrates, most IM models designed by academics, public administrations, technology centers, and consulting agencies emphasize the role performed by HR in innovation. With a degree of caution—our study was limited to twenty-two companies and, moreover, did not consider the impact of constraining variables such as the company's technological level, the sector to which it belonged, or its size—our examination of HR policies in these innovative companies in the Basque Country clarifies the fact that business reality is still rather removed from what the theoretical models propose.

Although it is true that the companies analyzed have incorporated many of the processes and routines permitting the development of an innovative capacity (the average score achieved in the application of the integral IM elements was 2.64 out of 4), certain opportunities for improvement were found in the area of HR.

First of all we would underscore the fact that, in contrast to the IM models, the innovative companies questioned did not grant such a significant role to HR. Contrary to the opinion of innovation experts, the Basque companies placed HR in ninth position among the twenty elements that were studied and considered *organization, financial resources*, and *measurement and monitoring*, among others, to be more important.

Furthermore, when it came time to implement the IM elements, the innovative companies relegated HR to the last positions, being more systematic in the *implementation of ICTs* and in the *use of IMT*, which indicated a real bias toward technology on the part of the companies analyzed.

The recognition and rewarding of innovative attitudes, as well as the appropriation of time and resources for innovation, were the practices where there was greatest room for improvement among the companies studied. Likewise, the effort made by this group of Basque companies in the design of evaluation policies that favored initiatives from their personnel still had room for improvement. The experience of innovative companies like those mentioned at the beginning of this chapter reflects the benefits derived from these types of initiatives and the wide variety of formulas that can be used to implement them.

A house of innovation is often designed from the top down, but if it is not built from below, from the involvement and the commitment of the people in it, this project will have little chance of progressing. From this perspective, HR policies can play a key role when taking on the challenge of innovation. The initiatives studied in the area of HR here favor the creation of a breeding ground for ideas, the promotion of initiative and creativity, and the involvement and motivation of personnel in order to move forward with projects. With these ingredients, a company will have greater chances of success in the innovation challenge. In short, Basque companies should move forward with their HR policies, while trying to be more proactive toward innovation in their design.

References

Andrew, James P., and Harold L. Sirkin. 2008. "Aligning for Innovation." *Global Business and Organizational Excellence* 27, no. 6 (September–October): 21–39.

Brand, Adam. 1998. "Knowledge Management and Innovation at 3M," *Journal of Knowledge Management* 2, no. 1: 17–22.

Chiesa, Vittorio, Paul Coughlan, and Chris A. Voss. 1996. "Development of a Technical Innovation Audit." *Journal of Product Innovation Management* 13, no. 2: 105–36.

Club Excelencia En Gestión. 2006. *Marco de referencia de innovación.* Madrid: Club Excelencia en Gestión.

Cotec. 1999. *Temaguide: pautas metodológicas en gestión de la tecnología y de la innovación para empresas.* Madrid: Fundación Cotec para la Innovación Tecnológica.

———. 2001. *Benitec, Gestión de la innovación y la tecnología en la empresa.* Madrid: Fundación Cotec.

Dobni, C. Brooke. 2008. "The DNA of Innovation." *Journal of Business Strategy* 29, no. 2: 43–50.

Escorsa, Pere, and Jaume Valls. 2003. *Tecnología e innovación en la empresa.* Barcelona: Edicions de la Universitat Politècnica de Catalunya.

Gobierno Vasco. 2005. Competitividad Empresarial e Innovación Social: Bases de la Estrategia y Líneas de Actuación. At http://212.8.99.31/web/docs/publicaciones/MemoriaSPRI-CAS.pdf.

Goffin, Keith, and Rick Mitchell. 2005. *Innovation Management: Strategy and Implementation Using the Pentathlon Framework.* Basingstoke: Palgrave Macmillan.

Hidalgo, Antonio, and José Albors. 2008. "Innovation Management Techniques and Tools: A Review from Theory and Practice." *R&D Management* 38, no. 2: 113–27.

Hidalgo Nuchera, Antonio, Antonio Vizán Idoipe, and Torres, M. 2008. "Los factores clave de la innovación tecnológica: claves de la competitividad empresarial." *Dirección y Organización* 36 (October): 5–22.

Johannessen, Jon-Arild, Johan Olaisen, and Bjørn Olsen. 1999. "Managing and Organizing Innovation in the Knowledge Economy." *European Journal of Innovation Management* 2, no. 3: 116–28.

Jonash, Ronald S., and Tom Sommerlatte. 1999. *The Innovation Premium: How Next-generation Companies Are Achieving Peak Performance and Profitability.* Reading, MA: Perseus Books.

Laursen, Keld. 2002. "The Importance of Sectoral Differences in the Application of Complementary HRM Practices for Innovation Performance." *International Journal of Economics of Business* 9, no. 1: 139–56.

Laursen, Keld, and Nicolai J. Foss. 2003. "New Human Resource Management Practices, Complementarities and the Impact on Innovation Performance." *Cambridge Journal of Economics* 27, no. 2: 243–63.

Leede, Jan de, and Jan Kees Looise. 2005. "Innovation and HRM: Towards an Integrated Framework." *Creativity and Innovation Management* 14, no. 2: 108–17.

Loewe, Pierre, and Jennifer Dominiquini. 2006. "Overcoming Barriers to Effective Innovation." *Strategy & Leadership* 34, no. 1: 24–31.

Morcillo Ortega, Patricio. 1997. *Dirección estratégica de la tecnología e innovación: Un enfoque de competencias.* Madrid: Civitas.

Muñoz-Nájar, José Antonio, and Joaquim Vilà. 2000. *Dirección integral de la innovación*. Technical Note IESE DGN 609. Barcelona: IESE Publishing.

Nieto, Mariano. 2003. "From R&D Management to Knowledge Management: An Overview of Studies of Innovation Management." *Technological Forecasting & Social Change* 70, no. 2: 135–61.

Organisation for Economic Co-operation and Development (OECD). 2005. *Oslo Manual: Guidelines for Collecting and Interpreting Innovation Data*. 3rd ed. Paris: OECD and Eurostat.

Ortt, J. Roland, and Ruud Smits. 2006. "Innovation Management: Different Approaches to Cope with the Same Trends." *International Journal of Technology Management* 34, nos. 3–4: 296–318.

Padmore, Tim, Hans Schuetze, and Hervey Gibson. 1998. "Modeling Systems of Innovation: An Enterprise-centered View." *Research Policy* 26, no. 6: 605–24.

Pérez López, Susana, José Manuel Montes Peón, and Camilo José Vázquez Ordas. 2005. "Human Resource Practices, Organizational Learning and Business Performance." *Human Resource Development International* 8, no. 2: 147–64.

Pollitt, David. 2006. "Toshiba Sparks a Wave of Innovation." *Human Resource Management International Digest* 14, no. 6: 5–7.

Rodríguez Castellanos, Arturo, Andrés Araujo De La Mata, Markus Hagemeister, Jon Landeta Rodriguez, Macarena Larrauri Estefanía, and Stanislav Ranguelov Youlianov. 2006. *Capacidad empresarial para la absorción de resultados de I+D: Un enfoque de conocimiento: principios, análisis empíricos y directrices de autoevaluación*. Bilbao: Servicio Editorial de la UPV.

Scarbrough, Harry. 2003. "Knowledge Management, HRM and the Innovation Process." *International Journal of Manpower* 24, no. 5: 501–16.

Shipton, Helen, Doris Fay, Michael A. West, Malcolm Patterson, and Kamal Birdi. 2005. "Managing People to Promote Innovation." *Creativity and Innovation Management* 14, no. 2: 118–28.

Shipton, Helen, Michael A. West, Jeremy Dawson, Kamal Birdi, and Malcolm Patterson. 2006. "HRM as a Predictor of Innovation." *Human Resource Management Journal* 16, no. 1: 3–27.

Tidd, Joseph, John Bessant, and Keith Pavitt. 2005. *Managing Innovation: Integrating Technological, Market and Organizational Change*. 3rd edition. Chichester: Wiley & Sons.

Velasco, Eva, and Ibon Zamanillo. 2008. "Evolución de las propuestas sobre el proceso de innovación: ¿Qué se puede concluir de su estudio?" *Investigaciones Europeas de Dirección y Economía de la Empresa* 14, no. 2: 127–38.

Von Stamm, Bettina. 2003. *The Innovation Wave: Meeting the Corporate Challenge*. Chichester: Wiley & Sons.

2

Vectors of Organizational Change in European Union Company Law

Juan Pablo Landa and Igone Altzelai

Translated by Jennifer R. Ottman

The aim of this chapter is to analyze the vectors of organizational change affecting businesses that can be extracted from European Union (EU) law. Our chronological field of analysis starts with the objectives set by the European Council of the heads of state and government of EU member states (European Council 2000) in the so-called *European Strategy for Growth and Jobs,* better known as the Lisbon Strategy, for the period from 2000 to 2010. These principles have been taken up again and reviewed by the European Commission (formerly the Commission of the European Communities and now the European Commission, since December 1, 2009) in its proposal for the next European Council summit, at which the EU's strategy for 2020, *Europe 2020: A Strategy for Smart, Sustainable and Inclusive Growth,* will be adopted, in the current context of the Stability and Growth Pact (European Commission 2010b).

Within the general framework of this European strategy, as it has been defined by EU authorities, we would like to highlight the continuity of two strategic objectives: jobs and competitiveness. These strategic objectives have been the motors of two significant vectors of organizational change in the business world: one with regard to the organization of work, based on the concept of "flexicurity" (European Commission 2007b), and the other with reference to improving the business climate, based on the "Think Small First" principle (European Commission 2008a).

The European Union's Strategies for Relaunching Economic Growth and the Competitiveness of Its Businesses in a Globalized Economy

The European Council (2000) set as the central objective of its Lisbon Strategy that by 2010 the EU would be "the world's leading and most dynamic knowledge-based economy, capable of sustainable economic growth together with a quantity and quality improvement of employment, greater social cohesion." Underlying this declaration was the idea that, in order to improve its standard of living and maintain its economic and social model, the EU needed to increase its productivity and competitiveness in the face of ever fiercer global competition, technological change, and an aging population. In addition, it acknowledged that reforms could not be successfully carried out only at the EU level. As in other areas, achieving this objective implied making use of powers that belonged to the individual member states, so that close collaboration between these states and the EU was necessary.

This division of powers between the EU and its member states—exacerbated even more by the specific federal or decentralized structure of many European countries, with particular powers assigned to regions or territorial administrations at different levels— resulted in a certain degree of confusion and dispersed activity, because it was often difficult to identify the intended targets of European action. For this reason, in addition to the excessive number of objectives and the relative vagueness of many of them, the Lisbon Strategy was relaunched in 2005 (European Commission 2005), following a midterm review, with a greater sense of priorities, and focused on four preferential areas: (1) research and innovation; (2) investing in people and modernizing labor markets; (3) unlocking business potential, especially that of small and medium-sized enterprises (SMEs); and (4) energy and climate change. At the same time, a new governance structure for relations among the member states and EU institutions was established, perfecting the open method of coordination.

The original application of the open method of coordination arose out of the *1997–2005 European Employment Strategy* (European Council 1997). The aim was to introduce a new collaborative framework among member states by "directing national policies towards common objectives in areas which fall within the competences of the Member States, such as employment." Subsequently, the idea was gradually extended to many other issues. *European Governance: A White Paper* (European Commission 2001) stated that the open method of coordination offered a perfect equilibrium between European integration and national diversity, seeking the convergence of objectives, results, and political approaches, but without the need for every member state to implement the same programs, rules, and institutions (Zeitlin 2005, 448).

The influence of the open method of coordination in the areas of employment policy, inclusion, and social protection was inevitable, explaining its exponential growth in these areas over the last ten years. This was noted, for example, in the Commission's *Green Paper: Modernising Labour Law to Meet the Challenges of the 21st Century.* As the text acknowledges, "Responsibility for safeguarding working conditions and improving the quality of work in the Member States primarily rests on national legislation and on the efficacy of enforcement and control measures at national level. At the EU level, the social *acquis* supports and complements the actions of the Member States in this sphere" (European Commission 2006, 6). By contrast, the open method of coordination works through references, indicators, peer review, and the exchange of best practices ("mutual learning and benchmarking"), which function as mechanisms for evaluating the degree to which member states fulfill the objectives recommended by the European Council and European Commission.

In 2010, when the Commission had to evaluate the results of the Lisbon Strategy, it focused on the essential element, its impact on economic growth and employment (European Commission 2010a). Nevertheless, this impact did not prove easy to measure, due to external events (the expansion of the EU from fifteen to twenty-seven members, the importance of the euro, and the growth of the Eurozone from twelve countries to sixteen) and to the fact that, on the other hand, the Lisbon Strategy had come to an end at a time of global economic crisis.

In effect, the impact of the financial crisis had wreaked havoc on the Lisbon Strategy's forecasts for 2010. In 2009, the EU's GDP decreased by 4 percent, unemployment was at 10 percent, the public deficit reached 7 percent of gross domestic product (GDP), and public debt increased by 20 percent. Nevertheless, according to data from 2008, before the outbreak of the financial crisis, the level of employment in the EU was at 66 percent, compared to 62 percent in 2000, and the unemployment rate had fallen to 7 percent, even if EU spending on R&D had increased by only .08 percent of GDP compared to 2000 (European Commission 2010a, 3).

Despite these adverse circumstances, the Commission judged that the Lisbon Strategy had had a positive impact on the EU. Considered as a whole, even if its most concrete objectives were ultimately not attained (an employment level of 70 percent of the active population and R&D spending of 3 percent of GDP), the strategy promoted significant common actions, in the Commission's view, that made it possible to open new paths toward addressing the EU's chief long-term challenges. The Commission also understood that the Lisbon Strategy had contributed to creating a broad consensus about the reforms needed both at the EU level and within the member states; these reforms prominently feature the two topics with which we are concerned: (1) more and better jobs through modernizing the labor market on the basis of flexibility and security ("flexicurity") and investing in people, and (2) unlocking business potential, especially that of small and medium-sized enterprises (SMEs). Nonetheless, even if the process of learning about effective reform policies and the exchange of best practices intensified after 2005, the Commission acknowledged that the Lisbon Strategy was quite unevenly applied due to extremely weak European governance structures.

This fact raises questions about the effectiveness of the open method of coordination. This is a significant issue, given the interdependence of EU countries (and particularly members of the Eurozone) as the consequence of a tightly integrated economic reality. It will only be possible to take advantage of the growth and employment potential proclaimed by the "crisis pact" if all the member states apply these reforms at more or less the same pace (European Commission 2010a, 5). The Commission's working document proposes correcting the European Employment Strategy's Integrated Guidelines so as to establish a greater degree of internal hierarchy among them, with clear and measurable objectives (priorities and headline targets). At the same time, the document also criticizes the fact that the partnership approach between member states and the EU has not been successfully replicated at the local and regional levels within the member states, despite the fact that these substate levels often have specific political powers and receive significant resources from European structural funds (European Commission 2010a, 6). Specific recommendations will be made to each member state, possibly accompanied by policy warnings in the event of inadequate response by a member state. According to the communication from the Commission, the European Council will direct the new strategy with full powers, and the European Parliament will have the mission of mobilizing citizens and will be a co-legislator on key initiatives (European Commission 2010a, 4).

To a great extent, the post-Lisbon strategy, known as Europe 2020 (European Commission 2010b), maintains the priorities defined in the Lisbon Strategy, especially subsequent to the review conducted on the occasion of the relaunch of the strategy in 2005. In its new form, the strategy introduces an approach based on thematic areas. Specifically, the Europe 2020 Strategy proposes three mutually reinforcing thematic priorities: smart growth: developing an economy based on knowledge and innovation; sustainable growth: promoting a more resource efficient, greener, and more competitive economy; and inclusive growth: fostering a high-employment economy delivering social and territorial cohesion.

Simultaneously, the strategy defines five headline targets for 2020, representing the three priorities of smart, sustainable, and inclusive growth: employment (75 percent of the population between twenty and sixty-four years old employed), research and innovation (3 percent of GDP), climate change (a 30 percent reduction in emissions) and energy (20/20/20: a 20 percent cut in carbon dioxide (CO_2) emissions, a 20 percent improvement in energy efficiency, and 20 percent of energy consumed drawn from renewable sources), education (40 percent of young people with post-secondary education qualifications), and the fight against poverty (twenty million fewer poor people). Finally, seven flagship initiatives are proposed in order to channel progress on each of the priority issues.

Upon examining these targets and flagship initiatives, we conclude that the EU is continuing to stake its future on the two vectors of organizational change in the business world that emerged with the Lisbon Strategy, summarized respectively in the "Think Small First" principle with regard to business creation and development and the "flexicurity" strategy for labor relations. On the one hand, the idea of improving the business climate and unlocking its potential persists among the targets and flagship initiatives proposed for the first two priorities (smart growth and sustainable growth), with special attention to SMEs and with the aim of developing a strong and sustainable industrial base that can compete worldwide. On the other hand, as far as the third priority (inclusive growth) is concerned, implementation of the principles of "flexicurity" is considered key to better managing transitions in the labor market, to fighting unemployment, and to increasing the rate of activity.

"Think Small First": Modernizing Company Law and Improving Firm Governance

The EU faces the challenge of managing the transition to a knowledge-based economy so as to become a more competitive and dynamic economy with more and better jobs and a higher level of social cohesion. In response to this challenge, the EU has chosen to think small first and pay special attention to SMEs. The EU has decided that this is the time for these enterprises to occupy a prominent position in its policies, with the aim that they will find the most favorable possible climate in the EU (European Commission 2008a).

SMEs play a fundamental role in the European economy, representing 99.8 percent of businesses in the EU, producing 60 percent of its GDP, and accounting for 67 percent of its private-sector jobs (over 80 percent of jobs in some sectors, such as metal-products manufacturing, construction, and furniture manufacturing).[1] To these telling figures we must add the advantages that these enterprises offer or can offer due to their particular character. SMEs, which employ so many people, are strongly rooted in their local or regional communities, making them guarantors of social cohesion and stability. They can also be more dynamic than large enterprises, potentially putting them in an especially favorable position for taking advantage of the opportunities offered by globalization and the acceleration of technological change. These two advantages in fact coincide with the objectives set by the Lisbon meeting of the European Council in 2000 and with the Europe 2020 Strategy (European Commission 2010b). Everything therefore points in the direction of European institutions making a special effort to take advantage of the potential for growth that SMEs represent. In a changing world context and under heavy competitive pressure, the role of SMEs in the economy is understood to be key, leading to the decision to create a favorable business climate for them.

Nevertheless, these enterprises suffer problems of competitiveness that are of concern to the firms themselves in the first instance and also to EU member states and EU authorities. The fact is that at the present time, as a general rule, SMEs in the EU have much lower productivity and a notably slower rate of growth than SMEs in the United States. Telling data also exists in this regard. For example, in the US, in the first seven years of existence of successful enterprises, the number of jobs grows by

---

1. See http://ec.europa.eu/enterprise/sme.

an average of 60 percent, while in the EU, this average is between 10 and 20 percent (European Commission 2008a). Moreover, SMEs in the EU find it more difficult to obtain financing and venture capital (a crucial element in creating innovative SMEs and ensuring their growth) than their US counterparts. Indeed, in Europe this market is only half the size of that in the US (European Commission 2007c, 11).

European SMEs generally have a much lower productivity than their American counterparts, a cause for worry in the context of a globalized economy. Furthermore, the authorities are conscious of the fact that SMEs face serious problems of competitiveness due to their market disadvantages or deficiencies in comparison to large enterprises. These problems of competitiveness and weakness in comparison to large enterprises have their chief impact in the form of an excessive administrative and regulatory burden, difficulties accessing financing, difficulties in engaging in research and innovation, and difficulties in addressing environmental issues. For every euro that a large enterprise spends per employee as a result of a regulatory obligation, for example, a medium-sized enterprise may spend four euros, and a small enterprise up to ten euros (European Commission 2007a, 4). EU authorities are conscious of the handicaps suffered by SMEs, and this concern was explicitly stated at the 2000 European Council in Lisbon itself. These problems have been to a large extent identified, and the institutions are continually at work studying them and the possible measures to be adopted.

For all these reasons, the EU has promoted the Small Business Act initiative (European Commission, 2008a), through which it aspires to change the global political approach to the entrepreneurial spirit. In this way, it is trying to establish the "Think Small First" principle as part of the formulation of its policies and to promote the growth of SMEs by helping them to confront the problems that continue to pose obstacles to their development.

Finally, the Commission some time ago defined the terms "enterprise," "micro-enterprise," "small enterprise," and "medium-sized enterprise" in order to prevent the proliferation of multiple definitions and apply a single definition throughout the EU (and the European Economic Area as well) (European Commission 2003, Annex, Art. 2). These definitions establish that:

- *Medium-sized enterprises* are considered to be those that employ fewer than 250 people and have an annual turnover not exceeding fifty million euros and/or an annual balance sheet total not exceeding forty-three million euros.

- *Small enterprises* are considered to be those that employ fewer than fifty people and have an annual turnover and/or an annual balance sheet total not exceeding ten million euros.
- *Micro-enterprises* are considered to be those that employ fewer than ten people and have an annual turnover and/or an annual balance sheet total not exceeding two million euros.

To this it must be added that an SME has to be an independent enterprise. This is an essential element, since these conditions do not apply if an enterprise, for example, is a subsidiary of another, larger one. These conditions have to apply to the enterprise as a whole, including subsidiaries located in other member states and outside the EU. In order to evaluate the real economic position of an enterprise and whether it should be classified as an SME, other concepts have also been defined, such as "autonomous enterprise," "partner enterprise," and "linked enterprise" (European Commission 2003, Annex, Art. 3).

Small Business Act for Europe

The *Small Business Act* (European Commission 2008a) is a general initiative that has the objective of creating a political framework to promote SMEs. It is a plan to respond to the needs of SMEs, promote their growth, and thereby take advantage of their potential. It acknowledges the central role of SMEs in the EU economy and articulates for the first time a political framework for the EU and its member states, through the establishment of a series of ten principles intended to guide policy formation and implementation (both at the EU level and at that of the member states) and the elaboration of five new legislative proposals to be adopted by the EU, guided by the "Think Small First" principle. These proposals are the following:

- A general block exemption regulation on state aids
- A regulation providing for a statute for a European private company
- A directive on reduced value-added tax (VAT) rates
- A legislative proposal to further modernize, simplify, and synchronize the rules on VAT invoicing

- A modification of Directive 2000/35/EC on late payments in commercial transactions to ensure that SMEs are paid on time in all commercial transactions

Despite its name, the "Small Business Act" is not a binding legal text elaborated under EU procedures (a directive or regulation), but rather a "soft law" initiative. Nevertheless, this symbolic name reflects the political will to change the EU's approach to business policy and create a new political framework for the EU and its member states.

With the passage of time since the Small Business Act was approved (on June 25, 2008), questions have arisen about its effective application and results (European Commission 2009c). Nevertheless, in this regard, one should note the existence of two distinct levels. On the one hand, evaluating the application of the principles contained in the initiative may be complex, even debatable, depending on the optimism or lack thereof of the observer. The national and local climates in which SMEs operate are highly diverse (including countries of the former socialist bloc), complicating the evaluation of the implementation and effectiveness of such principles, as well as the exchange of best practices carried out. Yet on the other hand, it is a simpler task to evaluate the extent to which the regulatory initiatives proposed by the Small Business Act have been put into place. In this regard, it should be specified that:

- We have Commission Regulation (EC) No. 800/2008, declaring certain categories of aid compatible with the common market (General Block Exemption Regulation) (European Commission 2008e), in effect from August 30, 2008, to December 31, 2013.
- With regard to the Statute for a European Private Company, there is a Draft Commission Regulation that has not yet been approved (European Commission 2008b).
- For its part, Council Directive 2009/47/EC, amending Directive 2006/112/EC as regards reduced rates of value-added tax, went into effect on June 1, 2009 (European Council 2009).
- In January 2009, the Commission adopted a proposal to modify Directive 2006/112/EC (the "VAT Directive") with regard to invoicing rules, for the purpose of aligning the treatment of paper and electronic invoices (European Commission 2009a).
- Likewise, in April 2009, the Commission adopted a proposed directive to combat late payment in commercial transactions,

amending the existing Directive 2000/35/EC (European Commission 2009b).

The Small Business Act has therefore served some purpose and, in addition to its principles being more or less applied, it has produced some tangible results encouraging a more favorable business climate for SMEs. Of the five regulatory suggestions put forward in the initiative, two have been implemented, and proposals in regard to the other three (in the form of one new regulation and the modification of two prior directives) have been introduced by the Commission and are working their way through the system.

In what follows, we will turn our attention specifically to an analysis of the draft regulation in regard to a Statute for a European Private Company, since it constitutes a significant novelty and a true vector of organizational change in European company law. As we will see, the European Private Company being proposed entails the creation of a new model of corporation that is going to expand the spectrum of company forms available to economic actors.

Draft Regulation for a European Private Company

The draft regulation for a European Private Company (*Societas Privata Europaea*), which proposes creating a new type of company, is part of the package of measures put forward in the Small Business Act. It is based on Article 352 of the Treaty on the Functioning of the European Union (formerly Article 308 of the Treaty Establishing the European Community), like the other existing types of European companies: the European Company or *Societas Europaea*, the European Economic Interest Grouping, and the European Cooperative Society.

Significance of the Draft

Numerous aspects of commercial companies have been the subject of synchronization among the various EU member states through EU directives in the area of company law. Directives are normative legal acts that bind member states with regard to the result to be obtained, leaving them free to choose the means and methods to be used. Consequently, in order for a directive to have an effect, it is necessary for the national legislative power to carry out an act of transposition in which national law is adapted to the objectives established in the directive. In this way, progress is made toward the approximation of the various national bodies of law. Nevertheless, the fact is that, despite the significant work done by the EU in this way, differences between the laws of different countries persist, implying the existence of obstacles for firms that operate across the EU market as a whole.

For this reason, after a long process pursued with the aim of preventing these problems, the EU initiated a new phase of drawing up regulations in the area of company law. This was the origin of several new company types created by EU law itself: the European Economic Interest Grouping (European Council 1985), the European Company or *Societas Europaea* (European Council 2001a), and the European Cooperative Society (European Council 2003a). These organizational types aim to facilitate and promote the operations of concentration and reorganization of those enterprises that carry out their activities in several EU countries, thereby enabling them to avoid being forced to adopt the organizational forms prescribed by national regulations.

These types of companies are created and governed by EU law itself (by the respective regulations); nonetheless, they are required to register and establish legal domicile in a member state, the laws and regulations of which apply as supplements to the Regulation on the Statute for a European Company on those issues not regulated by the latter. In addition, the *Societas Europaea* and the European Cooperative Society require the legislative implementation by member states of the respective EU directives on employee involvement in the firm. Consequently, even if they offer a European legal framework, they do not entail the establishment of a unitary and complete legal system applied in the same way throughout the EU.

For example, the legal system governing European Companies is made up of EU regulations and of the laws and regulations of the different member states that supplement the former in numerous areas (shares, obligations, modifications of share capital, and so forth). In addition, the *Societas Europaea* must necessarily establish its corporate domicile in the member state in which its central administration is located (the "real seat" principle), with the consequence that it is the laws of this state that apply to its formation and operations. To this it must be added that, even if the regulation governing the *Societas Europaea* dates from 2001, it went into effect on October 8, 2004, the date by which member states were to carry out the legislative implementation of Directive 2001/86 and make the necessary legal changes to adapt their respective national bodies of law. To the EU's disappointment, only six countries (Belgium, Austria, Denmark, Sweden, Finland, and Iceland) adopted the necessary measures for the creation of a *Societas Europaea* on their territory within the time period foreseen. As far as the Spanish state is concerned, the registration of a *Societas Europaea* in Spain became possible starting in October 2006, two years later, after the legislative implementation of the mentioned Directive 2001/86 and the provisions on employee involvement (Law 31 of October 18, 2006, on employee involvement).

This supplementary application of national law introduces elements that may erase the distinctiveness of these companies under EU law, since it is impossible to guarantee legal unity in this area. The supplementary law to be applied differs from one member state to the next, and as a consequence, the identical legal treatment of the European company types is not fully assured (Pastor 2009, 122). Since the regulations are configured as a flexible framework, in some cases the state where the company in question has its headquarters (whether that company is a European Economic Interest Grouping, *Societas Europaea,* or European Cooperative Society) may determine crucial elements of its legal make-up.

To a large extent, these three organizational types (the European Economic Interest Grouping, the *Societas Europaea,* and the European Cooperative Society) exist as part of a process of specialization of EU company law with the goal of meeting specific needs that are characteristic of inter-business cooperation. The three types refer to companies endowed with a specific legal character, but their usefulness centers basically on the creation of ties between enterprises. Even if a European Cooperative Society can be created by a minimum of five natural persons resident in at least two member states, the three types are ideal for carrying out mergers of enterprises or groups of companies. They are especially appropriate as legal ways to link preexisting enterprises (legally independent companies already in existence) for reasons of business integration or reorganization, with the aim of integrating their business policies under a single financial management. In this way, enterprises that operate in more than one EU member state can function within a single legal framework and have a unified system of management and administration, instead of constituting a network of subsidiaries subject to different national legal systems, a more complicated and costly option (Paz-Ares 2006, 1470).

In practice, these organizational types are not being used to the extent expected by European authorities, and the number of cases registered is very low. The European Economic Interest Grouping is the form that has existed the longest and has consequently consolidated its place on the scene, although enterprises that desire to cooperate on a transnational level still do not take full advantage of it. The *Societas Europaea* has shown a degree of popularity in some member states. Among the best-known examples are Allianz, BASF, Porsche, Fresenius, and Man in Germany; SCOR in France; Elcoteq in Luxembourg; and Strabag in Austria. Nevertheless, it has not taken hold in other member states, and the Commission has already initiated a study in order to determine whether changes in its statute are needed in order to encourage its use throughout the EU. As far as the European Cooperative Society is concerned, it has found practically no application. In addition, these organizational types do not match the needs of SMEs. They are excessively rigid for these enterprises, which need a more flexible tool. For example, a *Societas Europaea* requires a minimum capital of 120,000 euros, in addition to compliance with other conditions designed to protect shareholders, creditors, and workers, thereby limiting shareholders' room for maneuver.

Even if these three organizational types are especially appropriate for large enterprises and for forming groups of enterprises and have for that purpose a legal framework that does not include a single, uniform set of laws and regulations across the EU, then the *Societas Privata Europaea* (SPE) is something very different, as a consequence of which we believe that it constitutes a true vector of change in European company law.

First, it is worth highlighting that the SPE is not a type of company especially suited for inter-business cooperation or the formation of groups of enterprises. As the Explanatory Memorandum of the draft regulation on its statute (European Commission 2008b) states, this organizational type can be useful for enterprises of all kinds, large and small, and also for the formation of groups; the text also stresses, however, that this new European legal form is born with the vocation to facilitate the establishment and activity of SMEs in the European single market and thereby promote their competitiveness. The proposed SPE Statute has therefore been drawn up thinking specifically about the particular needs of SMEs and not the reverse, thinking about large enterprises, as was previously the case.

Second, this is the first time that any attempt has been made to create a new company type for the entire EU through a regulation. For this purpose, an organizational form has been designed that can be set up in accordance with a company law that is simple, flexible, and identical in all member states. In this way, the proposal aims to reduce the costs of legal and regulatory compliance arising from the disparities between national bodies of law with regard to both company formation and company operations. The proposal does not regulate aspects related to labor or tax law, accounting, or insolvency, nor does it concern itself with the contractual rights and obligations of the SPE or its shareholders, except for those deriving from its articles of association. These aspects will continue to be governed by national law, and if applicable, by existing EU law.

The creation of this new type of company aims to make it easier for economic actors to establish a subsidiary in another member state by allowing entrepreneurs to adhere to the same company law throughout the EU and maintain the same management structure independent of the enterprise's location. The aim is to save time and money, especially in the cost of the legal proceedings needed to establish different kinds of enterprises in different member states. Enterprises in the various member states will be able to make use of the SPE without the need for any cross-border element.

As a directly applicable legal instrument, the SPE Statute will be effective throughout the EU without the need for its legislative implementation as part of each state's national law; in other words, without a requirement to modify each state's company law, as was the case with the directives accompanying the *Societas Europaea* and the European Cooperative Society. Thus, a new type of company is going to be incorporated into each country's repertory through EU regulations, directly applicable in EU member states. In order to ensure its European character (independent of national law) and its requisite uniformity across the EU, the draft foresees resorting to each state's national law only for those aspects not covered by the regulation or addressed in the bylaws drawn up by shareholders. To this end, Annex I lists the areas that are to be regulated in the articles of association.

In this way, the SPE will be another organizational form, in addition to the legal forms provided for at the national level. It will be a new type of commercial company to which economic actors within a member state can turn in order to give legal form to their enterprises, entering into direct competition with similar types of companies in their respective countries (Viera 2008, 1341).

The first studies of the SPE go back to 1973 (Boucourechliev 1973); nevertheless, the EU gave preference to the regulation of other company types (European Economic Interest Grouping, *Societas Europaea*, and European Cooperative Society). As far as the SPE is concerned, from those first studies to the current proposed regulation, the objective has been to regulate a private, flexible, and European company type—a supranational corporate identity under EU law, without requiring any cross-border element, and with a simple legal statute adaptable to the scale and needs of SMEs and capable of providing legal security to foreign clients, collaborators, and investors. Taking into account the profile with which this new proposal has been designed, it reflects an authentic political will by the EU to encourage SMEs. This SPE regulation is expected to contribute to improving the SME business climate by reducing transaction costs and thereby promoting the external focus of SMEs (European Commission 2010b, 18).

Certainly, these objectives are beyond debate (European Commission 2008b, Explanatory Memorandum 6). However, problems and discrepancies arise when it comes to designing the SPE model, since this requires taking a position on issues such as the type and number of shareholders who can form an SPE, its capital, its cross-border element, its domicile, the application of national laws, distributions to shareholders, and employee participation (Boquera and Latorre 2009, 103).

Discussion of the Proposed Model

The proposal being debated in the EU to create the SPE resembles an entity similar to the Spanish Sociedad de Responsabilidad Limitada (SL), the French Société a Responsabilité Limitée (SARL), the German Gesellschaft mit beschränkter Haftung (GmbH), and the British Limited Company (Ltd.). It is a company with its own legal character and limited shareholder liability, although with a flexible regime for the transmission of shares. Below we highlight some of the most significant aspects of the draft regulation put forward by the Commission for debate 2008b).

The draft allows the opening of subsidiaries or branches in EU countries other than the country where the company was founded, without the need to comply with the specifics of each body of national law. This will enable a dramatic decrease in the cost of founding and operating a company. An SPE may be formed by one or several natural or legal persons. It may also be formed through the transformation, merger, or division of preexisting companies (Art. 5.2). Transnational activity is not required to form an SPE, so that companies that operate in a single EU state with national partners from the same state could use this form. This company form would thereby expand the list of company types available to economic actors in each state. This poses the problem of the competition that the SPE might entail for national types of private corporations (Hommel-hoff and Teichmann 2008, 900).

The company's legal domicile does not have to coincide with its real headquarters (its chief establishment or place of business or its administrative center), in agreement with the recent jurisprudence of the Court of Justice of the European Union. The two domiciles may be in different states, but both must be members of the EU (Art. 7). Provision is also made for a change of domicile within the EU without especial difficulty (Art. 35.1).

With regard to the formalities required to form an SPE, registration in the national registry corresponding to the place of legal domicile is a constitutive requirement for the company's foundation. To this end, the draft proposes a single oversight instance, which may be either the corresponding national administrative or judicial body or the notary who certifies the documents (Art. 10.4). As was to be expected, notarial organizations have protested energetically against the possibility of doing without notarial certification as a prerequisite to registration (Teichmann and Limmer 2009).

No minimum capital is required. An SPE could be formed with a capital of one euro (Art. 19.4). In addition, the establishment of reserves is unregulated; they could be created (or not) through the company's bylaws. This formula is in line with the most recent reforms implemented in some states, such as France (in 2003) and Germany (in 2008), following the lead of the English-speaking countries. Nevertheless, numerous criticisms have been made of the effectiveness of the alternatives to the capital maintenance regime (Hommelhoff 2009, 278; Otxoa-Errarte 2010, 46).

In contrast, the draft does include measures to protect the company's capital in the event of distribution among the shareholders, the acquisition of the company's own shares (Art. 23.2), or a reduction in share capital (Art. 24.2), all inspired by the text of the Second Directive with regard to capital. The distribution of dividends is unregulated so long as the remaining assets are sufficient to cover the company's debts (Art. 21.1). The bylaws may require a "solvency test" in which the management body states that following the test and during the entire subsequent year, the SPE will be in a position to pay its debts as they come due (Art. 21.2). Guarantees are provided for the system by establishing the liability of the shareholders for improper distributions, in the amount received, and of the company's directors for the damage to the company's capital (Art. 31.4).

The liability of members of the management body (except for the provisions of Art. 31.4 with regard to damage to the company) is left to national law. The Commission does not appear to have dared to seek a consensus among the varied formulas offered by the laws of the different member states, thereby missing a good opportunity to articulate a single regime of creditor protection that, if not centered on capital, must be centered on the liability of the management bodies (Otxoa-Errarte 2010, 46).

In the area of the company's internal organization, the draft grants a maximum of flexibility. The management structure, management bodies, and those bodies' functions are left to a great extent in the hands of shareholders. A management body capable of exercising all those powers that did not have to be exercised by shareholders is expected to be obligatory. It is thus left to the shareholders to specify whether they wish to reserve the right to issue instructions or make the adoption of decisions or resolutions on management matters subject to their authorization (Hommelhoff and Teichmann 2008, 902; Bücker 2009, 292). Further, the bylaws will have to determine the structure and composition of the management body. It is possible to opt for a unitary or for a dual model that includes an oversight council. A General Assembly is not required. Resolutions affecting the company's financing, its structure, the appointment of directors or auditors, and so on, are to be adopted by the shareholders, but it is not necessary that they meet physically in an assembly (Art. 27.3). The directors are required only to submit to the shareholders the proposed resolutions and the information needed to allow them to make a well-informed decision (Art. 28).

A non-exhaustive list of rights of the shareholders as owners is included (Art. 27.1). It is possible (even desirable) to include in the bylaws issues such as shareholders' ability to issue instructions or require their prior authorization for making decisions about the company's management, the procedure for adopting resolutions, the majorities required, the deadlines, the way in which shareholders are to be informed, the rules applicable to their representation, information about resolutions adopted, and so on. Two rights assigned to the minority of shareholders who hold 5 percent of the SPE's voting rights are also mentioned (Art. 29): the right to propose resolutions and the right to request that an independent expert be named when a serious violation of the company's legal regime or its bylaws on the part of the management body is suspected. The configuration of the obligations and rights corresponding to the shareholders in their capacity as such is equally flexible.

The SPE will be subject to the laws and regulations on employee participation that apply in the member state in which it has its corporate domicile (Art. 34.1). This may be an issue posing one of the greatest difficulties for achieving the consensus needed to approve the regulation. The draft (Art. 34.1 in relation with Art. 7.2) allows SPEs to ignore the laws and regulations regarding co-management that are in effect in several member states and constitute one of the pillars of their business culture. This is the case of Germany, Austria, the Netherlands, Denmark, Sweden, Finland, and so on. There is concern in these states that the SPE might be used as a way to escape co-management (Hommelhoff 2008, 677), something that both the Commission and the European Parliament affirm that they want to prevent (Considerandum 15). The problem of employee involvement in firm management was one of the issues that posed hurdles for the approval of the Statute for the *Societas Europaea* (Aguilar 2007, 89), and it is much the same now with the SPE. Simply referring the issue to national law, as the Commission's proposed text does, is not a solution for a question that has aroused so much debate in the recent past.

As can be seen, the proposed model is highly flexible and may generate some effects contrary to the draft objectives. The highly flexible nature of this new kind of company and the absence even of any soft law in the text that regulates it (which is to be supplemented by the company bylaws) demand that it be assessed and monitored closely.

Even if external relations, in order to ensure legal security, are regulated to a greater extent by obligatory provisions, the internal sphere is left entirely to the disposition of the shareholders, who are charged with the task of complementing this legal regime through a set of bylaws with the extensive obligatory content defined in Annex I of the draft statute. If the bylaws really have to comply in detail with all the areas assigned to them by the draft, the shareholders are going to have to take on a massive regulatory task that will perhaps make this company form less attractive, or else pay for expert advice, one of the costs that the proposal is precisely intended to avoid. Then there are difficulties as regards both assessment and monitoring. If, as has already been indicated, the task of monitoring an SPE's registration is left solely in the hands of the registering body (without notarial intervention), it will still as long or even longer to form the company.

These difficulties could be remedied if official model bylaws were available. In fact, those drawing up the draft in the first place did consider creating a number of official models, and the Commission charged the Advisory Group on Corporate Governance and Company Law with developing them. The text has circulated among experts, but the Commission has not officially presented it.

On March 10, 2009, the European Parliament approved the text, but it did so while introducing proposals for modifications that affect essential elements of the draft. The expectation was that the regulation might enter into effect on July 1, 2010. The Council would first have to approve the definitive text, after resolving such decisive issues as the requirement or lack thereof for a minimum capital, the requirement for a transnational element, and the treatment of employee participation in company management, which have been handled differently by the two European institutions. Nevertheless, it does not appear that this expectation will be fulfilled. The proposal presented to the Competitiveness Council by the Swedish Presidency in December 2009 has not achieved the required consensus (Hommelhoff and Teichmann 2010), and the Spanish Presidency has been urged by various interests not to act hastily in adopting a compromise that has generated no enthusiasm among the actors involved.

The final result is not easy to predict, but the level of deregulation presented by the SPE, together with the marked freedom of its shareholders and the possibility of its use by companies without a transnational dimension may pose obstacles to its definitive approval (Hommelhoff 2008, 671). These elements are viewed in some spheres as a threat to the significant heritage of business and legal culture accumulated to this point and to member states' competence to regulate private corporations.

Modernization of Labor Law for Growth and Jobs Based on the Principles of the Flexicurity Strategy

The European "flexicurity" strategy is the implementation of an idea that seeks to reinforce the beneficial interaction for all concerned between increased flexibility of market rules in order to improve business competitiveness and increased security of workers' individual positions in the labor market.

Before being introduced as an EU strategy, the concept was developed on both a theoretical and a practical level in Denmark and the Netherlands. In theory, the idea of flexicurity is defined as "A policy strategy that attempts, synchronically and in a deliberate way, to enhance the flexibility of labour markets, work organization and labour relations on the one hand, and to enhance security—employment security and social security—notably for weaker groups in and outside the labour market, on the other hand" (European Expert Group on Flexicurity 2007, 11).

This policy, theoretically speaking, would be applied on four levels corresponding to four possible content areas in the policy of increased flexibility on the one hand (internal numerical, external numerical, functional, and compensation flexibility) and the policy of security for employees on the other (job, employment, income/social protection, and combined security) (Wilthagen and Tros 2004). From the perspective of the organization of work within firms, the most significant aspects are functional flexibility and flexibility in compensation: geographical and functional mobility, polyvalence and adaptability, training, and anti-crisis measures in connection with salaries and the management of work hours. All these areas are interrelated, however, and have been studied in various combinations by labor sociologists.

Foundations for a European Flexicurity Strategy

This kind of study is significant because of its importance to designing a more efficient and effective labor-market reform policy, with the goal of achieving the objectives laid out by the European Strategy for Growth and Jobs; the implementation of which, in accordance with the EU Foundational Treaties, is the responsibility of each member state (the actors that have the requisite regulatory capabilities) with its national characteristics.

The guiding objective of the flexicurity strategy is to promote and defend a solid balance between social interests and goals, on the one hand, and economic objectives, on the other. This is a characteristic objective of the so-called European social and productive model. As we said at the outset, this objective was inseparable from the Lisbon Strategy for Growth and Jobs and continues to be so in the post-Lisbon era. The road to achieving this is to consider social and employment policies as an integral part of economic policy, the joint application of which is inseparable from the open method of coordination that guided the implementation of the European Employment Strategy until 2010.

This joint and not mutually exclusive consideration of EU social and economic policy thus constitutes a central characteristic of the current European social model, in the opinion of the Commission and of a leading sector of EU thought (Rogowski 2008, 82). Specifically, the Commission's approach to its flexicurity strategy has four components: (1) flexibility of conditions of work through modern labor legislation, collective agreements, and the organization of work; (2) a general strategy of lifelong learning; (3) an effective and active employment policy that helps people to adapt to change, reduces unemployment, and facilitates the transition to new jobs; and (4) the modernization of social security systems so as to provide adequate subsidies to the unemployed while simultaneously providing an incentive to return to work and facilitating mobility within the labor market.

The outbreak of the economic crisis in 2009 has not changed the perspective adopted in the Lisbon Strategy; rather, it has made the implementation of the structural reforms proposed in that strategy more urgent. The *European Economic Recovery Plan* (European Commission 2008d, section 2.3) calls for reforms to be centered on reinforcing internal flexibility, with the aim of forestalling business crises or reacting to them more efficiently. In the Europe 2020 Strategy, implementing flexicurity principles and enabling people to acquire new qualifications and adapt to changes and transitions in the labor market are considered key. Specifically, in the flagship initiative of the "Agenda for New Skills and Jobs," the Commission, together with European social partners, is charged with implementing the second phase of the "Flexicurity Agenda" in order to identify the best ways to manage economic transitions, fight unemployment, and increase activity rates, adapt the legislative framework to the new work modalities, and promote mobility within the EU (European Commission 2010b, 20).

As we can see, despite the context of severe economic crisis in which we find ourselves, European political interest in the flexicurity strategy persists. Its aim is to shape a strategy of smart, sustainable, and inclusive growth toward a new economic model of production that is more politically and socially sustainable, capable of overcoming the crisis's financial costs with greater social cohesion, more active solidarity, and more dialogue and understanding among the protagonists of production in the real economy.

In sum, the objectives of the Lisbon Strategy and the European Employment Strategy for 2010, which included the modernization of labor law and the defense of the European flexicurity strategy, remain essentially intact in the current Europe 2020 Strategy. To that end, the European governance mechanisms for this strategy have been reviewed and improved, at least in theory, by the incorporation of additional tools, a more integrated approach to the structural funds, and a defense of the principles of flexicurity in its original meaning. In other words, this is a strategy focused primordially on reinforcing flexibility at the margins, especially the transition between losing one job and searching for another, as well as balancing work and family life, with or without loss of a job, by affirming security in the labor market, but not in holding onto a job.

Certainly, there are other issues and other possible approaches to the flexicurity strategy that are especially relevant to making the organization of work more productive and more favorable to increasing a firm's competitiveness and even to innovative strategies within a firm. These include functional and salary flexibility, lifelong learning, and active aging, all policies adopted in their case in the context of corporate social responsibility (another, no less important EU strategy). On this topic of functional flexibility within a given enterprise, the Commission merely echoes the Expert Group's report, which confirms that countries that have adopted integrated flexicurity policies are usually those in which dialogue—and above all, trust—among social partners, on the one hand, and between social partners and public authorities, on the other, has played a significant role (European Expert Group on Flexicurity 2007, 5). For the rest, these issues have been basically transferred by the Europe 2020 Strategy to social partners, the European social dialogue, and national or transnational collective bargaining.

At present, the implementation of the flexicurity strategy in the form proposed by the Commission in the Europe 2020 Strategy appears to be oriented more toward exiting the crisis than toward realizing the goal of full employment (which was the slogan of the Lisbon Strategy in its day). More realistically, the chief objective of the flexicurity strategy would now be to find the most effective way to handle the transitions between periods of employment and periods without work over an individual's entire cycle of activity. In the short term, it would be a matter of learning the lessons of this crisis and its effects on jobs. The objective would be to try to anticipate the negative repercussions on a labor market in ongoing transition between old and new formulas of labor relations and between different job opportunities for workers, which do not always guarantee stability in the same position, nor a situation of full employment, especially in times of economic crisis.

In any event, this strategy continues theoretically to also seek to improve the security of individual workers in the market and better protect basic labor rights on the job. In its conception, it is not solely limited to seeking the regulatory framework for the labor market and the organization of production that would be most efficient for business competitiveness, but also seeks to ensure some kind of security for workers. In this regard, one should recall that beyond its economic objectives, the ultimate reason for the Europe 2020 Strategy, together with the *Renewed Social Agenda* (European Commission 2008c), is the human development of European citizens, and by extension, the citizens of the rest of the world (an objective aligned with the UN Development Programme). The effective practice of the social and humanist values inscribed in the EU Charter of Fundamental Rights and the new Treaty on the Functioning of the European Union requires this (Euzéby 2008, 565).

In the form in which this strategy is being proposed in the EU, there is no single pathway for achieving this win-win outcome. Rather, at least in theory, there are as many paths as its member states desire to take, since the flexicurity strategy is to be realized through the specific policies and regulations implemented by each member state.

New Challenges for Implementation

The problem, then, is how the member states are going to implement the European flexicurity strategy so as to continue along the path laid out by the review of the Lisbon Strategy in 2010 (European Commission 2010a) and advance in the direction of inclusive, sustainable, and smart growth, in a context of crisis and protectionism focused on national interests within the member states. Today, throughout Europe, all signs appear to indicate that is not sufficient to concentrate efforts on developing an organizational capacity in European enterprises that is suitable for favoring their competitiveness. Rather, it is necessary to seek out mechanisms that can improve the productivity of the human factor, actions that can mobilize the capabilities and the greater adaptability of the labor force employed, as well as achieve a better management of hours worked and systems of compensation based on real productivity. In addition to this, however, EU foreign policy, in the name of its member states, needs to be capable of winning respect for its social and productive model in the forums of international governance (the WTO, G-20, and so on), first of all, and subsequently in the greatest possible number of economies, through bilateral and multilateral agreements. This is a major challenge that does not presently seem to be within the reach of EU foreign policy, although it will undoubtedly have to be attempted if the aim is the success of European economic policy over the medium and long term. The challenge will be met to the extent that the integration of the EU's social policy finds the same success.

From our perspective, the challenge of globalization requires the EU to move forward boldly, to sign the major international social agreements in that capacity. This would be a significant step forward in the European strategy to achieve greater economic integration and stronger social cohesion among the EU member states. The agenda for the 2010–2011 European Presidencies (Spain, Belgium, and the Netherlands) presented to the European Council on December 7, 2009, addressed the subject of how to facilitate the practical and balanced application of the general principles of flexicurity in the revised Lisbon Strategy (known as the Europe 2020 Strategy). In addition, however, it examined the exterior dimension of the European social model, with the aim of reinforcing this dimension and promoting the Decent Work Agenda of the International Labour Organization (ILO). Likewise, with the new Treaty on the Functioning of the European Union, in effect since December 1, 2009, the Spanish Presidency began the process of EU adhesion to the Council of Europe's Convention for the Protection of Human Rights and Fundamental Freedoms.

All these actions by the European Presidency are indispensable, even if the EU could still move further in the direction of a greater European commitment to the defense of a social model for the era of economic globalization. Along these lines, the defense of the European social model demands EU ratification of the ILO Declaration on Social Justice for a Fair Globalization, adopted at the Ninety-seventh Meeting of the International Labour Conference in 2008. In this way, it could more effectively contribute to promoting a more universal conception of social justice in accordance with the 2008 Declaration, which invites states to apply an integrated approach to their policies, in consonance with the Decent Work Agenda, the four strategic objectives of which are repeated in the 2008 Declaration: job creation, the defense of fundamental rights and principles on the job, social dialogue, and social protection (Moreau 2010, 332). In particular, the Declaration stresses the development of an institutional and economic framework that can ensure the objective of developing each individual's capabilities, businesses' growth and profits, jobs, and society as a whole by pursuing economic development at the same time as social progress.

As indicated in the Lisbon Strategy's 2005 revision, the Integrated Guidelines of the European Employment Strategy, and the Broad Economic Policy Guidelines, the need for the EU to move forward on economic integration is even more evident in the current context. Even if the need to coordinate and supervise tax and budget policies that are part of member states' powers is most often mentioned in this regard, in order to make progress on the desired economic integration—which will only be achieved by improving EU governance—similar progress in the reciprocal integration of the various systems of labor relations in the different member states must also be a priority.

The ILO's above-mentioned 2008 Declaration affirms that the different member states' labor laws and regulations should not be the cause of competitive advantages for European enterprises because of the state in which their company headquarters is located. The flexicurity strategy, then, in addition to having served to define the scope of the European Employment Strategy in what were certainly vague terms, should now represent an ongoing and sustained attempt by the Commission to improve the integration of national labor regulations, through the use of the typical techniques of open methods of coordination, such as best practices and the consequent regulatory alignment.

Following this method, increasing similarity between member states' labor-relations systems will result from a gradual extension of formulas put into practice by those member states that have demonstrated greater comparative success in the context of the objectives pursued by the Europe 2020 Strategy. Definitively speaking, despite all the criticism received, it is a matter of continuing to effectively apply the open method of coordination, since it is at the present time the only means of ensuring, with full respect to the principle of subsidiarity inscribed in the Treaty on the Functioning of the European Union, the preservation of member states' social traditions and regulatory powers. At the same time, these same member states may find themselves launched on a dynamic of social and economic progress coherent with the EU social and economic model.

A positive example of how this open and minimally coercive EU strategy in social affairs can work in practice is the current labor-market reform process now underway in Spain. Within the framework of the four general actions laid out by the European flexicurity strategy, the Spanish government's reform initiative addressed to social and economic partners in a context of social dialogue (Ministerio de Trabajo e Inmigración 2010) on April 12, 2010, *Diálogo Social sobre actuaciones en el mercado de trabajo* [Social Dialogue on Interventions in the Labor Market], proposed to incorporate into the Spanish regulatory framework the German experiment known as *Kurzarbeit*. This is a system of reducing the working day with a corresponding pay decrease, compensated for by unemployment insurance while the situation lasts. Fundamentally, it would be an alternative to mass dismissals of a firm's workers in situations of economic crisis. This measure could be extended to enterprises of all kinds, independent of the number of workers affected (Ministerio de Trabajo e Inmigración 2010, 13).

The possibility of incorporating the reform of dismissal regulations adopted in Austria in 2002 is likewise under study with the aim of assisting enterprises in difficulties, especially SMEs (Ministerio de Trabajo e Inmigración 2010, 4). One Austrian reform created a fund financed by firms themselves, through which they guarantee the legal indemnity to be paid out in the event of dismissal. Each worker has an individual account financed by the firm (in the amount of 1.5 percent of his or her ordinary pay). The account is individual and in the name of the employee, who can take it to a new firm in the event of changing jobs. If, on the other hand, the worker retains his or her ties to a single firm until retirement, the accumulated funds will serve to complement his or her retirement pension.

Also under study is the future of public aid for firms that hire workers, with the aim of making this more effective, to which end it is expected that such aid will be focused on a particular type of enterprise or on enterprises of a particular size, a measure that would also favor SMEs (Ministerio de Trabajo e Inmigración 2010, 12).

Conclusions

As regards EU strategies and initiatives for the future relaunching of its economy and the competitiveness of its businesses in the context of a globalized economy, in this time of economic crisis the EU is continuing to stake its efforts on the two vectors of change in the business world stated in the Lisbon Strategy and formulated in terms of the "Think Small First" principle with regard to business creation and development and in terms of the "flexicurity" strategy for the functioning of labor relations.

In both cases—encouraging SMES and promoting flexicurity—the EU has turned to an original method of governance. From the beginning, the fundamental problem of the Lisbon Strategy was precisely its governance. With the open method of coordination, member states are invited to collaborate on a voluntary basis and to take advantage of the best practices of other countries in order to reform their national policies. In the context of the Lisbon Strategy, this idea did not work sufficiently well in practical terms, most likely because member states were not willing to comply and there the EU did not have the sufficient coercive means to enforce its reform proposals.

Everything indicates that the open method of coordination, the effectiveness of which continues to be debated, will only be successfully implemented if its application is improved and complemented with new techniques, such as more individualized recommendations and more peer reviews, but also the approval of true commercial and labor standards by means of regulations and directives—in other words, also making use of the traditional method of creating European law. Indeed, the EU has even more legitimacy for these traditional regulatory interventions following the institutional reforms introduced by the Treaty on the Functioning of the European Union, especially as a result of the increased and determining role assigned to the European Parliament by the new treaty.

Despite the criticism levied against the use of the open method of coordination, as opposed to the traditional EU method for adopting regulations, it constitutes a necessary and useful resource in areas in which the EU has little or no scope for making legislative decisions, as in the case of labor law.

Yet even in those areas in which the use of the EU method is a possibility, as in the case of company law, success is still not assured. It is equally costly to achieve a level of consensus and move forward on regulatory development on that basis. In practice, it will be difficult to improve European governance with bolder and more integrative steps forward by its political systems in the absence of the firm support of most citizens mobilized in the member states. Regarding our subject, if citizens do not perceive the importance of EU strategies, national governments—which make up the European Council—will not feel impelled to modify their internal policies or to defend more pro-European positions, independent of the method applied at that particular time, be it the open method of coordination or the Community method.

References

Aguilar, María Cristina. 2007. "La aplicación en España de las normas comunitarias sobre la participación de los trabajadores en la Sociedad Anónima Europea y en la Sociedad Cooperativa Europea." *Justicia Laboral* 32: 89–120.

Boquera, Josefina and Nuria Latorre. 2009. "La Sociedad Privada Europea." *Revista de Derecho de Sociedades* 33: 97–128.

Boucourechliev, Jeanne. 1973. *Pour une SARL Europeenne*. Paris. Presses Universitaires de France.

Bücker, Thomas. 2009. "Die Organisationsverfassung der SPE." *ZHR-Zeitschrift für das gesamte Handelsrecht und Wirtschaftsrecht* 173: 281–308.

European Commission. 2001. *European Governance, A White Paper.* COM (2001) 428 Final.

———. 2003. Recommendation, of 6 May 2003, Concerning the Definition of Micro, Small and Medium-sized Enterprises. *Official Journal* L 124: 36–41.

———. 2005. *Communication to the Spring European Council: Working Together for Growth and Jobs; A New Start for the Lisbon Strategy; Communication from President Barroso in Agreement with Vice-President Verheugen.* COM (2005) 24 final.

———. 2006. *Green Paper: Modernising Labour Law to Meet the Challenges of the 21st Century.* COM (2006) 708 final.

———. 2007a. Report of the Expert Group, *Models to Reduce the Disproportionate Regulatory Burden on SMES*, at ec.europa.eu/enterprise/policies/sme/business-environment/administrative-burdens.

———. 2007b. *Communication from the Commission to the European Parliament, the Council, the European Economic and Social Committee and the Committee of the Regions: Towards Common Principles of Flexicurity: More and Better Jobs through Flexibility and Security.* COM(2007) 359 final.

———. 2007c. *Communication from the Commission to the Council, the European Parliament, the European Economic and Social Committee and the Committee of the Regions: Removing Obstacles to Cross-border Investments by Venture Capital Funds.* COM (2007) 853 final.

———. 2008a. *Communication from the Commission to the Council: the European Parliament; the European Economic and Social Committee and the Committee of the Regions; Think Small First; A Small Business Act for Europe.* COM (2008) 394 final.

———. 2008b. *Proposal for a Council Regulation on the Statute for a European Private Company.* COM (2008) 396 final.

———. 2008c. *Communication from the Commission to the European Par-*

liament: the Council, the European Economic and Social Committee and the Committee of the Regions; Renewed Social Agenda; Opportunities, Access and Solidarity in 21st Century Europe. COM (2008) 412 final.

————. 2008d. *Communication from the Commission to the European Council: A European Economic Recovery Plan.* COM (2008) 800 final.

————. 2008e. Regulation (EC) Nº 800/2008 of 6 August 2008 declaring certain categories of aid compatible with the common market in application of Articles 87 and 88 of the Treaty (General block exemption Regulation). *Official Journal of the European Union* L 214: 3–47.

————. 2009a. *Proposal for a Council Directive Amending Directive 2006/112/EC on the Common System of Value Added Tax as Regards the Rules on Invoicing.* COM (2009) 21 final.

————. 2009b. *Proposal for a Directive of the European Parliament and of the Council on Combating Late Payment in Commercial Transactions (Recast) Implementing the Small Business Act.* COM (2009) 126 final.

————. 2009c. *Working Document: Report on the Implementation of the SBA.* COM (2009) 680 final.

————. 2010a. *Commission Staff Working Document Lisbon Strategy Evaluation Document.* SEC (2010) 114 final.

————. 2010b. *Communication from the Commission: Europe 2020; A Strategy for Smart, Sustainable and Inclusive Growth.* COM (2010) 2020.

European Council. 1985. Regulation (EEC) Nº 2137/85 of 25 July 1985 on the European Economic Interest Grouping (EEIG). *Official Journal of the European Union* L 199: 1–9.

————. 1997. Luxembourg European Council, November 1997, Presidency Conclusions. At www.europa.eu/european-council.

————. 2000. Lisbon European Council, 23 and 24 March 2000, Presidency Conclusions.

————. 2001a. Council Regulation (EC) Nº 2157/2001 of 8 October 2001 on the Statute for a European company (*Societas Europaea* or SE). *Official Journal of the European Union* L 294: 1–21.

————. 2001b. Council Directive 2001/86/EC of 8 October 2001 supplementing the Statute for a European company with regard to the involvement of employees. *Official Journal of the European Union* L 294: 22–32.

——. 2003a. Council Regulation (EC) N° 1435/2003 of 22 July 2003 on the Statute for a European Cooperative Society (SCE). *Official Journal of the European Union* L 207: 1–24.

——. 2003b. Council Directive 2003/72/EC of 22 July 2003 supplementing the Statute for a European Cooperative Society with regard to the involvement of employees. *Official Journal of the European Union* L 207: 25–36.

——. 2009. Directive 2009/47/EC, of 5 May 2009, amending Directive 2006/112/EC as regards reduced rates of value added tax. *Official Journal of the European Union* L 116: 18.

European Expert Group on Flexicurity. 2007. *Flexicurity Pathways: Turning Hurdles into Stepping Stones.* At http://ec.europa.eu/social.

Euzéby, Alain. 2008. "Le développement humain, une référence majeure pour la Stratégie de Lisbonne." *Revue du Marche Commun et de l'Union Européenne* 522: 565–71.

Hommelhoff, Peter. 2008. "Bruchstellen im Kommissionsentwurf für eine SPE-Verordnung." In *Festschrift für Karsten Schmidt zum 70 Geburtstag das gesamte Handelsrecht und Wirtschaftsrecht,* edited by Georg Bitter, Marcus Lutter, Hans-Joachim Priester, Wolfgang Schön, Pand Peter Ulmer. Köln: Otto Schmidt.

Hommelhoff, Peter and Christoph Teichmann. 2008. "Eine GmbH für Europa: Der Vorschlag der EU-Kommission zur Societas Privata Europaea (SPE)." *GmbH Rundschau* 17: 897–911.

——. 2010. "Die SPE vor dem Gipfelsturm: Zum Kompromissvorschlag der schwedischen EU-Ratspräsidentschaft." *GmbH Rundschau* 7: 337–48.

Ministerio de Trabajo e Inmigración. 2010. *Documento de Trabajo: Diálogo Social sobre actuaciones en el mercado de trabajo.* At www.lamoncloa.es.

Moreau, Marie-Ange. 2010. "Autour de la justice social: perspectives Internationales et communautaires." *Droit Social* 3: 324–33.

Otxoa-Errarte, Rosa. 2010. *La responsabilidad de los socios por la infracapitalización de su sociedad.* Cizur Menor: Thomson-Aranzadi.

Pastor, Carmen. 2009. "La sociedad cooperativa europea domiciliada en España." *Revista de Estudios Cooperativos* 97: 117–44.

Paz-Ares, Cándido. 2006. "Uniones de empresas y grupos de sociedades."

In *Curso de Derecho Mercantil I*, edited by Rodrigo Uría et al. Cizur Menor: Aranzadi.

Rogowski, Ralf. 2008. "Governance of the European Social Model: The Case of Flexicurity." *Intereconomics-Review of European Economic Policy* 43, no. 2: 82–91.

Teichmann, Christoph and Peter Limmer. 2009. "Die Societas Privata Europaea (SPE) aus notarieller Sicht: eine Zwischenbilanz nach dem Votum des Europäischen Parlaments." *GmbH Rundschau* 10: 537–40.

Viera, A. Jorge. 2008. "La Sociedad Privada Europea: Una alternativa a la Sociedad de Responsabilidad Limitada." *Revista de Derecho Mercantil* 270: 1331–92.

Wilthagen, Ton and Frank Tros. 2004. "The Concept of Flexicurity: A New Approach to Regulate Employment and Labour Markets." *Transfer: European Review of Labour and Research* 10, no. 2: 166–86.

Zeitlin, Jonathan. 2005. "The Open Method of Coordination in Action: Theoretical Promise, Empirical Realities, Reform Strategy." In *The Open Method of Coordination in Action: The European Employment and Social Inclusion Strategies*, edited by Jonathan Zeitlin, Philippe Pochet, and Lars Magnusson. Brussels: P.I.E.-Peter Lang.

3

Company Stakeholder Responsibility (CSR)

Jose Luis Retolaza, Leire San-Jose, and Andrés Araujo
de la Mata

Translated by Lauren DeAre

The objective of this chapter is not purely theoretical; it is intended to contribute toward creating a culture and values where employee participation in corporate governance[1] is a necessity. In the new economy, new values and forms of organization are emerging, such as the shift in importance of fixed to intangible assets; from a more or less decentralized pyramidal structure to that of a network; and from ownership of the means of production to outsourcing. And yet, with respect to participation in corporate governance, the theory of ownership rights continues to be used, confining participation to the operational level.

In recent decades, influential theories have emerged that, while not disputing the right of ownership, equate it with the rights of other groups

---

* This chapter provides a more extensive analysis of company participation. It also includes anthropological, sociological, and neo-Marxist perspectives and was financed by the Department of Social Economy of the Basque Government. A previous version of this chapter received the FESIDE (Emilio Soldevilla Foundation for Research and Development of Business Economics) Award for Best Methodology (European Academy of Management and Business Economics [AEDEM] 2009 Annual Conference; Seville, Spain) and was published in the journal *Universitas Psychologica*.

1. Defining this concept has become more problematic since its process, nature, or method was developed. There are at least six different interpretations of governance (see Rhodes 2005), among which is corporate governance, and it is in this sense that the term is used in this chapter.

that participate in a company. This new perspective has come to be called a "normative revolution" (Donaldson 2008), and it revolutionizes not only the social character of a company but also the way that relationships between its components are understood and, in particular, what the very concept of participation means.

The objective of this chapter is to analyze the importance of stakeholder participation in the corporate governance framework by examining corporate governance theories (Clarke 2005) with specific reference to stakeholder theory (Freeman 1984), multifiduciary theory (Boatright 2002), and corporate citizenship theory (Néron and Norman 2008a, 2008b). Specifically, we propose breaking away from the assumption that corporate governance is intrinsically tied to ownership or capital shareholding (Ayuso and Argandoña 2007). In general, corporate governance refers to the system by which corporations are directed and controlled. It specifies the distribution of rights and responsibilities among shareholders and executives, as well as the regulations and procedures used for corporate decision-making. However, in a broader sense, corporate governance also includes relationships with a wider range of company stakeholders, both internal (employees) and external (customers, suppliers, and so on). Along these lines, Jean Tirole (2001) proposes defining corporate governance as a corporate design that induces or forces management to internalize stakeholder well-being. This idea departs from the classic definition based on the theory of the firm (Alchian and Demsetz 1972) and on the fringe benefits associated with investment risk. Concurrently, we should point out that the argument for stakeholder participation is also a departure from two other conceptions: one taken from Marxism wherein capital gain is solely linked to work, and the other from certain conceptions of the social economy wherein employee ownership of the means of production is considered the distinguishing element.

Throughout this chapter, we argue for the need to promote an evolution of the nature of participation. It must move toward increasingly institutional and larger-scale implementation consistent with stakeholder theory, which proposes this participation as a necessary condition and a natural consequence of the conception of the company as a network of relationships. Likewise, it expands upon management theories that encompass a participatory model and, conversely, the competency demands that participation requires, including teamwork; vision; analytical, communication, and negotiation skills; and a proactive attitude as well as a shared culture.

Participation in Corporate Governance Based on Ownership Theory

Employee participation in a company is a recurring theme in HR management (Navarro 2007), and its fundamentals can be approached from both normative and instrumental perspectives. This chapter is based on corporate social responsibility (CSR) and, more specifically, on stakeholder theory as proposed by Freeman (1984) and subsequently developed by many other authors (Agle et al. 2008).

Stakeholder theory, to a certain degree, "opposes" the shareholder theory (Freeman, Harrison, and Wicks 2008) that, to our understanding, is nothing more than a reformulation of the theory of ownership rights, which proposes that a company's fundamental responsibility is to its owners. On the other hand, the cooperative approach, although from the radically opposing notion of empowering workers over capital, accepts the premises of ownership theory by considering that it is the employees' ownership of the means of production, and therefore, the company, that makes it possible for the capital gains generated to be redistributed among them.

The fundamental principle of the theory of ownership can be defined as follows: ownership of the company (understood as ownership in terms of the organization's capital) generates, at the least, two exclusive rights: the right to obtain the benefit generated by the company's activity and the right to decide. The first right comes from the identification between the company and capital, meaning whoever holds the capital owns the company and, therefore, has exclusive rights over the company's results. The second is derived from the first by way of risk factor and can be described in a logical syllogism wherein $A \wedge B \rightarrow C$: given that shareholders receive a variable benefit according to the company's results and these results are affected by the management of the company. Shareholders have the right to make decisions in the company, which affects corporate governance. The remaining participants in the company—employees, suppliers, customers, and others—will receive a benefit or contracted compensation according to contractual theory (Coase 1937; Williamson 2002).

The so-called shareholder theory approach, generally attributed to Milton Friedman (1962), is based on this dual approach to the theory of ownership rights and contractual theory. Company decisions are made by its owners; therefore, it is assumed that only shareholders are at risk in the formation of the company, and it is their responsibility to make decisions because corporate governance should be linked to assumption of risk. However, in corporations, owners do not manage the company directly but rather through directors who are given the right to manage (agency theory) (Jensen and Meckling 1976). This means that the directors, named agents, actually manage the company in representation of the owners, named principals; from which we can assume that the responsibility of the agents is to optimize the interests of the principals, although sometimes and illegally, they may put their own interests first. The agency theory is of particular interest because it is at the root of any theory or approach related to participation.

One should make special mention of the social economy, wherein participation is an abiding value to the concept itself. However, upon further examination, we find ourselves with two very different rights of action, which are even in conflict with the phenomenon itself. One might be termed the legal perspective because it is tied to the legal status of the company, and the other the ideological perspective because it is linked to the values of the cooperative movement, updated to present reality.

In regards to the legal perspective, it is rooted in ownership rights theory because it assumes that what gives rights to participation in the directive bodies and benefits is holding an ownership share in the company, and therefore, employee participation requires their incorporation as shareholders. This idea, far from proposing an alternative to the shareholder theory, accepts it, transforming employees into stakeholders. Consequently, it does not resolve the participation of those employees who are not part of the ownership and all other participants in the company who are not directly tied through ownership shares. The origin of this problem lies in the implicit continued existence of the outdated Marxist concept of "ownership of the means of production."

For its part, the ideological perspective has been fundamentally focused on social value over economic participation, although the values stated by the International Co-operative Alliance (ICA)[2] are very ambiguous: voluntary and open membership; democratic member control; member economic participation; autonomy and independence; education, training and information; cooperation among cooperatives; and concern for community. Among the aforementioned, the idea that participation is reserved solely for members would seem to have been discarded, which

---

2. See www.ica.coop/al-ica/.

is nevertheless inconsistent with the inclusion of the third sector in the social economy.

Potentially, the third sector includes more than any other the aspirations of justice and creation of social value that gave life to the cooperative movement at its foundation. However, in almost all of its manifestations, member economic participation in the traditional sense does not exist, and there is even a disconnection between the role of member and employee. And in our field of concern, potential participation or lack thereof is not justified in any case by capital ownership. Foundations are the exception, and agency theory could possibly be applied in a representative manner so that the owner of founding capital decides who will be the trustees, and therefore, the principals of the organization.

Participation in Corporate Governance Based on Stakeholder Theory

Stakeholder theory, from our point of view, assumes an evolution from a company-centered perspective. Looking back just a few decades, various approaches have been developed that have integrated prior theories, and although we possibly still do not have enough perspective to know exactly where the evolutionary track of these theories will lead, in figure 3.1 we propose a method for representing the evolution of different strategic focuses toward a focus on stakeholders.

Figure 3.1. Evolution of strategic approaches in companies

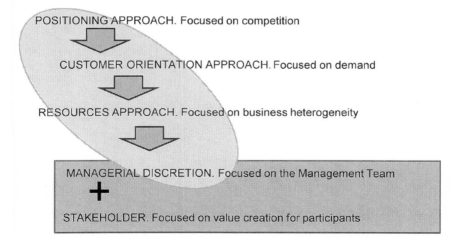

Although Michael E. Porter's five forces theory (1985) highlights the competitiveness of a company, almost in parallel, a customer-oriented focus (Kotler 1988; Narver and Slater 1990) emphasizes the role that customers' needs should have in the company strategy and how the company's goals should be to generate value for customers. Subsequently, the resources and capabilities theory (Wernerfelt 1984) refocuses the centrality toward the company's idiosyncratic resources that could become a sustainable competitive advantage over time. And more recently, in the managerial discretion (upper-echelons) theory (Hambrick and Mason 1984), the center of attention becomes the role that company management plays in the organization of resources within its competitive context in order to increase the value generated for customers. All of these ideas emphasize diverse interest groups within the company: competition, customers, resources (with many of them understood to be intangibles linked to personnel), and management. The logical evolution of this theory has brought about stakeholder theory, which emphasizes the importance of all interest groups, and, in addition to those already mentioned adds suppliers, the government, and society in general.

Building on Friedman's concept of corporate social responsibility (1962), instrumental concern for groups in the company other than shareholders has become standard; but not until the appearance of the stakeholder theory (Freeman 1984) did the company's responsibility to all of the interest groups make a normative perspective possible. The current concept of social responsibility in business (Carroll 1999) is presented as a continuum that goes from concern about special interest groups at its most instrumental application to, at its most radical, concern even for non-stakeholders, becoming a commitment to interest groups. Both extremes are normative in nature. From this perspective, the company is just the result of the relationship between all of these groups over time.

Stakeholder theory opposes Friedman's shareholder theory (1962), with one becoming the antithesis of the other in what could be called the "Friedman-Freeman debate" (Freeman, Harrison, and Wicks 2008). Part of Friedman's argument has come to include the idea that a company is affected by different interest groups, including employees, suppliers, customers, administration, or pressure groups; and in order to continue to maintain medium and long-term benefits for the company, the interests of these groups must be satisfied in some way. However, the directors' responsibility, ultimately, is to generate benefits for shareholders, and satisfying other interests is just a means or an instrument to improve or maintain those benefits over time. This approach, which serves as an introduction to the concept of social responsibility, is fundamentally focused on pressure groups or those that can affect the results of the company with their actions. In this sense, we find ourselves faced with an instrumental argument regarding the concept of social responsibility, wherein its justification is not in its ethical or ontological character but its utilitarian application. Social responsibility is necessary because it can improve benefits in the medium and long term and therefore benefit owners. In this sense, social responsibility must be understood more as an aspect of business marketing.

In contrast, the normative approach to business social responsibility includes all interest groups as constituents and inherent to the company. The company's and therefore its management team's objective (agency theory) is to satisfy all of their interests in the best way possible. Because these interests differ and in some cases conflict with one another, the company management must try to satisfy them in a balanced manner without prioritizing one group continuously over time. Thus, while in the instrumental perspective the final interest is directed toward shareholders, in the normative it is directed at all participants. This is based on a modification of two proposals, one on the importance of capital and the other on the importance of the assumption of risk.

Shareholder theory accepts that the only absolutely necessary element in the constitution of a company is monetary capital and that the other value-creating elements are acquired through transactions explicable by contractual theory. In this new approach, other assets—including intellectual capital, workforce competences, customer or supplier trust, administrative or societal support—are considered as important as monetary capital. Second, whereas in shareholder theory, shareholders are the only ones considered to take on risk, in stakeholder theory, which comes closer to reality, all participants, more or less, take on risk. Employees assume the risk of dismissal, or opportunity cost; suppliers risk default; customers risk the non-performance of guarantees or delivery times; administration and society, in turn, assume an ecological risk or the risk of bail out. Therefore, neither assets nor risk belong exclusively to shareholders but to the participants as a whole, and a company should not act only for shareholders but for all who invest and assume risks so that the company may exist and so that benefit creation is possible. Consistent with this, the company's objective and therefore the directors' responsibility is not maximizing benefit but satisfying the interests of the various participants.

Nevertheless, stakeholder theory is itself contested and involves a spectrum of opinion ranging from rational self-interest to altruistic interpretations,[3] fundamentally based on what is understood as an interest group. Thus, we can find three ways of defining interest groups:

1. Based on a restricted interpretation, they would include pressure groups, or those that can perform organized actions that affect the company.

2. Based on an intermediary interpretation, they would include those that invest and assume risks in the company and, by action or omission, can develop coordinated or individual activities, planned or spontaneous, that will affect the company.

3. Based on a broad interpretation, they would, in addition to those mentioned above, also include affected groups, or those that are actively influenced by the company's actions, independent of whether they can or cannot, in turn, affect the company.

Within the limits of stakeholder theory, it is also important to discuss non-stakeholders, which are understood as those who are passively affected by the company or by companies in a sector as a whole, but they are unable to exercise any activities that place pressure on or can influence the company (Néron and Norman, 2008a).

The Theoretical Foundation of Stakeholder Participation in Corporate Governance

The theoretical foundation of stakeholder participation in corporate governance can be explained by three theories: stakeholder theory, multifiduciary theory, and corporate citizenship theory.

Stakeholder theory and a company's responsibility seem to demand that the right and necessity of stakeholder participation in the company's development be considered and that it is not perceived as just a network of relationships between different groups of participants, risking adhering

---

3. The altruistic extreme that we refer to, which is located on the maximum commitment end of the spectrum, should not be confused with philanthropy, which, according to Néron and Norman (2008), would be found in the minimalist model (the end with least social commitment) of the classification proposed by Matten and Crane (2005).

to the enlightened absolutism saying *tout pour le peuple, rien par le peuple* [all for the people, and nothing by them]. Based on this theory (Freeman, Harrison, and Wicks 2008), the company is seen as a combination of relationships whose objective is the maximization of value for the stakeholders as a group (this argument is explained in the previous section).

Multifiduciary theory, proposed by John R. Boatright (2002, 2008), is based on contractual theory, and, more specifically, on agency theory, granting the category of principal not only to shareholders but to the stakeholders as a group, generating an obligation for the agent to create value for all of them. One could say that Boatright's multifiduciary theory (2008) came about as a solution to the Goodpaster paradox (1991), in which the author argues that, based on agency theory, directors or agents are not just trustees for the principals, meaning the shareholders. It goes on to explain that because an agent's rights are granted in the transfer of rights by owners, an agent is not authorized to make any decision that the principal would not take, or which the principal would feel was not in his or her best interest. This is especially important because the stakeholder theory contends that management be responsible for balancing satisfaction of the group of stakeholders' interests and for resolving conflicts of interest that may arise between them. The outcome would be that the agent would be likely to give more to other stakeholder groups than what the principal would most likely grant, which would violate the fiduciary principle, creating an ethical and legal problem.

Faced with this problem, multifiduciary theory emerges with a solution framed within agency theory. Its primary contribution is taking into consideration not just shareholders but all groups of stakeholders in the company as principals; therefore, the agent must respond to these legitimate interest groups as a whole and not just the shareholders, and the agent must become a facilitator for the interests of each and every one of them.

Michael C. Jensen (2002, 2008), meanwhile, argues that the multifiduciary theory is incompatible with corporate governance, due to the existence of a group of principals with divergent and opposing interests. Agents become arbitrators for satisfying interests, and there is no means of controlling them because they do not have to defend their actions before any governing group. In practice, agents in fact become principals, although not legally, and agents' actions become uncontrollable. Boatright's response (2002) is based on the consideration that control of the agent by the principal is, in most cases, fictitious and that in reality, the agent actually acts as a trustee for the principal only in terms of the agent's ethical responsibility. Consequently, this same responsibility must be placed on the agent before a heterogeneous group of principals. In our opinion, the problem of control is not associated as much with a conflict of interest between different stakeholders as with dispersion of power among principals. Conflicts of interest are the same between the shareholders themselves and, in the event that majorities do not exist or ownership shares are very scattered, this power truly lies with the CEO (Chief Executive Officer) of the corporation. Apart from the quantitative factor of increase and dispersion of interested parties, the multifiduciary theory introduces a new qualitative factor: the non-existence of legal structuring for the participation of the remaining stakeholders.

The third approach that we are going to analyze is the idea of corporate citizenship. While this theory does accept several interpretations—minimalist, equitable and extended—we are going to examine it from the latter, following James E. Post and Shawn L. Berman (2001, 28), who state that "corporate citizenship is the process of identifying, analyzing and responding to the company's social, political and economic responsibilities as defined through law and public policy, stakeholder's expectations, and voluntary acts flowing from corporate values and business strategies. Corporate citizenship involves actual results (what corporations do) and the process through which they are achieved (how they do it)."

Pierre-Yves Néron and Wayne Norman (2008b) persuasively scrutinize the concept of corporate citizenship and potentially resolve one of the primary problems left by corporate social responsibility and the stakeholder theory: the company's ethical responsibility to non-stakeholders.

Fundamentally, stakeholders are understood as an assembly of groups that have a legitimate interest in a firm, but there are very different interpretations of "legitimate interest." In a restrictive (instrumental) definition, they are understood to be those groups that could affect the company; while in a broader (normative) definition, they could also include all "groups who can affect or [are] affected by the achievement of the firm's objectives" (Freeman 1984, 25). However, even in the broadest definition, it seems that the firm is only responsible to those groups who are affected by its actions. In fact, when stakeholder groups are identified (Freeman, Harrison, and Wicks 2008)—customers, suppliers, employees, funders, community, government, competitors, consumer and environmental groups, special interest groups, and the media—it seems that the people that are not directly affected by the company just have to fit into

the interest group categories attributed to the community or special interest groups.

We find the antithesis of the stakeholder concept in the idea of non-stakeholders, meaning those groups or people who have no legitimate interest in the operation of the company because they are unable to affect it or be affected by it. However, the significance of the term "affected" is also extremely complex, as we can see in the following example: When a company plans to move from one location to another, those affected would include the current employees who could lose their jobs but also the potential employees for the new plant who could then obtain those jobs. Here lies a normal problem of conflict between stakeholders, or at the least, between current and potential stakeholders. However, one might also question whether or not employees on strike in other geographical areas that the company is neither leaving nor moving to are also stakeholders. On a theoretical level, one could consider those affected as another group of stakeholders by default, but this would broaden stakeholder groups so much that managing their interests would be utterly impossible for the company. Therefore, there are non-stakeholders, groups of people affected entirely by default, whose interests—based on corporate social responsibility that has its foundations in stakeholder theory—cannot be the responsibility of specific companies.

In order to better understand the problem, let us further examine financial exclusion. That a certain person would be financially excluded is not the responsibility of any specific financial entity, since this person does not belong to any stakeholder group for any entity. However, the problem of financial exclusion is a real problem that affects many citizens and merits a solution. Who should provide the answer? Companies? Or the government, in the form of subsidies?

The idea of corporate citizenship could resolve the problem of non-stakeholders because it emphasizes interdependence between the company and the community where it operates (Néron and Norman 2008a). From this perspective, the company's responsibility goes beyond its legal obligations because it has a commitment to develop the society in which it participates. The community also appears as a stakeholder in stakeholder theory, but only in a very limited form, primarily as a geographically close local community and perhaps, in a slightly broader sense, as a "community of interest" or "virtual community" (Freeman, Harrison, and Wicks 2008).

At this point, Néron and Norman (2008a) contribute to resolving a major fundamental problem. Nevertheless, when facing global problems, a question about the limitations of the concept of citizenship arises. Richard T. De George (2008) refers to this problem but from a different perspective, arguing that good citizenship has a strong cultural component and therefore differs from one country to another. For us, the problem is different; it is the limitation of citizen responsibility to the country where one is a citizen. Clearly, citizenship is a duty and a right that is tied to a specific country and the same is true of companies. If so, their commitments would be exclusively to the country where the company is located. We assume that the potentially opposing interests of the different countries where a company may do business could be resolved as legitimate conflicts of interest between stakeholders. Yet "corporate citizenship" would not have responsibility over those non-stakeholders in countries outside the company's interests, with the very concept of citizenship limiting its responsibility territorially.

These three arguments are not without problems. Concerning stakeholder theory, the Goodpaster paradox (1991) is well known, and Boatright has attempted to provide an answer. His answer, however, does not resolve the corporate governance problem raised by Jensen (2002, 2008) regarding the idea of multifiduciary agents with interests that are both different and antagonistic: the agent becomes both judge and jury, making control by the principal impossible. It criticizes what Boatright protests as the illusion of a sense of control in classic agency theory. Meanwhile, Nerón and Norman's argument draws diverse criticisms as well, from it being a metaphorical interpretation (Wood and Logsdon 2008) to the variability of the concept of "good citizenship" according to cultures in different countries (De George 2008), to the identification of only corporate philanthropy in their minimalist view (Saiia 2001), which leads to the limitations that the concept of citizenship places on a globalized world, and to which we have already referred.

Despite these criticisms, the three theories offer very interesting viewpoints in regards to the participation of stakeholders as a group in company management, and they are consistent with the theoretical conceptions that are accepted as standard in a capitalist economy as a whole. Thus, the multifiduciary theory brings a solid foundation for the right of participation, based on contractual and agency theories, pillars of the current economic system. Further, R. Edward Freeman, Jeffrey S. Harrison, and Andrew C. Wicks (2008), by labeling it stakeholder capitalism, make

"Managing for Stakeholders" as an intermediary between capitalism and the social economy. In addition, Freeman provides a foundation, a methodological theory for developing management based on the stakeholder group, and therefore for participation of those stakeholders in all areas of the company. Finally, the conception of "corporate citizenship" justifies the legitimate interest of non-stakeholders, and therefore their potential (direct or representative) inclusion in corporate governing bodies.

Participation Mechanisms

After demonstrating the need for participation by the stakeholder groups in corporate governance based on stakeholder theory and two of its subsequent theories (multifiduciary theory and corporate citizenship theory), we now propose ideas on the keys to stakeholder participation.

More precisely, and following Freeman, Harrison, and Wicks (2008, 60), we consider there to be ten guiding principles for managing for stakeholders.

1. Stakeholder interests need to go together over time.
2. Solutions must be found that satisfy multiple stakeholders simultaneously.
3. Never trade off the interests of one party over others continuously over time.
4. Action should be taken with the goal of satisfying the expectations of all stakeholders.
5. Stakeholders should not be allowed to participate in the corporate government.
6. Continuous interaction and dialogue with all stakeholders is necessary.
7. Stakeholders are real people with names and faces.
8. A general marketing approach is necessary.
9. Attention must be given to both primary and secondary stakeholders.
10. Processes must be constantly monitored and redesigned to make them better serve stakeholders.

Of these ten principles, the fifth is radically different from the others. In the other nine, it is the agent who should be concerned about the stakeholders, yet in the fifth principle, the idea of incorporating stakeholders in the corporate government beginning at the company's incorporation—possibly as principals—changes the nature of their participation.

There are multiple ways of participating in a company, principal among which are: shareholder meetings, generally linked to ownership rights; the board of directors, based on the concept of representation and trust, which has typically been linked to the concept of ownership but with the possibility of redirecting it based on the multifiduciary theory; the executive team, traditionally considered an agent (agency theory), but with the potential for including representatives for other stakeholders; management teams, which make natural participation possible through various methodological proposals from employees; improvement teams, which facilitate incorporating the interests of a larger number of stakeholders in the company strategy; and, lastly, the systematic individual, through informal and non-standardized channels for gathering and managing information. However, these mechanisms do not grant equal amounts of power to the participants. Therefore, the participation of systematic individuals or improvement teams could simply refer to more participatory management by HR; while participation in the board of directors introduces stakeholders to the "heart" of business decision-making.

No matter which participatory option is chosen, it seems that any possibility for stakeholder groups managing is based on the potential of identifying the interests of these stakeholders, and here there are major methodological limitations. The most common approaches—including Michel Godet's MACTOR methodology (2006), that of Freeman, Harrison, and Wicks (2008), or that of Jose Luis Retolaza, Maite Ruiz, and Leire San-Jose (2009)—propose a deductive view, and identifying specific stakeholder interests tends toward a quasi-infinite regression; or at the least, it is too broad to be incorporated as an aspect of management. Another major limitation comes from using traditional logic wherein all people who make up an interest group share the same level of interest in that group. In reality, this is not achieved because membership in an interest group is far from a dichotomy (yes/no–0/1), but instead works on a continuum between 0 and 1, with varied levels of interest intensity.

The goal in this field is to develop new methodologies that might bring together the inductive perspective and a more "blurred" conception of interest groups. This would allow agents to identify and systematize various interests in order to optimize their satisfaction.

Ethical Leadership

As stated in our analysis of the various theories, in one way or another, all of them refer to a predominant role of the agent in management, the difficulty for principals to control them, and consequently, the importance of the manager's responsibility to satisfy participants' interests. This is especially prevalent in the multifiduciary theory (Boatright 2002), and moreover, this problem provides even more basis for stakeholder participation in corporate governance and is consistent with agency theory and contractual theory. In this context, the concept of ethical leadership (Werhane 1999) becomes even more relevant because it would be difficult for any other type of leadership to manage, without strict control, in a way that would benefit the stakeholders instead of to their own benefit.

Without expanding into the topic of leadership, which would require extensive further analysis, we will now discuss the six principles formulated by Freeman, Harrison, and Wicks (2008), and Carlos María Moreno's seven Cs of leadership (2004), because we consider them to be integral to stakeholder participation at the highest levels of corporate governance. Without these principles to support ethical leadership, Jensen's problem of non-governance (2002, 2008) would possibly become an endemic problem in a multifiduciary agency relationship.

The six principles of ethical leadership (Freeman, Harrison, and Wicks 2008) are as follows:

1. Leader principle: The leader is a member of the organization and the group of stakeholders and the leader's actions must benefit the stakeholders as a whole.

2. Participants principle: The leader does not view the participants as separate entities but as a whole and attempts to develop a whole-team culture (Gutierrez 2006).

3. Results principle: The organization's objectives must be connected to individual participants' interests.

4. Process principle: Work must be done in an open manner, integrating participants' points of view, values, and opinions.

5. Context principle: Leadership must be based on ethical principles but should be flexible in complex decisions.

6. Ethical principle: Actions and proposals must be debated in ethical terms.

The six principles indicated here complement Moreno's seven Cs of ethical leadership (2001, 2004): Character, willpower and habits; Courage to know when to say no; Credibility: consistency, consequence, and confidence; Communication: clear and concise; Cognition: competence and capability; Compromise: work and organization; and Comprehension.

Conclusions

Employee participation in a company has been a recurring topic for a long time and is based on several theories. Currently, stakeholder theory provides the basis for the participation of both employees and all others who participate in a company. While there have been some problems and paradoxes with this theory, the solutions it provides place it among the most powerful theories today concerning corporate governance.

Right now the greatest problem lies in finding the mechanisms that might facilitate such participation. Existing legal, social, and management challenges make true integration of stakeholders into a company's effective management difficult, and as a result, practical actions have mostly been centered on the role of ethical leadership that agents should take. However, although this is relevant and necessary, it should not hide the need for changes in corporate governance that would give stakeholders legal access to this level of management.

The current challenge and the most pressing research areas involve the task of defining and comparing models of participatory corporate governance that could be legally sustained or that could identify necessary legislative amendments.

References

Alchian, Armen A., and Harold Demsetz. 1972. "Production, Information Cost and Economic Organization." *American Economic Review* 62, no. 5: 777–95.

Ayuso, Silvia, and Antonio Argandoña. 2007. "Responsible Corporate Governance: Towards a Stakeholder Board of Directors?" *IESE Business School Working Paper* 701: 1–18.

Agle, Bradley R., Thomas Donaldson, R. Edward Freeman, Michael C. Jensen, Ronald K. Mitchell, and Donna J. Wood. 2008. "Dialogue: Toward Superior Stakeholder Theory." *Business Ethics Quarterly* 18, no. 12: 153–90.

Boatright, John R. 2002. "Contractors as Stakeholders: Reconciling Stakeholders Theory with the Nexus-of Contracts Firm." *Journal of Banking and Finances* 26, no. 9: 1837–52.

———. 2008. *Ethics In Finance*. 2nd ed. Malden: Blackwell.

Carroll, Archie B. 1999. "Corporate Social Responsibility: Evolution of a Definitional Construct." *Business and Society* 38, no. 3: 268–95.

Clarke, Thomas, ed. 2005. *Theories of Corporate Governance: The Philosophical Foundations of Corporate Governance*. London: Routledge.

Coase, Ronald H. 1937. "The Nature of the Firm." *Economica* 4, no. 6: 386–405.

De George, Richard T. 2008. "Reflections on Citizenship, Inc." *Business Ethics Quarterly* 18, no. 1: 43–50.

Donaldson, Thomas. 2008. "Two Stories." In Bradley R. Agle, Thomas Donaldson, R. Edward Freeman, Michael C. Jensen, Ronald K. Mitchell, and Donna J. Wood. 2008. "Dialogue: Toward Superior Stakeholder Theory." *Business Ethics Quarterly* 18, no. 12: 172–76 (153–90).

Freeman, R. Edward. 1984. *Strategic Management: A Stakeholder Approach*. Boston: Pitman.

Freeman, R. Edward, Jeffrey S. Harrison, and Andrew C. Wicks. 2008. *Managing for Stakeholders: Survival, Reputation, and Success*. New Haven: Yale University Press.

Friedman, Milton. 1962. *Capitalism and Freedom*. Chicago: University of Chicago Press.

Goodpaster, Kenneth E. 1991. "Business Ethic and Stakeholder Analysis." *Business Ethics Quarterly* 1, no. 1: 53–73.

Godet, Michel. 2006. *Creating Futures: Scenario Planning as a Strategic Management Tool*. Paris: Economica.

Gutierrez, Eduardo. 2006. "Cultura, organizaciones e intervención." *Universitas Psychologica* 6, no. 1: 115–29.

Hambrick, Donald C., and Phyllis A. Mason. 1984. "Upper Echelons: The Organization as a Reflection of its Top Managers." *Academy of Management Review* 9, no. 2: 193–206.

Jensen, Michael C. 2002. "Value Maximization, Stakeholder Theory, and the Corporate Objective Function." *Business Ethics Quarterly* 12, no. 3: 235–56.

———. 2008. "Non-Rational Behaviour, Value Conflicts, Stakeholder

Theory, and Firm Behaviour." *Business Ethics Quarterly* 18, no. 2: 167–71.

Jensen, Michael C., and William H. Meckling. 1976. "Theory of the Firm: Managerial Behavior, Agency Costs and Ownership Structure." *Journal of Financial Economics* 3, no. 4: 305–60.

Kotler, Philip. 1988. *Marketing Management: Analysis, Planning, Implementation, and Control.* Englewood Cliffs, NJ: Prentice Hall.

Matten, Dirk, and Andrew Crane. 2005. "Corporate Citizenship: Toward Extended Theoretical Conceptualization." *Academy of Management Review* 30, no. 1: 166–79.

Moreno, Carlos María. 2001. "El liderazgo ético fundamentado en virtudes." *Papeles de Economía, Ética y Dirección* 6: 1–8.

———. 2004. "Las 7 C del liderazgo ético." *Capital Humano* 183: 84–89.

Navarro, Juan Antonio. 2007. "Críticas y apoyos hacia la responsabilidad social de la empresa: una aproximación etnográfica desde la vivencia del trabajador y una propuesta metodológica cualitativa." *Universitas Psychologica* 6, no. 1: 59–68.

Narver, John C., and Stanley F. Slater. 1990. "The Effect of Marketing Orientation on Business Profitability." *Journal of Marketing* 54, no. 4: 20–35.

Néron, Pierre-Yves, and Wayne Norman. 2008a. "Citizenship, Inc.: Do We Really Want Businesses to Be Good Corporate Citizens?" *Business Ethics Quarterly* 18, no. 1: 1–26.

———. 2008b. "Corporations as Citizens Political not Metaphorical." *Business Ethics Quarterly* 18, no. 1: 61–66.

Porter, Michael E. 1985. *Competitive Advantage: Creating and Sustaining Superior Performance.* New York: Free Press.

Post, James E., and Shawn L. Berman. 2001. "Global Corporate Citizenship in a Dot.com World: The Role of Organisational Identity." In *Perspectives on Corporate Citizenship*, edited by Jörg Andriof and Malcolm McIntosh. Sheffield: Greenleaf Publishing.

Retolaza, Jose Luis, Maite Ruiz, and Leire San-Jose. 2009. "CSR in Business Start-ups: An Application Method for Stakeholder Engagement." *Corporate Social Responsibility and Environmental Management* 16, no. 6: 324–36.

Rhodes, Rod A.W. 2005. "La nueva gobernanza: gobernar sin gobierno."

In *La gobernanza hoy: 10 textos de referencia*, edited by Agustí Cerrillo. Madrid: Instituto Nacional de Administración Públicas.

Saiia, David H. 2001. "Philanthropy and Corporate Citizenship: Strategic Philanthropy is Good Corporate Citizenship." *Journal of Corporate Citizenship* 2: 57–74.

Tirole, Jean. 2001. "Corporate governance." *Econometrica* 69, no. 1: 1–35.

Werhane, Patricia H. 1999. *Moral Imagination and Management Decision Making*. Oxford: Oxford University Press.

Wernerfelt, Birger. 1984. "A Resource-based View of the Firm." *Strategic Management Journal* 5, no. 2: 171–80.

Williamson, Oliver E. 2002. "The Theory of the Firm as Governance Structure: From Choice to Contract." *Journal of Economic Perspectives* 16, no. 3: 171–95.

Wood, Donna J., and Jeanne Logsdon. 2008. "Business Citizenship as Metaphor and Reality." *Business Ethics Quarterly* 18, no. 1: 51–59.

4

Origins and Development of Industrial Clusters in the Basque Country: Path-Dependency and Economic Evolution

JESÚS MARÍA VALDALISO, AITZIBER ELOLA, MARÍA JOSE ARANGUREN, and SANTIAGO LÓPEZ

Translated by Lauren DeAre

Economists, geographers, and sociologists who have, from various approaches, analyzed the localization of industrial activity and the competitiveness of companies, clusters, and regions are recognizing the importance of history as an explanatory factor in the processes of economic development. Companies are organizations that learn from experience and are determined by their previous historical path (path-dependency). Clusters and regions, however, can build their competitive advantage on factors that are difficult to replicate. These include knowledge, institutions, and social capital, which are very region-specific and historically constructed, dependent both on the past (path-dependent) and on geographic location (place-dependent) (Porter and Sölvell 1998; Enright 1998; Lawson and Lorenz 1999; Westlund 2006; Boschma 2004; Martin and Sunley 2006; Lagerholm and Malmberg 2009). As Michael Porter (1990, 175) notes, "the process of creating and sustaining competitive advantage is one

* This study is included in Research Project HAR2009-03264, funded by the Ministry of Science and Innovation (MICINN). J. María Valdaliso and S. López are also grateful to the Basque Government Consolidated Research Group IT-337-10 for financial support.

where history matters."[1] Competitive advantages are dynamic by nature, and forging them can sometimes depend on chance and on the creation of specific social and business structures. These structures are closely linked to the particular history of the industry and region in which the companies are located (which includes the very specific conditions of local factors; characteristics inherent to local demand; distinct features of the sectors related to or pertaining to institutions in the geographic location; policies enacted by governments; and even pure chance). For these reasons, industrial activity tends to be concentrated geographically into clusters that group firms from the same sector or closely related sectors, specialized suppliers, service providers, customers, and supporting institutions.[2] Despite obviously recognizing the importance of history in explaining the current location and competitiveness of industries, clusters, and regions, very few studies of the different trends related to these phenomena have included in-depth historical studies.[3]

In this chapter we present the results of an ongoing research project focused on the historical origins of industrial clusters in the Basque Country and their legacy for present day competitiveness. Our goal is to analyze history's influence on the competitiveness of both companies and the region as a whole. We will examine when and how companies, sectors, and the entire Basque economy have created and developed their competitive advantages; which factors served as their foundations; and the development experienced over time. We take as our unit of analysis the current industrial clusters in the Basque Country that belong to a cluster association—twelve in total. The firms associated with these clus-

---

1. With varying results, other fields have also acknowledged the importance of history, including: new economic geography, Krugman (1991); evolutionary economic geography, Boschma and Martin (2007); and studies on organizational change and learning, Fear (2001).

2. Clusters promote cooperation and competition between firms and member institutions, increase firms' productivity, coordinate the rate and direction of innovation, stimulate the creation of new firms and, in short, improve the competitiveness of both firms and also the regions where these companies are located, Porter (1990), (1998a), (1998b), and (2003); Enright (1998 and 2003).

3. On an international level, Porter's pioneering work (1990) includes a brief preliminary historical analysis for each of the countries and sectors studied, an approach that is also followed by one of his collaborators, Enright (1995 and 1998). See also Saxenian (1994), Mowery and Nelson, eds. (1999), and Feldman (2001), among others. Nevertheless, most studies in the field of economics focusing on current clusters and other industrial conglomerations recognize that the information available concerning their origins is very limited or does not exist, Bresnahan, Gambardella, and Saxenian (2001), Feldman, Francis, and Bercovitz (2005), and Bergman (2009).

ters represented a third of both the region's employment and industrial value-added base (VAB) in 2006 (Orkestra 2009). We established a series of development phases for each cluster by considering variables such as the industry life cycle, the number of companies, and the employment provided. Within each, a study of competitive position was performed based on the four vectors of what is known as the Porter Diamond (factor conditions, demand conditions, firm structure and rivalry, and related supporting industries, in addition to the role of the government).[4] Then in the second phase of this research, based on a meta-study of existing case studies,[5] we sought comparable results on three points: the factors that have led to the formation of competitive advantages for clusters in the Basque Country; the factors that currently determine them; and, on a more aggregate basis, the economic development of the region.

The Basque Country is a suitable focus of study for such a project for several reasons. The region experienced early industrialization and, in the 1980s, suffered a serious economic and industrial crisis. In 1990, it implemented a competitiveness policy based on cluster promotion that was groundbreaking within the EU. These policies produced verified and recognized results for the objectives of promoting R&D, innovation, and business competitiveness (Monitor Company 1991; Ketels 2004; Aranguren and Navarro 2003; Iturrioz et al. 2005; OECD 2007; Orkestra 2009). In 2008, the Basque Country was ranked among the top forty European regions, with a per capita GDP that was much higher than the Spanish average (134 per 100) and the EU-27 average (137 per 100). R&D expenses were 1.65 per 100 of the GDP in 2007, higher than the Spanish average and close to the European average of 1.83 per 100. The Basque Country's inventive activity in 2008, measured by the number of patents registered at the European Office per million inhabitants, was the highest in Spain (OEPM-MITC 2009). It is also the European region with the highest pro-

---

4. To date, three case studies have been published that use a longitudinal (historical) analysis and qualitative methodology to examine the following clusters: paper, electronics and ITCs, and the maritime industry (Valdaliso et al. 2008, 2010a; López et al. 2008), and a fourth study on the aerospace and space cluster is at an advanced stage. The methodology used does not always allow us to establish clear cause and effect relationships, but it is possible to compare and even reject many already established theories and explore new ideas based on historical analysis.

5. There is a description of meta-study methodology in Van der Linde (2003). In addition to this, other works that employ a similar methodology include Belussi and Sedita (2009) on Italian industrial districts; Breshahan, Gambardella, and Saxenian (2001) on innovation clusters, and a study by the research group Elola et al. (forthcoming 2011) on four clusters in the Basque Country.

portion of graduates in science and technology and ranks sixth in human resources dedicated to science and technology (Eustat and Eurostat). Like many other early industrialized European regions, the Basque Country has been able to renovate its industrial network by improving older industry clusters and promoting new ones (Trippl and Tödtling 2009; Hassink 2005).

This chapter is composed of three main sections. First, we present some theoretical foundations, analyzing the primary factors that have shaped the development of clusters and the regional economy as a whole. Next, we describe the Basque Country's economic development trajectory in the nineteenth and twentieth centuries. Our approach focuses on the region's primary industries and clusters, with the goal of identifying both the historical roots of regional path-dependency and potential future development paths. Finally, based on a comparative analysis of the four clusters for which we have in-depth studies, we highlight some meso- and micro-economic factors that seem to have guided its development. At the end of the chapter, we include some conclusions.

The Economic Development of Clusters and Regions: An Evolutionary Perspective

Competitiveness is a complex and systemic phenomenon wherein multiple interrelated factors intervene: macro-, meso-, and micro-economic factors as well as social and institutional factors. Some of these factors (low-skilled workforce, natural resources, capital, freely accessed and encoded information and technology) are easy to replicate and therefore can be transferred easily from one place to another. Others, such as entrepreneurial initiative, unique industrial specialization, the institutional framework, knowledge, and social capital, are very specific to each region and have been established and developed though a historical process subject to increasing returns to scale and diverse dynamic externalities.[6] Therefore, they are dependent on both the previous trajectory of the region (path-dependent) and the geographical area (place-dependent), and for precisely this reason, they are very difficult for other competitor regions to replicate (Porter and Sölvell 1998; Lawson and Lorenz 1999; Boschma

---

6. Glaeser et al. (1992) describe three types of dynamic externalities: MAR (Marhall, Arrow, Romer), Porter, and Jacobs. The first two are external to companies but internal within an industry, whereas the latter is external to both companies and industry, and stems from more diverse environments.

2004; Kitson, Martin and Tyler 2004; Asheim and Gertler 2005; Martin and Sunley 2006). Their importance is obvious today given that, despite the unrelenting expansion of globalization (which would seem to reduce the importance of national and regional individuality), industrial activity continues to be unequally dispersed and is highly concentrated in specific regions and even localities (Porter 1990, 1998a, and 1998b; Enright 1998 and 2003).

Our main argument is that "regional competitiveness" is affected by the companies' and the entire region's knowledge, resources, and capabilities base. This base is accumulated in the routines and powers of the firms (subsequently replicated and reproduced) and of the region's institutions—both formal, such as its government, educational system, and R&D infrastructures, and informal, such as its social networks, culture, and conventions (Boschma 2004; Kitson, Martin, and Tyler 2004; Lagerholm and Malmberg 2009). Learning, replication, and innovation (change of routines) in firms are affected by current routines and powers that have been accumulated and developed historically (Nelson and Winter 1982; Dosi 1988); and by their dynamic capabilities, which define the ability of a company to change, integrate, or build powers—internal or external—in order to face situations of technological breakdown or radical market changes (Teece, Pisano, and Shuen 1997; Winter 2003).[7] The same also applies to institutions, defined by Paul A. David (1994) as "carriers of history";[8] technology (Rosenberg 1982; Dosi 1988); and knowledge and social capital (Asheim and Gertler 2005; Westlund 2006). Regional competitiveness is determined by the competitiveness of the firms and industries that are located there. Nonetheless, there are two ways that regions can also play an important role in the competitiveness of their companies and industries: (1) by developing a region-specific knowledge and capabilities base that functions as an incentive and selection mechanism, thereby promoting the diffusion of knowledge and skills and stimulating (related) variety and diversity; and (2) by creating a region-specific institutional environment that favors entrepreneurship, learning, and innovation (Boschma 2004; Asheim and Gertler 2005; Lagerholm and Malmberg 2009).

---

7. A variation on these would be companies' ability to integrate external knowledge; see Cohen and Levinthal (1990).

8. Nelson and Nelson (2002) define institutions as "social technologies" in order to highlight the similarities between their development and the development of physical technologies.

When explaining the current competitiveness of a region, the assumption that "history matters" or that history is "embedded in the present" does not imply rigid historical determinism (or past-dependency). It simply means that the choices made in the past by economic agents (related to adopted technology, investments in specific assets, and specialization of the firms' workforce; or, on a regional level, in economic and/or industrial specialization, government, education, and research institutions, and social capital) will influence, affect, and even limit the choices available to companies and the region as a whole in the present, favoring a certain range of potential paths and making others difficult or even impossible. In other words, the path-dependency argument implies understanding the regional economic development process not as linear, inevitable, and predetermined, but as one that is probabilistic and contingent (Martin and Sunley 2006; Martin 2009; Lagerholm and Malmberg 2009). Path-dependent trajectories, through processes subject to increasing returns to scale, may reinforce the industrial specialization of clusters and the region as a whole and end up leading to lock-in situations. These situations make adaptation to potential technology, market, or competitor changes difficult or impossible and, in the end, deteriorate or eliminate competitive advantages and lead to economic decline.[9] The local or region-specific nature of path-dependent processes demonstrates that the economic development of clusters and industry must also be place-dependent, and this characteristic must be understood in the same way as the former: The inclusion of a company or cluster in a region defines, through regional industrial specialization, allotment of resources, institutions, and other variables, the range of possible choices available and paths to follow (Martin and Sunley 2006; Lagerholm and Malmberg 2009).

However, the existence of increasing returns to scale and regional path-dependency does not mean that lock-in is the only possible outcome. This is further corroborated by the large diversity of trajectories followed in the regions: Through improvement and change processes, existing clusters, companies, and industries can avoid a lock-in situation and reinstate their competitive advantages. The very process of

---

9. The classic explanation of a situation that exemplifies these characteristics is in Grabher (1993). Based on an approach that focuses on clusters, Porter (1990) warns of the dangers of "insularity" or isolation of a cluster, and Maskell and Malmberg (2007) use the term "myopia" to describe similar conditions.

regional economic development can, through increasing returns to scale, knowledge spillovers, and Jacobs' dynamic externalities, increase diversity and related variety or drive inter-industry diversification processes that would open the range of possibilities for regional development in new sectors and industries. In addition to a historical trajectory, other elements that are contingent upon (accidents of history) or relatively exogenous to the cluster or the region in question (technological and industrial breakdowns, windows of opportunity resulting from the emergence of new technologies, products and/or markets) can radically alter its economic developmen; Boschma 2004; Martin and Sunley 2006; Martin 2009).

Some works have begun to apply these insights to individual studies of clusters, attempting to analyze the factors involved in their transformation and development. In general, all authors agree on the existence of multiple development paths that allow companies and clusters as a group to escape the dominant determining factors of the industry life cycle or of the cluster itself and escape many local (endogenous) and global (exogenous) factors (Lorenzen 2005; Belussi and Sedita 2009; Bergmann 2009; Martin 2009; Menzel and Fornahl 2009). We are going to focus on three variables, observable on micro- and meso-economic levels, that directly affect the methods for escaping the lock-in situations and that increase the development paths available to clusters and regions as a whole: companies' dynamic capabilities to face changes and the various strategies adopted; the external knowledge integration capability of firms, clusters, and/or specific institutions in the region (universities, research centers); and the existence of social capital that encourages entrepreneurship, external knowledge acquisition and integration, and innovation.[10]

---

10. Dynamic capabilities and external knowledge integration capability can influence the creation of endogenous processes or can improve existing industries and facilitate the transfer of external technology and knowledge; see Teece, Pisano and Shuen (1997), Winter (2003), and Cohen and Levinthal (1990). Although one can see these at the company level, they may also be transferred to a cluster or the industry as a whole; see Giuliani (2005). Belussi and Sedita (2009) have shown the importance of the strategies that firms adopt to escape dependence on the life cycle of a particular industry or cluster to which they belong. Social capital is defined as a group of social networks, standards, and values that promote confidence and facilitate cooperation between individuals and organizations. It is intangible, historically constructed in specific places and regions, and very difficult to replicate, and regions can build competitive advantages based on it; see Nahapiet and Ghosal (1998), Porter and Sölvell (1998), and Westlund (2006).

Industrialization and Regional Path-Dependency: The Economic Development of Basque Industry in the Nineteenth and Twentieth Centuries

In this section, we offer a long-term overview of the process of growth, change, and diversification that industry in the Basque Country underwent during the nineteenth and twentieth centuries. It is based on a selection of the industrial clusters that were most influential at the beginning of the industrialization process and an analysis of their subsequent development. We base our information on the numerous studies available on the economic and business history of the region.[11] However, for certain years, we also offer the sectoral distribution of the population employed in the industry, using the statistical sources available (the Instituto Nacional de Estadística or INE, the Spanish National Statistics Institute, and Eustat, the Basque Statistics Institute). This long-term overview focuses on the roots of regional path-dependency and on the possibilities for escaping the lock-in conditions described in the previous section.

Along with Catalonia, the Basque Country was one of the regions that led the industrial revolution in Spain in the nineteenth century. Until the end of the twentieth century, industrial development was the primary driving force for economic growth in the region. It was much greater than the Spanish average in terms of the per capita GDP and close to the average for the fifteen most developed countries in the EU. Even today, the relative importance of industry in the Basque economy (based on contribution to the GDP and employment) is greater that the average in Spain, although the service sector now supersedes it.[12]

On the eve of the nineteenth-century industrial revolution, the Basque Country had a longstanding manufacturing and business tradition that was very much centered around iron, maritime trade and shipping, and related industrial activities such as shipbuilding. Basque commercial and manufacturing activities dated from medieval times, which explains why the region had business experience and entrepreneurship, capital, a

---

11. This section was greatly influenced by Boschma's work (1999) on the development of industrial clusters in Belgium. In this long-term overview, the term "cluster" solely refers to the spatial grouping of firms that undertake similar activities. Recent analyses of the Basque Country's economic and business historiography include Fernández de Pinedo (2001), Valdaliso (2002, 2003), Catalán (2002), and Torres (2006).

12. On regional GDP development in the twentieth century, see Alcaide (2003). On the development of the Basque economy in the last thirty years, see Orkestra (2008). For a territorial overview of Spanish industrialization, see Nadal (2003).

highly skilled workforce, and institutions that supported economic development. Industrialization of the Basque Country began in the 1840s after its inclusion within Spain's customs borders. Tariff protection facilitated the emergence of modern industry in the maritime provinces of Bizkaia (Vizcaya) and Gipuzkoa (Guipúzcoa), created by native entrepreneurs who introduced new outside technologies. Industrial specialization inside the Basque Country itself was established on the basis of certain factors including the existence of natural resources (ore, water), skilled labor, entrepreneurship, and a prior history of manufacturing, some of which was inherited from the region's past. Industrial development in Bizkaia was initially concentrated around Bilbao and its estuary, and was primarily focused in three closely related sectors: iron and steel manufacturing, iron mining, and maritime transportation. Although less influential, a consumer goods industry also emerged. In Gipuzkoa, the primary sectors in this first industrialization were the consumer goods industries (textiles, paper, food and beverage, and firearms), and they were spread throughout the province, along the coast, and along major rivers that provided water and hydraulic power. During this first industrialization, which lasted until the end of the nineteenth century, several industrial clusters emerged: one near Bilbao for iron and steel manufcaturing and metal industries; clusters for paper, textiles, and firearm manufacturing in Gipuzkoa; and a maritime transportation and services cluster comprised of companies providing those services that operated in the port of Bilbao (Fernández de Pinedo 2001; Valdaliso 2002 and 2003).

A second industrial revolution began in the region in 1891, characterized by the introduction and diffusion of new technologies, new power sources (electricity), and new production sectors. During this period, which lasted until 1936, the existing industrial clusters strengthened their specializations and their participation in Spanish industry as a whole through a process of increasing returns to scale and by benefiting from the appearance of external and agglomeration economies. The process of regional economic development itself also drove industrial diversification and increased related variety in Basque industry. A metal product and machinery manufacturing industry in Bizkaia emerged in the 1890s, driven by companies in the iron and steel cluster. At the beginning of the twentieth century, the shipbuilding and auxiliary industry emerged around the Bilbao Estuary in order to meet the demands of the maritime cluster. In the 1920s and 1930s, manufacturing industries for bicycles, sewing machines, and machine tools emerged in the Eibar region (Gipuzkoa) due to the industrial restructuring of the firearms cluster. The existence of strong market potential, entrepreneurship, and available investment capital during the early twentieth century explains the creation of the Basque Country's major electricity production and distribution companies, which in turn launched the emergence of an electrical machinery and equipment manufacturing industry. The crisis and disappearance of traditional sectors also prompted diversification processes. Thus, ships' carpenters who were unemployed due to the crisis and the disappearance of a large portion of the traditional shipyards for wooden hulled vessel construction created the first furniture businesses in the Urola region (Gipuzkoa), around which a small cluster was established in the 1920s.

The region's small size, close proximity of industries, relatively concentrated financial system, and close associative network all contributed to reduce information and transaction costs in the businesses and capital markets. The earlier commercial and manufacturing tradition and relatively highly trained Basque entrepreneurs, many of them educated abroad, resulted in an open attitude that encouraged importing external technology and knowledge into learning and innovation (which, in turn, increased the "integration capacity" of the region's companies). Industrialization of the Basque Country demanded increases and improvements in transportation and communication, educational institutions and workforce training, and a more developed financial system that, once available, would also encourage and drive economic growth and development in the region. Last but not least, as a result of its speciifc historical trajectory and integration into the Spanish tax system, the Basque Country retained a number of local and provincial (*Diputaciones* or provincial councils) institutions that were very much engaged in the fixed social capital infrastructures and the creation of human capital (Valdaliso 2002 and 2003).

In the decades after the Spanish Civil War (1936–39) the Basque Country strengthened its industrial specializations in the following industries: iron and steel, metal products, and vehicle and transportation equipment manufacturing. Indeed, these sectors represented more than 45 per 100 industrial jobs in the region during those years. Other sectors that experienced significant growth were non-electrical machinery manufacturing, electrical and electronic machinery and equpiment manufacturing, the chemical industry, and rubber and plastics. The Basque Country's industrial specialization was concentrated in all of these sectors, whose participation in Spanish industry as a whole was much greater than average. On the other hand, consumer goods industries like textiles and footwear declined in absolute and relative terms, as did others (more or less) like the food and beverage or furniture industries, whereas the paper and graphic arts industry maintained its level of participation. In this period, diversification of metal-related industries into new sectors provided a boost for specialized clusters such as machine tools, home appliances, and the automotive components industry. New electrical and electronic product and machinery manufacturing companies also emerged and prompted the formation of a specialized cluster in the 1980s. In the four cases cited, specialized industries and clusters emerged as the result of already existing capability and knowledge within companies in related sectors. This occurred either because these companies replaced an already mature market with another that had greater growth potential (or combined the two), or because some of the skilled partners, leaders, or employees of those companies decided to create new firms (spin-offs) in order to take advantage of the windows of opportunity opened by the new market and/or technology. In short, entrepreneurship and skilled labor were typically resposnible for the appearance of these new industries and clusters (Fernández de Pinedo 2001; Catalán 2002). Furthermore, due to saturation in the most industrialized regions of Bizkaia and Gipuzkoa, some companies relocated to the interior province of Araba (Álava), whose industrialization process began at that time.

Industrial development in this period was still based on several common factors handed down from the past: entrepreneurship; a relatively abundant, inexpensive, and highly skilled labor supply; and high rates of investment provided by a financial system that was able to channel private savings into productive investment. Training of human capital was carried out within a framework of technical and higher education that, during this period, experienced significant development, at least when compared to the Spanish average. In the early 1970s, the Basque Country had the highest number of professionally trained students per inhabitant, with Gipuzkoa heading the ranking with figures almost three times the Spanish average. The same occurred with graduates of non-university post-secondary technical training (experts, technical engineers, site superintendents, and so on). At the same time, there was greater choice and better quality options in university education . However, higher education in the Basque Country still lagged behind that of Western Europe as a whole, if not in the number of university degrees relative to the population (a ratio similar to the European average in the early 1970s) then in the number of science and engineering degrees and in education spending relative to the GDP (Valdaliso 2010).

Like other European regions that were industrialized early and came to specialize in heavy industry (the Rhur in Germany, Northeast England, Wales, Scotland, and so on), between the late 1970s and mid-1980s the Basque Country faced a serious economic and industrial crisis deepened by the progressive opening of the Basque and Spanish economies to foreign competition. This was accelerated by incorporation into the European Economic Community (1986) and competition from other non-European regions. This crisis was moreover accompanied by a large-scale institutional and political process of change involving both a change of political regime in Spain between 1975 and 1977, and, after 1981, the creation of a regional Basque government with broad powers in fiscal and economic matters; as well as a social crisis marked by terrorist violence and labor conflict. Together, this all led to a significant reduction in the Basque Country's GDP and a major industrial restructuring in sectors like metalworking, metal processing, shipbuilding, and home appliances, and also acted as a kind of external shock that shook up the regions' actors (companies, institutions, employees), leading to major change and adaptation (Navarro, Aranguren, and Rivera 2004; Valdaliso 2010).

In 1981, the new autonomous Basque administration implemented a technological and industrial policy directed at improving competitiveness of those companies and industries in the region that had survived the crisis and industrial restructuring. Its purpose was to build on the capabilities and resources that existing companies and industries had already accumulated over time, rather than promote new fields. The autonomous government's fundamental priority during the 1980s was to "introduce and spread R&D culture throughout the industrial spectrum of the Basque Country" through the creation of an infrastructure of technological opportunity (technology centers and parks) and technology promotion and development within companies. A good example of this policy is the Plan de Estrategia Tecnológica (PET, Technology Strategy Plan, 1980–1992). The regional administration, companies, and other institutions collaborated in its design, along with an external auditor, the Stanford Research Institute. The PET defined a technology strategy that was "selective, integrated and based on existing realities," specifically related to the metal processing industry, the most influential industrial sector in the Basque Country. It prioritized three areas of technology: new materials technologies, production technologies, and information technologies, and encouraged collaboration between technological supply and demand in these three areas.[13] Indeed, the Basque government introduced a new competitiveness policy based on Michael Porter's cluster model in the 1990s that was a groundbreaking initiative at the European level. It was designed to inspire improvement and renovation of older industrial clusters (the value-added steel, machine tools, home appliances, automotive, port of Bilbao, maritime industries, and paper clusters) and promote the creation of new clusters in emerging industries and sectors (the electronics, aerospace, environment, energy, and audio-visual sectors). This policy also intended to build on existing strengths, encouraging the transformation of existing business associations into cluster associations (Monitor Company 1991; Aranguren and Navarro 2003).

In 1985, the Basque economy began a period of economic recovery and growth that continued until the early 1990s. Later, after a crisis from 1991 to 1993, there was a new period of growth that lasted until the end of the century. In general terms, between 1985 and 2005 the Basque economy grew faster than both Spanish and European averages. This explains the growing differences between the Basque Country and Spain in terms of per capita GDP and its convergence with the most advanced EU countries. Although during this period the service sector gained influence in terms of both the GDP and employment, the relative importance of industry in the Basque economy continued to be greater than Spanish and European averages (Orkestra 2008; www.politicaindustrialvasca.net).

The distribution of employment and the VAB in Basque industry for 2007 (with slight variations due to variety in statistical classifications) shows that, despite the serious crisis that Basque industry experienced between 1975 and 1985, it continued to follow a regional development path that was very focused on the same hegemonic sectors as before. In other words, metallurgy and metal products and transportation equipment represented almost 44 percent of industrial employment for the region in 2007, machinery and electrical product manufacturing together represented 21 percent of jobs, followed by rubber and plastics, food and beverage, and paper and graphic arts, which together comprised almost

---

13. Public policies, although also path-dependent (Woolcock, Szreter, and Rao 2009), can nonetheless be a powerful transformational factor. On the Basque government's industrial and technology policy at this time, see www.politicaindustrialvasca.net. See also Díez and García (1990), Navarro (1992), and Plaza (2000).

another 20 percent of all employment. Although the sectors have not changed, there have been significant improvements in the technological level of both production in general and exports in particular. Between 1990 and 2004, high-tech level exports increased from 1 to 2 percent, and medium-high-tech level exports grew from 27 to 50 percent (Eustat).

Significantly, in 2007, Basque industry represented 9 percent of Spanish industrial employment, a figure similar to that of the late 1950s. The same sectors continued to have above-average relative participation: metallurgy and metal product manufacturing, machinery and mechanical equipment, electrical and electronic products and equipment, transportation equipment, and rubber and plastics. Only the paper and graphic arts industry fell out of the group of leading sectors in the Spanish economy. The INE's classification system, based on large groups of sectors from Spain's official national classification of economic activities, does not allow for further desegregation, but the figures provided by Basque industrial associations show much higher percentages in more specific sectors.[14]

The work of identifying the clusters in the Comunidad Autónoma del País Vasco/Euskal Autonomia Erkidegoa (CAPV/EAE, Autonomous Community of the Basque Country) carried out by the Basque Institute of Competitiveness shows, from a different perspective, the same, persistent reality: namely, that metals and manufacturing, automotive, and production technology clusters represented 55.5 percent of CAPV/EAE exports. If to those we add motors and heavy equipment and machinery clusters, the total comes to 67 percent. These are all competitive clusters, with a market share of worldwide exports that is greater than the average for Basque exports (Aranguren 2008).

In summary, this synthetic overview of the Basque Country's economic development shows a path of growing and persistent specialization around a number of industries and clusters related to iron and metals, built on factors inherited from the past and accumulated in companies' resources and capabilities base and routines. The region's prior history, through agglomeration economies, increasing returns to scale, and economies derived from industrial specialization, has defined the direction

---

14. Figures from the Basque Development Agency (SPRI) at app3.spri.net/Investing//en-index.html show the percentages of Basque industry within Spanish industry for the most prominent sectors to be: 90 percent in specialized steel, 80 percent in machine tools, 75 percent in drop forging, 50 percent in capital goods manufacturing and casting, and 40 percent in steel, home appliances, and professional electronics.

of the Basque industrial development path. However, the past has also provided, by means of the aforementioned factors and others including inter-industrial diversification processes and the creation of a social and institutional environment that is very welcoming to entrepreneurship (endogenous creation) and to technological change and innovation, paths that have allowed the region (and its companies and industries) to escape a situation similar to the lock-in experienced between 1975 and 1985, thereby improving the technological base of existing industries and promoting the creation of new industrial initiatives. The creation of these new paths is closely linked to the choices and behaviors of economic agents, specifically as related to the firms, as we will see in the following section.

The Economic Development of Several Industrial Clusters in the Basque Country and Their Determining Factors

Among the clear micro-level variables that have affected the Basque regional economic development path, we have highlighted companies' dynamic capabilities in the face of change and the diverse business strategies adopted; their ability to integrate external knowledge into firms, clusters, and/or specific institutions in the region (universities, research centers); and the creation of social capital that supports entrepreneurship, learning and knowledge integration, and innovation. In the previous section we examined Basque industry as a whole. Here, we will focus on the four industrial sectors for which in-depth studies have already been completed: paper, the maritime industry, electronics and information and communication technologies (ICTs), and the aerospace industry. The first two date from the first industrial revolution in the late nineteenth century, although they were based on older local traditions and have subsequently undergone a complete life cycle of development, maturity, and decline. The origins of the second pair are more recent: The first major companies in the electronics cluster were established in the 1940s and 1950s, and aerospace and space industries were created in the 1980s and are still in a development phase. An initial analysis of the factors that have guided the origins and development of the four clusters provides interesting results (Elola et al. forthcoming 2011). The development of these clusters can only be explained by multiple factors. Their origins can be attributed to a combination of local factors (factor endowment, local demand, past conditions, entrepreneurship) in addition to the integration of outside knowledge and technology. In subsequent stages, along with the existence of local demand, new factors emerged that were linked to the previous path, such as the development of cluster-specific factors (human capital, social capital, training and research centers) and the strategic capabilities developed by firms. Meanwhile, the two most important universal factors aiding development of these clusters have been growth in international demand and global competition, both of which were widespread from the 1980s on.

Companies' strategic capabilities were developed according to two very different competitive strategies: cost leadership (accomplished through economies of scale) and differentiation, and product improvement and diversification. The former implied greater specialization and, therefore, higher probability of leading the firms (and the cluster as a whole) to a lock-in situation in their maturity stage, as was the case with companies in the paper and maritime industries clusters. They were incapable of facing the new scenario of global competition in the last quarter of the twentieth century. Only small and medium-sized shipyards in the maritime cluster, which in previous stages had followed a strategy of product differentiation and diversification, were capable of surviving the crisis of the 1970s and 1980s, leading to a new stage of restructuring that began in the late 1990s. For the younger clusters, which were much more R&D and knowledge intensive, when they were established companies had constructed a solid resources and capabilities base and had adopted a strategy of technological innovation, improvement, and differentiation of products and solutions (and, in one case, related diversification). These various strategies alone do not explain the varied nature and condition of the clusters analyzed; historical factors also had an impact. Companies in the paper and maritime industries clusters emerged and were developed in an economy that was relatively protected from external competition. In contrast, firms in the electronics and aerospace clusters have had to face, practically since their creation, a highly competitive global market in which, given its relatively small size, technological innovation and product differentiation were the only possible growth strategies.

A second fundamental variable in the development of these clusters was their ability to creatively integrate, spread, and exploit outside knowledge ("integration capability"), thereby avoiding situations of isolation, insularity, and myopia that lead clusters to their decline and disappearance. This is evident in the knowledge base of the firms in this cluster, but also in the various knowledge diffusion and transference mechanisms that exist within them (technical and scientific communities, social networks, interactions between companies, labor mobility and spin-offs, shared research projects, collaborative institutions, and so on), and in the existence of channels to bring in this outside knowledge (foreign firms, technical assistance contracts, international projects, internationalization of the cluster firms themselves). Obviously, the incentives for companies to integrate external knowledge and exploit it depend on their competitive position and the level of rivalry in the markets to which they belong. From the outset, firms in the paper and maritime industries clusters operated in a protected market that they were able to dominate with very little competition due to their lower costs. The electronics, ICT, and aerospace companies, however, operate within global markets and must compete in innovation and quality. The internationalization process undergone by firms in the latter two clusters and, since the late 1990s, by companies in the Basque maritime industry, is functioning as an active entry mechanism for outside knowledge (Valdaliso et al. 2010a and Elola et al. forthcoming 2011).

The final variable of note is social capital. Our case studies on the four clusters mentioned suggest the existence of a direct relationship between social capital and integration capability and between social capital, knowledge creation and transfer, and innovation. In the electronics and ICT clusters, a high level of social capital has been established that has led to active cooperation between firms and institutions in forming skilled human capital, R&D activities, and the internationalization process, coordinated through an institution like a cluster association. In the aerospace cluster, social capital has been established based on close collaboration between three key companies (Sener, Gamesa, and ITP) that have pushed for the creation of a cluster association. This social capital has increased the ability for knowledge integration for both clusters and strengthened and differentiated their competitive advantages. On the contrary, levels of social capital in the paper cluster are much more limited and cooperation between firms is scarce. In the Basque maritime industry cluster, inter-firm cooperation (and cluster association labor) is greater than in the paper cluster and has been able to encourage strategies of product innovation, differentiation, and improvement, and, in the most recent restructuring phase, company internationalization (Elola et al. forthcoming 2011; Valdaliso et al. 2010a and 2010b).

Conclusions

History plays an important role in the creation of competitive advantages for companies, clusters, and regions and one should take account of the past in order to fully understand the competitiveness phenomenon. However, the assumption that history matters does not imply a rigid historical determinism (past-dependency) from which firms, clusters, and regions cannot escape. Processes of economic development for clusters and regions are path-dependent, which means that the choices and paths currently available to firms and regions are dependent on the decisions made in the past and the paths followed up to present.

Empirical evidence cited for the Basque Country indicates that, in a similar way to many other regions, the development of both its industry and its clusters provides numerous and varied paths for escaping the cycle of life of the industry or cluster, lock-in situations, and economic decline. History, through agglomeration economies, increasing returns to scale, and economies derived from industrial specialization, has defined the direction for the path of industrial development in the Basque Country. Nevertheless, the past has also provided opportunities, which include both the aforementioned factors and others like inter-industrial diversification processes and the creation of a social and institutional environment that greatly supports entrepreneurship and innovation. These paths have allowed the Basque Country (and its companies and industries) to escape a lock-in situation similar to the conditions between 1975 and 1985, and have instead improved the technology base for existing industries and promoted the creation of new industries. The behaviors of economic agents and specifically, of the companies in question, together with their resources and capabilities base (which includes their dynamic capabilities and external knowledge integration capabilities) and growth strategies have the potential to lead these clusters or the region as a whole toward new development paths. The accumulation of social capital, with proven positive effects on collective knowledge acquisition, integration, and diffusion, acts as an intermediary between the region and the firms and also widens the range of possible paths in economic evolution.

References

Alcaide Inchausti, Julio. 2003. *Evolución económica de las regiones y provincias españolas en el siglo XX*. Bilbao: Fundación BBVA.

Aranguren, María Jose, and Itziar Navarro. 2003. "La política de clusters en la Comunidad Autónoma del País Vasco: una primera valoración." *Ekonomiaz* 53: 90–113.

Aranguren, María Jose, ed. 2008. *Identificación de clústeres en la CAPV.* Bilbao: Publicaciones de la Universidad de Deusto.

Asheim, Bjørn T., and Meric S. Gertler. 2005. "The Geography of Innovation: Regional Innovation Systems." In *The Oxford Handbook of Innovation*, edited by Jan Fagerberg, David C. Mowery, and Richard R. Nelson. New York: Oxford University Press.

Belussi, Francesca, and Rita Sedita. 2009. "Life Cycle vs. Multiple Path Dependency in Industrial Districts." *European Planning Studies* 17, no. 4: 505–28.

Bergmann, Edward M. 2009. "Cluster Life-cycles: An Emerging Synthesis." In *Handbook of Research on Cluster Theory*, edited by C. Karlsson. Cheltenham: Edward Elgar.

Boschma, Ron A. 1999. "The Rise of Clusters of Innovative Industries in Belgium during the Industrial Epoch." *Research Policy* 28, no. 8: 853–71.

———. 2004. "Competitiveness of Regions from an Evolutionary Perspective." *Regional Studies* 38, no. 9: 1001–14.

Boschma, Ron A. and Ron Martin. 2007. "Constructing an Evolutionary Economic Geography." *Journal of Economic Geography* 7, no. 5: 537–48.

Bresnahan, Timothy, Alfonso Gambardella, and AnnaLee Saxenian. 2001. "'Old Economy' Inputs for 'New Economy' Outcomes: Cluster Formation in the New Silicon Valleys." *Industrial and Corporate Change* 10, no. 4: 835–60.

Caja Laboral Popular. 2002. *Economía vasca: Evolución sectorial (1976–2001).* Arrasate: Caja Laboral.

Catalán, Jordi. 2002. "La madurez de una economía industrial, 1936–1999." In *Historia del País Vasco y Navarra en el siglo XX*, edited by José Luis De la Granja and Santiago de Pablo. Madrid: Biblioteca Nueva.

Cohen, Wesley M., and Daniel A. Levinthal. 1990. "Absorptive Capacity: A New Perspective on Learning and Innovation." *Administrative Science Quarterly* 35, no. 1: 128–53.

David, Paul A. 1994. "Why are Institutions the 'Carriers of History'? Path Dependence and the Evolution of Conventions, Organizations and

Institutions." *Structural Change and Economic Dynamics* 5, no. 2: 205–20.

Díez, María Angeles, and Inés García. 1990. "La política tecnológica vasca en la década de los ochenta." *Ekonomiaz* 19: 140–53.

Dosi, Giovanni. 1988. "Sources, Procedures and Microeconomic Effects of Innovation." *Journal of Economic Literature* 26, no. 3: 1120–70.

Elola, Aitziber, Jesús María Valdaliso, María Jose Aranguren, and Santiago López. "Cluster Life Cycles, Path Dependency and Regional Economic Development: Insights from a Meta Study on Basque Clusters." *European Planning Studies* (accepted 2010, forthcoming 2011).

Enright, Michael J. 1995. "Organization and Coordination in Geographically Concentrated Industries." In *Coordination and Information: Historical Perspectives on the Organization of Enterprise*, edited by Naomi Lamoreaux and Daniel M.G. Raff. Chicago: The University of Chicago Press.

———. 1998. "Regional Clusters and Firm Strategy." In *The Dynamic Firm: The Role of Technology, Strategy, Organization, and Regions*, edited by Alfred D. Chandler, Jr., P. Hagstrom, and Ö. Solvell. New York: Oxford University Press.

———. 2003. "Regional Clusters: What We Know and What We Should Know." In *Innovation Clusters and Interregional Competition*, edited by J. Bröcker, D. Dohse, and R. Solwedel. Heidelberg: Springer.

Fear, Jeffrey P. 2001. "Thinking Historically about Organizational Learning." In *Handbook of Organizational Learning and Knowledge*, edited by M. Dierkes et al. Oxford: Oxford University Press.

Feldman, Maryann P. 2001. "The Entrepreneurial Event Revisited: Firm Formation in a Regional Context." *Industrial and Corporate Change* 10, no. 4: 861–91.

Feldman, Maryann P., Johanna Francis, and Janet Bercovitz. 2005. "Creating a Cluster While Building a Firm: Entrepreneurs and the Formation of Industrial Clusters." *Regional Studies* 39, no. 1: 129–41.

Fernández de Pinedo, Emiliano. 2001. "De la primera industrialización a la reconversión industrial: La economía vasca entre 1841 y 1990." In *Historia económica regional de España, siglos XIX y XX*, edited by Luis Germán et al. Barcelona: Crítica.

Giuliani, Elsa. 2005. "Cluster Absorptive Capacity: Why do Some Clusters Forge Ahead and Others Lag Behind?" *European Urban and Regional Studies* 12, no. 3: 269–88.

Glaeser, Edward L., Heidi D. Kallal, José A. Scheinkman, and Andrei Shleifer. 1992. "Growth in Cities." *Journal of Political Economy* 100, no. 6: 1126–52.

Grabher, Gernot. 1993. "The Weakness of Strong Ties: The 'Lock-in' of Regional Development in the Rhur Area." In *The Embedded Firm: On the Socio-Economics of Industrial Networks*, edited by Gernot Grabher. London: Routledge.

Hassink, Robert. 2005. "How to Unlock Regional Economies from Path Dependency? From Learning Region to Learning Cluster." *European Planning Studies* 13, no. 4: 521–35.

Iturrioz, Cristina, María Jose Aranguren, Cristina Aragón, and Miren Larrea. 2005. "¿La política industrial de cluster/redes mejora realmente la competitividad empresarial? Resultados de la evaluación de dos experiencias en la Comunidad Autónoma de Euskadi." *Ekonomiaz* 60: 10–61.

Ketels, Christian H.M. 2004. "European Clusters." In *Structural Change in Europe 3 — Innovative City and Business Regions*. Boston: Harvard Business School. At www.isc.hbs.edu/pdf/Ketels_European_Clusters_2004.pdf.

Kitson, Michael, Ron Martin, and Peter Tyler. 2004. "Regional Competitiveness: An Elusive yet Key Concept?" *Regional Studies* 38, no. 9: 991–99.

Krugman, Paul. 1991. *Geography and Trade*. Cambridge: The MIT Press.

Lagerholm, Magnus, and Anders Malmberg. 2009. "Path Dependence in Economic Geography." In *The Evolution of Path Dependence*, edited by Lars Magnusson and Jan Ottosson. Cheltenham: Edward Elgar.

Lawson, Clive, and Edward Lorenz. 1999. "Collective Learning, Tacit Knowledge and Regional Innovative Capacity." *Regional Studies* 33, no. 4: 305–17.

López, Santiago, Aitziber Elola, Jesús María Valdaliso, and María Jose Aranguren. 2008. *Los orígenes históricos del clúster de la electrónica, la informática y las telecomunicaciones del País Vasco y su legado para el presente*. San Sebastián: Dpto. Industria-ORKESTRA-Eusko Ikaskuntza.

Lorenzen, Mark. 2005. "Why do Clusters Change?" *European Urban and Regional Studies* 12, no. 3: 203–8.

Martin, Ron. 2009. "Rethinking Regional Path Dependence: Beyond Lock-in to Evolution." *Papers in Evolutionary Economic Geography 09.10.* Utrecht University.

Martin, Ron, and Peter Sunley. 2006. "Path Dependence and Regional Economic Evolution." *Journal of Economic Geography* 6, no. 4: 395–437.

Maskell, Peter, and Anders Malmberg. 2007. "Myopia, Knowledge Development and Cluster Evolution." *Journal of Economic Geography* 7, no. 5: 603–18.

Menzel, Max-Peter, and Dirk Fornahl. 2009. "Cluster Life Cycles–Dimensions and Rationales of Cluster Evolution." *Industrial and Corporate Change* 19, no. 1: 205–38.

Monitor Company. 1991. "La ventaja competitiva de Euskadi: Fase I: Identificación del potencial de competitividad." *Ekonomiaz* 21: 156–209.

Nadal, Jordi, ed. 2003. *Atlas de la industrialización de España 1750–2000.* Barcelona: Crítica-Fundación BBVA.

Nahapiet, Janine, and Sumantra Ghoshal. 1998. "Social Capital, Intellectual Capital, and the Organizational Advantage." *Academy of Management Journal* 23, no. 2: 242–66.

Navarro, Mikel. 1992. "Actividades empresariales de I+D y política tecnológica del Gobierno Vasco." *Ekonomiaz* 23: 118–59.

Navarro, Mikel, María Jose Aranguren, and Olga Rivera. 2004. *La crisis de la industria manufacturera en la CAPV: Aspectos estructurales.* Bilbao: Manu Robles-Arangiz Institutoa.

Nelson, Richard R., and Katherine Nelson. 2002. "Technology, Institutions, and Innovation Systems." *Research Policy* 31: 265–72.

Nelson, Richard R., and Sidney G. Winter. 1982. *An Evolutionary Theory of Economic Change.* Cambridge, MA: The Belknap Press.

OECD. 2007. *Competitive Regional Clusters: National Policy Approaches.* París: OECD.

Oepm-Mitc. 2009. *Estadísticas de propiedad industrial.* Volume I. Madrid: OEPM-MITC.

Orkestra. 2008. *Informe de competitividad del País Vasco: hacia una propuesta única de valor.* Bilbao: Orkestra-Instituto Vasco de Competitividad y Fundación Deusto.

———. 2009. *II Informe de competitividad del País Vasco: hacia el estadio competitivo de la innovación.* Bilbao: Ediciones Deusto.

Plaza, Beatriz. 2000. "Política industrial de la Comunidad Autónoma del País Vasco, 1981–2001." *Economía Industrial* 335-36: 299–314.

Porter, Michael E. 1990. *The Competitive Advantage of Nations*. London: MacMillan.

———. 1998a. "Clusters and the New Economics of Competition." *Harvard Business Review*, (November–December): 77–90.

———. 1998b. *On Competition*. Boston: Harvard Business Review.

Porter, Michael E., and Ö. Sölvell. 1998. "The Role of Geography in the Process of Innovation and the Sustainable Competitive Advantage of Firms." In *The Dynamic Firm: The Role of Technology, Strategy, Organization, and Regions*, edited by Alfred D. Chandler, Jr., P. Hagstrom, and Ö. Solvell. New York: Oxford University Press.

Rosenberg, Nathan. 1982. *Inside the Black Box: Technology and Economics*. Cambridge: Cambridge University Press.

Saxenian, AnnaLee. 1994. *Regional Advantage, Culture and Competition in Silicon Valley and Route 128*. Boston: Harvard University Press.

Teece, David, Gary Pisano, and Amy Shuen. 1997. "Dynamic Capabilities and Strategic Management." *Strategic Management Journal* 18, no. 7: 509–33.

Torres, Eugenio. 2006. "La empresa en el País Vasco (siglos XIX y XX)." In *Historia empresarial de España: Un enfoque regional en profundidad*, edited by José Luis García Ruiz and Eugenio Torres. Madrid: LID Editorial.

Trippl, Michaela, and Franz Tödtling. 2009. "Cluster Renewal in Old Industrial Regions: Continuity or Radical Change?" In *Handbook of Research on Cluster Theory*, edited by C. Karlsson. Cheltenham: Edward Elgar.

Valdaliso, Jesús María. 2002. "La industrialización en el primer tercio del siglo XX y sus protagonistas." In *Historia del País Vasco y Navarra en el siglo XX*, edited by José Luis De la Granja and Santiago de Pablo. Madrid: Biblioteca Nueva.

———. 2003. "El factor empresarial y la industrialización del País Vasco (1841–1914)." In *Modernización, desarrollo económico y transformación social en el País Vasco y Navarra*, edited by Francisco J. Caspistegui and María Mar Larraza. Pamplona: Ediciones Eunate.

———. 2010. *La evolución económica de los clústeres industriales del País Vasco: Historia, competitividad y desarrollo económico regional*. Bogotá: Cátedra Corona 16.

Valdaliso, Jesús María, María Jose Aranguren, Aitziber Elola, and Santiago López. 2008. *Los orígenes históricos del clúster del papel en el País Vasco y su legado para el presente.* San Sebastián: ORKESTRA-Eusko Ikaskuntza.

Valdaliso, Jesús María, Aitziber Elola, María Jose Aranguren, and Santiago López. 2010a. *Los orígenes históricos del cluster de la industria marítima vasca y su legado para el presente,* San Sebastián, ORKESTRA-Eusko Ikaskuntza.

———. "Social Capital, Internationalization and Absorptive Capacity: The Electronics and ICT Cluster of the Basque Country." *Entrepreneurship and Regional Development* (2010b accepted, in press).

Van der Linde, Claas. 2003. "The Demography of Clusters—Findings from the Cluster Meta-Study." In *Innovation Clusters and Interregional Competition,* edited by J. Bröcker, D. Dohse, and R. Solwedel. Heidelberg: Springer.

Westlund, Hans. 2006. *Social Capital in the Knowledge Economy: Theory and Empirics.* New York: Springer.

Winter, Sidney G. 2003. "Understanding Dynamic Capabilities." *Strategic Management Journal* 24, no. 10: 991–95.

Woolcock, Michael, Simon Szreter, and Vijayendra Rao. 2009. "How and Why Does History Matter for Development Policy?" *Brooks World Poverty Institute Working Paper* 68.

5

A Systemic and Multilevel Approach to Organizational Analysis

NEKANE BALLUERKA

Translated by Julie Waddington

Since its inception, social psychology has been forced to adopt the role of mediator between intrapersonal and social processes. In this difficult role, which tends to be criticized for its excessive scope, theories that focus on systems and on the multilevel perspective have provided an interpretative framework for the intermediate space between the individual and the social level. Furthermore, group psychology and organizational psychology, which both stem from social psychology, have attempted to use these approaches in their interpretation of reality. From the perspective of group dynamics, the role of social psychologists has been viewed more positively by adopting an intermediate position that links intrapersonal and contextual factors (Munich 1993). Currently, there is wide acceptance of the idea that an approach that is focused exclusively on contextual and structural factors ignores the experiences of individuals and their relations with others, obviating the effects of composition processes (Chan 1998), in the same way that analyses that are exclusively based on the individual isolate the subject from their group contexts and social meanings.

On the basis of these assumptions, this study has two key aims. The first of these is twofold: On the one hand, it attempts to integrate the principles that regulate complex systems that have traditionally been considered separately. And on the other, it deals with the integration of the classical systems approach (von Bertalanffy 1968; Agazarian 1989) and contemporary multilevel organizational theory (Rousseau 1985; Kozlowski and Klein 2000), through a consideration of the principles of isomorphism, hierarchization, and relative autonomy in a multilevel theory of organization. The second aim is to propose a methodological approach that is coherent with the theoretical approach developed throughout the chapter. To this end, I am critical of both the theories and methodologies that are characteristic of single vision approaches, and concludes by calling for the use of a multilevel analysis as a methodological alternative that is more appropriate for analyzing complex systems (Posser, Rasbash, and Goldstein 1991).

Systems Thinking

The Gestalt psychologist Kurt Lewin (1935, 1951) established the basis for systems thinking in his theoretical fieldwork. According to his theory, group behavior is determined by its interaction with the surrounding environment. The group is a system imbued within a hierarchy of systems. The first applications of the systems approach to organizations came from the Tavistock Institute of Human Relations that, in its attempt to regenerate the failing post-war British economy, applied Wilferd Bion's principles of the conception of the-group-as-a-whole (1976). But what do we actually understand by system? James Grier Miller (1978, 16) offers the following definition: "A system is a set of interacting units with relationships among them. The word 'set' implies that the units have some common properties. These common properties are essential if the units are to interact or have relationships. The state of each unit is constrained by, conditioned by, or dependent on the state of other units. The units are coupled. Moreover, there is at least one measure of the sum of its units which is larger than the sum of the measure of its units."

Systems thinking and conceptions provide us with a metatheory that facilitates the understanding of complex systems. The core of this thinking can be summed up in a widely used concept: the isomorphism. The roots of this concept can be found in Ludwig von Bertalanffy's "general systems theory" (1968), which highlights that fact that, as well as being interconnected, systems have a dynamic structure and are organized into hierarchical levels that are increasingly more complex. The isomorphism is reflected in the fact that, starting from the lowest level (the cellular) up to the highest and most complex levels of society, all systems possess the same structures and have functions with similar organizational principles and processes. More than a mere system, von Bertalanffy's general systems theory constitutes an epistemological principle because it is uncontestable. It is a scientific theory insofar as it provides us with a way of understanding events.

Helen Durkin (1972) carried out one of the most important attempts to systematically apply systems thinking and, in particular, the principles of the general systems theory. With the help of a committee of experts, and after several years searching for a way in which systems theory could improve group therapy practices, Durkin (1981) and her collaborators extracted various illuminating principles. In particular, they observed that von Bertalanffy's isomorphism was reflected as much in group structures as it was in subgroup and individual ones. Furthermore, they highlighted the principle of the relative autonomy of systems, meaning systems' capacity to change themselves and to have an influence on other systems.

Subsequently, and on the basis of her system-based theory, Yvonne M. Agazarian (1992) delved further into the possible practical implications of the previous research. System-based theory constitutes a framework for applying the constructs of the general systems theory and the principles extracted from Durkin's research (1981) to human systems. Therefore, Agazarian (1992) claims that the structure and function of the member in a subgroup, of the subgroup in a group, and of the group in a society can be observed, defined, and explained from one single perspective; in other words, from the perspective of the group in the organization and of the organization in the society. Because of this, as a meta-theory, it may be useful for all groups regardless of their characteristics.

Systems theory implies overcoming a perspective in which the unit of analysis (individual, group, or organization) is considered to be the nucleus around which the other processes revolve and a replacement of that perspective with an acceptance that this unit is located within a hierarchy of complex and inter-related systems (Whitehead 1952). Therefore, the focus of analysis is now directed at individuals, groups or organizations as a whole; the systems approach allows us to understand that the way in which these three systems function is very similar (Agazarian 1989). As W.E.E.C. Spronck and T.H.L. Copernolle (1997, 152) argue, "systems theory not only looks at wholes of interacting parts, it also looks at different levels of organization . . . The systems view is like a zoom lens . . . keeping us aware of the fact that one can study a problem, such as violence, on many different levels . . . Going from one level to another does not imply an increase or reduction of complexity. On each level it is interesting and inspiring to be aware of the interaction with the levels below and above."

Following the principles of systems theory, one should not just focus on the widest, highest, or macro-level. Neither does systems theory necessarily mean that by analyzing the individual level we are simultaneously considering the group level, or that by analyzing groups we are considering the organizational level, or that by analyzing organizations we are thereby considering societies:

> Thinking 'systematic' means that one is willing to take into account information about the other levels, the higher as well as the lower ones . . . Working with families, for example, one is ready to take into account information about the culture, as well as about the individual and the brain. Therapists as well as researchers, however, cannot address all these levels together at the same time. They have to choose. The level you choose to study and intervene on depends on your interest, your goal, your knowledge, your tools, capacities, power, and so on (Spronck and Copernolle 1997, 153).

In any event, we should not forget that the formulation of a hypothesis, at group level for example, does not exclude other hypotheses at different levels.

Regulatory Principles of Complex Systems

One of the regulatory principles of the systems-based theory is that the different systems that are the object of analysis are isomorphically related, which is to say "the systems of the member, the subgroup, and the group as a whole are similar in structure, function, and the dynamic principles of operation. The hypothesis is that . . . influencing the dynamics of any one subsystem influences all the systems (Agazarian and Janoff 1993, 43). Therefore, the dynamic principles that regulate the functioning of an organization, of groups, and of individuals tend to run in parallel and aspire toward ensuring the internal balance of the system. For example, an extremely hierarchical organizational structure will mean that the functioning of the groups will be hierarchical just as the individuals will tend to develop the habit of thinking in line with official thought and of submitting to the norms imposed.

A second regulatory principle is the hierarchical organization of systems. In all hierarchies or nested sets, each system exists within the environment of the higher system (the group exists in the environment of the organization) and, at the same time, constitutes the environment of the lower system (the individual). "Every living system is influenced by its environments (inputs) and, in turn, influences its environment (outputs)" (Agazarian and Janoff 1993, 39).

Third, among the most significant principles of systems-based theory is the principle of the relative autonomy of systems, which reveals that groups and individuals have a certain capacity to influence each other reciprocally and to bring innovations to the organizational system. In other words, the different subsystems in the higher unit have the capacity to exert an emerging influence. An emerging influence is understood to be the process that goes from bottom to top, one that becomes a higher characteristic generated by a combination of inferior characteristics. In this way, the processes of change may be started by individuals, groups, or by the organization.

Integration of the Regulatory Principles of Complex Systems

The movement toward more organizational decentralization has highlighted the key importance of individuals as active, autonomous subjects with creative abilities and emerging influence. However, this conception of the individual is not new but has been present in the sociological tradition from Hobbes to Parsons. Concerned about the relation between the actions of the social system (macro) and those of human social action (micro), sociologists separated both systems in order to better understand them. However, when they tried to relate them again, this led to a negation of the person's autonomy. Because of this, on the basis of individual autonomy, the sociological tradition has ended up establishing the (necessary and inevitable) predominance of a higher-order and hierarchical system that determines values and imposes decisions on individuals: Put another way, "Leviathan has come home to roost and crow in triumph" (Dawe 1978, 408). The hierarchical organizations of the industrial revolution thus found their supreme ally in *Leviathan*.

Nevertheless, neither hierarchy nor relative autonomy should be understood as two separate principles in organizational life; if we separate them, we run the risk of decontextualizing them from their meaning, their reality: "life is never a material, a substance to be moulded. If you want to know, life is the principle of self-renewal, it is constantly renewing and remaking and changing and transfiguring itself, it is infinitely beyond your or my theories about it" (Boris Pasternak, cited in Dawe 1978, 414). Life is dialogue and communication. Paraphrasing Martin Buber, it can be argued that the fundamental fact of human existence is neither the individual as such, nor the organization, but rather "the conversation between Man and Man," which is constantly reconstructed by organizations.

This "conversation between Man and Man" refers to the dominant system of communications in an organization. This is where we need to locate the current tension in any organization, between hierarchization and relative autonomy, which determines two important aspects of isomorphism: one, its existence, and two, the kinds of explanations offered to account for it. It has been argued that the absence of isomorphism is a reflection of the tension and change in subsystems and processes at different levels. If the tension between both principles is significant, it is likely that there will be no isomorphism. By contrast, if there is an alignment between both principles, two kinds of explanation for the isomorphism can be found that are similar to the framework of analysis for episodic and continuous types of change proposed by the theory of organizational change (Weick and Quinn 1999).

The first, in which one of the two principles regularly prevails over the other, brings about an explanation of the isomorphism (from the hierarchy) different from that which would be produced if the dominant principle was the contrary one. For example, in a strict culture, with unequal relations, hierarchization will determine organizational, group, and individual processes, while in an organizational culture, defined as flexible and with equal relations, the principle of autonomy will take precedence over hierarchization. In each case, the explanation of the isomorphism will be defined by the dominant principle (Cameron and Quinn 1999).

The second case, in which both principles are aligned in a way not defined by the predominance of either one of them, constitutes a dynamic process whereby the organization constantly adapts to the outside environment and to internal needs. In this case, the isomorphism is defined by the processes of adaptation at an individual, group, and organizational level, which present themselves simultaneously, producing a balanced exchange between the organizational hierarchy and the individuals' autonomy. This process of exchange between both principles can be clearly seen in an organization with a strong outward-looking approach where constant changes are produced. The management may establish new norms and adaptation procedures, but simultaneously, individuals and groups redefine these in order to achieve a balance between the needs of the organization and the needs of individuals.

Therefore, the isomorphism must be understood as a process of adaptation between the needs of the organization—the survival of the organization and its development in a competitive environment—and individuals' needs, which is to say their material survival and social, affective, and cognitive development. As a result of this, we can conclude that the principles of isomorphism, hierarchization, and relative autonomy form part of a sole regulatory principle of social systems: interpersonal communication that, based on the interaction and social action of people, contributes toward the constant reconstruction of the organizational system.

When information flows in a top-down way due to the lack of existing two-way channels, the organization regulates communication between people through interpretations imposed by the managers. When numerous channels of communication exist and nobody holds sufficient power to be able to impose decisions, it is interpersonal communication that defines the values and constructs the organizational system.

Working groups, when they function with relative autonomy, facilitate the development of people's autonomy, thereby having an impact on the modification of the organization's communications system. Channels of communication are created that facilitate the integration of individuals' needs with those of the organization, with new interpretations being constructed with regard to the realities of the organization and the function of its people. The development of autonomy enables integration between people's needs and those of the organization, and between the knowledge held by workers and that of managers.

Consequently, the dynamics of the communication present in an organization will affect the alignment between the three principles discussed, which enables us to integrate the multilevel and systems approach into the study of organizations, not, however, as separate principles, but rather as principles that are integrated within and adapted to a changing organizational reality in which the social action of individuals, interacting with the influence of the macro-system, regulates organizational performance.

Multilevel Organizational Theory

The aim of this section is to demonstrate that, from a multilevel organizational approach, the principles that regulate complex systems, as well as represent valid principles in organizational theory, can also be applicable and open to analysis. This is one of the significant contributions of this theoretical approach. With this in mind, I summarize here some of the proposals of multilevel organizational theory in an overall consideration of micro and macro variables and in understanding isomorphism, hierarchies, and relative autonomy.

From an integrated perspective in which all social psychology is individual and all individual psychology is social, organizational theory has attempted to develop both theoretical and methodological perspectives that allow for improved operability of the regulatory principles of complex systems (Katz and Kahn 1966; Coleman 1986; Taylor and Spencer 1989). Those who pursued these goals might be considered the precursors and initiators of so-called multilevel organizational theory (Klein and Kozlowski 2000), which entails great effort on a complex path. Based on the definition and joint consideration of the information deriving from variables located at individual, group, and organizational level, this theory gives way to proposals that attempt to make the analysis of complex systems more operational.

Before carrying out this task, however, it is important to consider some of the difficulties that may be presented by research that focuses its attention on one sole level of analysis. Denise M. Rousseau and Robert House (1994) argue that such single vision approaches may be subject to, at least, two biases. First, they may generalize the conclusions obtained at one level in an inappropriate way to other levels. Similarly, they may assume that the existing relation between two specific constructs at one level will be similar at higher levels (in other words, assume the isomorphism unduly). Second, if there are cross-level effects, research at one single level will not take these into account. In other words, studies of individuals may not consider the effects of the group on the individuals' behavior, and studies of groups may fail to take into account the influence of the individual on their environment or situation.

In itself, the macro perspective does not take into consideration the significance of and the influence exerted by the behavior, perceptions, affects, and interactions between individuals on the development of phenomena at higher levels. Similarly, an exclusively micro perspective does not take into account contextual factors that may reduce or alter relations between variables at an individual level. The multilevel approach, besides integrating both perspectives, seeks to avoid both ecological as well as atomistic fallacies (Kozlowski and Klein 2000).

Robert House, Denise M. Rousseau, and Melissa Thomas-Hunt (1995) suggest a formulation that offers a theoretical framework for guiding, coding, accumulating, and integrating multilevel research on the basis of different proposals requiring empirical verification: the meso paradigm. This paradigm simultaneously refers to the study of at least two levels of analysis in which (1) one or more levels refer to individual or group processes and variables, (2) one or more levels refer to organizational processes and variables, and (3) the processes through which the levels of analysis are related (defined as points "a" and "b") are analyzed as connections or relations between propositions (House, Rousseau, and Thomas-Hunt 1995, 73).

In this way, and as a multilevel theoretical proposal, the meso perspective involves approaching organizational analysis as a complex system. This perspective enables an understanding of how phenomena vary at different levels and permits an examination of their common aspects, thereby reflecting the organizational realities in a more appropriate way.

The Principle of Isomorphism from the Perspective of Multilevel Organizational Theory

The notion of isomorphism from multilevel organizational theory suggests that the same relation or process may be used to represent a specific construct at more than one level (Kozlowski and Klein 2000; Rousseau 1985). In this way, isomorphism has been considered as the degree to which the constitutive components of a phenomenon (such as self-efficacy) and the relations between this and other phenomena—for example the relation between self-efficacy and individual performance—are similar at different levels; in other words, the same relation or dynamics between collective efficacy and group performance can also be observed.

The proposal for the inclusive interaction between the micro and macro highlights the importance of intermediary structures in organizations (for example, teams and working groups) as elements that increase the likelihood of isomorphism. These intermediary structures channel the information and the influence of the macro level and are spaces in which individuals create new ideas and develop their autonomy, enabling an alignment between the needs of management and the needs of individuals.

The importance of working groups from the perspective of multilevel theory is exemplified in the meso paradigm of House, Rousseau, and Thomas-Hunt (1995). Here, the authors define the meso processes that encourage the inclusion of individuals in organizations, thereby increasing isomorphism. Both the processes defined by the meso paradigm and the understanding of isomorphism from the perspective of multilevel organizational theory enable a better analysis and greater application of this paradigm.

House, Rousseau, and Thomas-Hunt (1995) define *inclusiveness* as the proportion of activity carried out by a unit within the set of activities included in another higher unit (such as the members of a working group). Inclusiveness between the different levels increases the likelihood of isomorphism in organizations given that it increases the alignment between higher and lower levels. The more inclusive a unit is in relation to another, which is to say, the more activities a unit carries out within the activities characterized by another unit, the more influence it will have on that unit. This phenomenon is related to Karl E. Weick's concept of *strong coupling* (1976), which indicates the extent to which the units of an organization at different levels are, or are not, related.

The *construction of a collective meaning* constitutes another phenomenon that augments isomorphism between units at different organizational levels. This is defined as "the creation of interpretations for ambiguous environments and events" (House, Rousseau, and Thomas-Hunt 1995, 93). Through this process, groups and individuals collectively construct shared ideas or mental models in order to understand and interpret real situations (Weick 1992). This is a process that allows individual knowledge to be transformed into collective knowledge, bringing about a set of beliefs, norms, and values that enable the creation of shared meanings. These shared beliefs define the reality of the units to which individuals belong and have an effect upon variables at different levels.

Because of this, it is more likely that isomorphism will arise in organizational systems in which individual activities are located within significant higher units. In these units, shared collective meanings tend to be constructed due to the stability of each unit's members, a shared history, frequent interaction, a high level of interdependence, and other shared processes. As noted, this enables an alignment between individual needs and organizational ones, reducing the tension between hierarchization and autonomy and allowing for the existence of isomorphism.

We will now see how the principles of hierarchization and relative autonomy can be understood from the perspective of multilevel organizational theory.

Principles of Hierarchization and Relative Autonomy in Multilevel Organizational Theory

From the strict point of view of Parson's theory, to understand the organization as a complex and nested system requires explanatory models to analyze the influence of higher structures on lower structures. The hierarchical nesting of subsystems is a principle that is present in organizations, and failing to take this into account may lead us to draw only partial conclusions.

Nevertheless, both the principle of hierarchization as well as that of relative autonomy should be understood together. One important reason for integrating both principles lies in the transformation of the concept of organizational hierarchy. In recent years, the number of organizational structures has been reduced significantly. The organizational hierarchy, which is less bureaucratized and has fewer levels, has gone from identifying the position occupied by individuals within an organigram to identifying a series of functions related to the personal characteristics of the individuals and the needs of the organization. This kind of functional hierarchy in an organization responds to the needs of the different systems that it is composed of, which, conversely, present a high degree of interdependence. In this way, insofar as this reflects a movement from the exclusive predominance of hierarchization toward a greater emphasis on individuals' autonomy, the theoretical models of mutual influence become essential in order to understand organizational phenomena.

In this sense, Steve W.J. Kozlowski and Katherine J. Klein (2000, 10–11) make this twofold claim: "group and organizational factors are contexts for individual perceptions, attitudes, and behaviors and need to be explicitly incorporated into meaningful models of organizational behavior." They go on to highlight that "individual social-psychological processes can be manifest as group, subunit, and organizational phenomena and need to be explicitly incorporated into meaningful models of organizational behavior." With both claims, these authors recognize that the two principles should be considered together in an analysis of levels that takes into account bottom-up, top-down, and cross-level effects.

With this being necessary, and although there is some evidence to suggest that individuals may have a key influence on macro organizational phenomena (House 1988), organizational theory lacks theoretical arguments and empirical evidence relating to the way in which individuals, small groups, and organizational units affect the scope, behavior, processes, and dimensions of organizations. In this respect, Barry M. Staw and Robert I. Sutton (1992) suggest various processes on the basis of which the micro dimension could exercise macro effects. For example, (1) when individuals act as intermediaries for organizations and represent them before third parties; (2) when individuals have significant power in terms of the implementing of strategic managerial decisions; and (3) when individuals' joint attributes, their beliefs and emotions, determine the culture and climate of the organization. The composition models analyzed below attempt to conceptualize and put forward coherent theoretical frameworks that respond to the third idea here.

In an attempt to provide suitable theoretical frameworks for organizational analysis and to simplify the intrinsic complexity of the multilevel approach, David Chan (1998) outlines five emerging models of constructs at different levels. Underpinning the concept of emerging constructs is the need to understand how bottom-up processes are developed; in other words, how the dimensions measured at an individual level are combined to reflect dimensions of higher units. To a certain extent, Chan highlights individuals' ability to have an influence on organizations (for example to create the concept of organizational culture based on the measure of individual values). As such, this represents an approach that enables the validation of constructs based on what Chan calls composition models.

Chan describes different models: additive, direct consensus, referent-shift consensus, dispersion, and process. For each model, Chan analyzes the existing functional relation between the constructs of higher and lower levels, the operational combination that is necessary to apply the composition, and the specific empirical support for each composition.

The additive model is the simplest of the proposals. The meaning of the constructs at the higher level is derived from the total or the mean of the lower unit scores: for example, if we think of the construct *group cooperation* as the mean value of a set of questions that measure individual conduct (such as "When faced with a conflict with my colleagues, I try to analyze the situation and find a solution acceptable to everyone"), in a way that is independent of within-group variability.

In the direct consensus model, definitions of the construct that are of interest at both levels (individual and group) are required, and it is important that the definition that refers to the higher unit level (the group) reflects the need for the perceptual agreement between units at lower levels. Chan provides the clearest example of this model with the *psychological climate* and *group climate* constructs. The researcher, in this case, draws on the individual measures of the psychological climate construct and the within-group agreement index ($\mathbf{r}_{wg(j)}$) of the scores (James, Demaree, and Wolf 1984) and reveals the degree to which these scores are shared within the groups (Kozlowski and Hattrup 1992). It is this agreement that constitutes the functional equivalent of the *climate* construct at the two levels.

The referent-shift consensus model is the same as the previous model except for the fact that a change of referent of the construct measured is produced at an individual level. The example provided by Chan (1998, 238) is presented here in order to explain this model. Let us consider the construct *self-efficacy* to be a score upon which, among others, the assertion "I am confident that I can perform this task" is based. Another form of the construct at the same level is "I am confident that my team can perform this task." This second form refers to the collective construct of *collective efficacy,* which is added to the higher level to represent the value of the construct known as group efficacy. The basic content of the original construct of efficacy is maintained in the concept of *collective efficacy,* although it no longer refers to oneself but to the team. This would be the shift of referent. The way in which the constructs of interest are analyzed has an influence not only on how the information is dealt with, but also on the theoretical conclusions that are drawn from these analyses.

Unlike the consensus models, the dispersion model sees within-group variance as a key indicator for the operationalization of the construct in question: "Dispersion is by definition a group-level characteristic" (Chan 1998, 239). The logic of this model lies in its capacity to provide a theory relating to constructs in which the indices of dispersion are coherent with the operationalized constructs. For example, from the perspective of group development, consensus models may initially reflect group constructs such as the *group climate.* However, as processes of individuation and personal autonomy become increasingly more relevant, the dispersion model could be of great help in making certain constructs operational, such as *group competition,* which is defined as the struggle for individual interests. In any event, more than the indices of dispersion, it is the theoretical definition of the construct that needs to be prioritized given that a high level of within-group disagreement may indicate the existence of subgroups rather than the absence of consensus. The kurtosis indices of the distributions are indicators of low (unimodal platykurtic) and high (unimodal leptokurtic) within-group agreement and should therefore be taken into consideration.

The previous models can be understood from a static point of view. The process model, however, should be considered in a dynamic and temporal way, in other words, from a perspective that is interested in how constructs change under the conditions established. For example, with regards to the development of working groups, the processes according to which specific perceptions are developed at an individual level are outlined in the first place (for example, how the acquisition of individualistic values comes about from collectivist values). Subsequently, the process of change may be composed at a higher level in order to specify the emerging process of the change from collectivist values to individualist ones in the team, or in the organization as a whole. The processes of transformation observed at an individual level are analogous to the processes of transformation produced in teams. The initial and final status of the higher-level units is similar to that of the lower level units.

When it comes to deciding which model is most appropriate, it is important to take into account the operational nature of the construct in question. If we consider that the organizational climate should be conceived as a construct separate from the perceptual agreement between the members of an organization, the use of the additive model will be appropriate (clearly positioning us in opposition to tested theories and committing an atomistic fallacy). However, if we believe that the agreement in individual perceptions within an organization is the basis for defining the concept of organizational climate, then we should use the direct consensus model.

These composition models encourage the search for mechanisms whereby lower level constructs can be combined with higher level ones, which is to say they facilitate the analysis of the principle of the relative autonomy of the functioning of complex systems.

Methodological Considerations of Multilevel Analysis

Having presented the idea of an integrated theoretical approach to analyzing organizational systems, as a means of sustaining this approach I now offer a multilevel framework of methodological analysis that is consistent with previous theoretical thinking. In order to achieve this goal, I will first outline the methodological limitations of single vision analyses in order to examine a wide array of organizational phenomena. I will then describe the different threats that the aggregation may be subject to when trying to consider the influence of multiple levels on the constructs analyzed. Finally, I develop a multilevel analysis perspective, establishing a comparison between models of variable coefficients with those of random coefficients.

I previously noted how research at one single level presents conceptual limitations in the way that isomorphisms are falsely assumed and cross-level effects are underestimated or not taken into consideration. I will now focus on the methodological limitations presented by single vision analyses. Evidently, both types of limitations are intrinsically related. Furthermore, here I will also describe the characteristic principles of multilevel regression analysis and highlight its advantages in relation to traditional models of regression analysis. This description is essential because it constitutes a highly appropriate methodological approach for analyzing the data of a nested structured and because it is a necessary complement to the theoretical approach I previously described.

Multilevel analysis (Bryk and Raudenbush 1992; De Leeuw and Kreft 1986; Goldstein 1995) is a methodological approach that takes into consideration complex variability patterns and those of a nested character (for example, workers in teams, teams in organizations, students in classes, teachers in departments, departments in faculties, and so on). As we will see shortly, the statistical model of multilevel analysis is the multilevel linear regression model, which is to say an extension of the linear regression model to a model that includes nested random coefficients at different levels. The basic idea of multilevel analysis is that the data is structured in a nested way that includes unexplained variability at every level of the nesting. In this way, when analyzing the structures of data that shape any kind of nesting (for example, workers in teams and teams in organizations), we find the patterns of unexplained variability at level 1 (workers), at level 2 (teams), and at level 3 (organizations). In this way, the variability patterns at lower levels may be explained by variables at higher levels, taking into account the existing variability at different levels.

As Juan C. Oliver, Jesús Rosel, and Pilar Jara (2000) argue, one of the consequences of using ordinary regression with nested data is that biases can be generated in the typical measuring error and, as a result, the likelihood of committing statistical interference errors is thereby increased. Multilevel models outweigh traditional statistical techniques through their ability to explicitly model social contexts. This introduces a degree of realism that is usually absent from single level models such as multiple regression.

Traditional models break down the variance of the data of the within-group and between-group parts and, consequently, tend to ignore the variation between groups when focusing on within-group variance, or the within-group variation when analyzing data from an aggregate perspective. The advantage of multilevel contextual models is that they examine individual and contextual variability at the same time. Classical regression models assume that the intensity of the relation observed at the lowest level is constantly maintained across all groups, which is to say that they assume homogeneity along the regression slope. This assumption may be problematic given that it is highly likely that the contexts will have a significant effect on the groups analyzed. Carrying out a regression using all the data at level 1 (for example, sample individuals) is only acceptable when there are no significant contextual effects, in other words, when the correlation coefficient for the whole sample analyzed is equal to the within-group correlation coefficient, or when the between-group correlation coefficient is equal to zero. To assume the absence of contextual effects is to defend the idea that the relation between (X) and (Y) is the same in all contexts, something which would be highly unlikely in a real situation.

Aggregation: An Incomplete Solution

When analyzing data from one single level, we should ask ourselves several questions: What are the consequences of ignoring the hierarchical structure of the data? What kinds of errors may be committed if the data are analyzed from a single level perspective when the data come from significant groupings? Frequently, in social research carried out at two levels, data aggregation procedures from the lower level are often used in the higher level. The fact that the reliability of the aggregate data is directly related to the number of units at the micro level (level 1) is, however, often ignored. In other words, the greater the number of subjects (level 1) that belong to the different groups (level 2), the more reliable the measurement of the variables considered at the higher level will be. Furthermore, if the researcher is interested in questions related to both micro and macro variables, aggregation can produce significant errors (Snijders and Bosker 1999).

The first potential error is called "change of meaning" (Hüttner 1981, cited in Snijders and Bosker 1999). A micro variable that is aggregated to the macro level will refer to the macro unit and not directly to the micro unit. For example, if we use a direct consensus composition model and aggregate the scores of the *psychological climate* to the group level, thereby obtaining the *group climate* construct, this will refer to the climate in the group and not to the psychological climate of the individuals belonging to these groups.

A second potential error is the "ecological fallacy." This relates to the fact that a correlation between variables at a macro level cannot be used to make claims about the relations between such variables at a micro level; the importance of realizing that it is not possible to carry out predictions at an individual level on the basis of aggregate scores (Robinson 1950). For example, finding a correlation between two macro variables in a certain country—such as individualism and collective emotional stress—does not allow us to make predictions nor to extract conclusions with regards to the relation between emotional stress and the individualistic values held by the people of that country.

The third kind of error is related to the lack of consideration of the possible cross-level interactions generated by the potential effects of variables at a macro level on relations that exist between variables at a micro level. If the data is aggregated without having analyzed potential cross-level interactions, we will be unable to answer questions such as whether the relation observed between the level of self-management and group participation is maintained regardless of the kind of team (cooperative or not very cooperative) in which the individuals work.

Finally, the fourth potential error refers to changes in the structure of the original data, especially when certain types of analysis, such as the analysis of covariance, are used. For example, let us consider that we are interested in examining the differences that exist between different working groups concerning workers' level of work satisfaction (Y), once the scores between the groups have been adjusted to take into account their workload (X). In order to do this, an analysis is carried out of the covariance from which we obtain the results given in figure 5.1. In this figure, the real situation of four different teams, each composed of five people, can be seen.

Now let us suppose that we want to find out if the differences that exist between the teams in the dependent variable (Y) are statistically significant. A micro level approach, which adjusts the within-group regression of the variable (Y) according to the variable (X), leads us to a line of

Figure 5.1. Micro-level versus macro-level adjustments

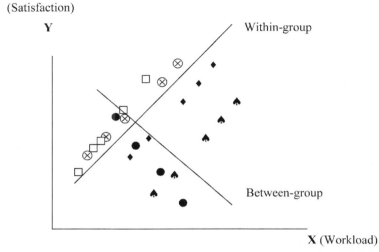

(X, Y) values for four groups indicated by □, ⊗, ♦, ♠. Group averages represented by ●.

Source: Adapted from Snijders and Bosker 1999, 14.

regression with a positive slope. All the members of the first team in the top part of the figure (□), are shown to be above the within-group regression line, whereas all the members of the team shown in the lower part of the figure (♠) are below the within-group regression line. Therefore, approaches carried out from a micro perspective lead us to conclude that there are significant statistical differences between the four teams, given that an adjustment has been made with regards to the variable (X).

By contrast, now let us suppose that we take the position of aggregating scores and carry out a regression of the average of ($\bar{Y}$) on the average of ($\bar{X}$). This situation is shown in figure 5.1 by way of a regression line with a negative slope. The averages for each group coincide almost exactly with the regression line, which is to say that we can accurately predict the averages of ($\bar{Y}$) based on the averages observed in ($\bar{X}$), leading us to conclude that, after having adjusted the scores with regards to the average of ($\bar{X}$), there are hardly any differences between the four teams. T.A.B. Snijders and Roel Bosker (1999, 26–31) have developed an example that illustrates how the within-group relation and the between-group relation may be completely different depending on the level at which the data is analyzed.

This alteration in relations can be clearly observed, not only in the area of regression, but also in the field of correlations between variables. In fact, the within-group correlations observed may be completely different from the between-group correlations. This should not surprise us if we take into account, for example, that work processes at a within-group level may be completely different from those between groups. Nevertheless, we should take into account that the total correlations, which is to say, the correlations obtained at a micro level—when the groupings of individuals in groups or of groups in organizations are obviated—represent a value that includes the relation between within-group and between-group averages. Therefore, it is essential to consider the within-group and between-group relations together as long as the grouping of the micro units in the macro units is significant and inherent to the phenomenon studied.

Consequently, considering the organization as a complex system made up of nested structures at different levels, a single level perspective may not capture important aspects of the reality. In such circumstances, the real relation between (Y) and (X) can only be perceived when the within-group and between-group relations are considered together, for example, through multilevel regression—in other words, from a multilevel perspective of organizational analysis.

A Multilevel Perspective of Regression

Having exposed the limitations of single level analyses, the risk posed by the use of aggregation, and the contribution that multilevel analysis can bring to this field of study, I will now briefly outline the statistical formulation upon which this analysis is based. My aim here is to highlight the point that this kind of analysis may respond more accurately to the research questions posed by systems and multilevel theory than traditional regression models of analysis.

Traditional regression models are based on the assumption that the linear regres sion of a dependent variable (Y) on an explanatory variable (X) is the linear function of (X) that provides the best prediction of (Y): in other words, the prediction that presents the least mean square error, known as the "least squares criteria." When the bivariate distribution of (X,Y) is known and the structure of the data has only one level, the formula which the regression function takes is widely recognized:

$$Y_i = a + bx_i + e_i \qquad \text{(equation 5.1)}$$

In which the regression coefficients are expressed by:

$a = E(Y) - E(X)$,

$$b = \frac{\text{cov}(X, Y)}{\text{var}(X)}$$

The constant term (a) is known as the intercept, whereas (b) is called the regression coefficient. The term (e_i) is the residual value or the error component and expresses the variability of the dependent variable (Y) that cannot be represented through a (Y) linear function. The terms E(Y) and E(X) refer to the average populations expected from (Y) and (X).

Nevertheless, adopting a single vision perspective means that either between-group or within-group variability can be overlooked. Therefore it is important to have models that are capable of analyzing data at the level at which they are measured and to take into consideration the within-group and between-group variability patterns together. These are termed *random coefficient models* (RCMs) of multilevel analysis (De Leeuw and Kreft 1986; Posser, Rasbash, and Goldstein 1991). RCMs are an extension of those known as *variable coefficient models* (VCMs), which provide as many predictions or regression lines as the contexts or groupings contained in the data (for example, ANCOVA).

An example will help illustrate the procedure through which RCMs are constructed. Initially, one starts from the VCMs in order to then analyze the RCMs. Let us suppose that we obtain data from N individuals ($i = 1, \ldots, N$) who are part of J groups ($j = 1, \ldots, J$). In this way, the subindexes ij can be assigned to each individual. At an individual level, the model includes a response variable (Y_{ij}) that, in this example, measures *work satisfaction* and one or several explanatory variables (X_{ij}). In order to present a parsimonious model, one single explanatory variable called *perceived self-management* is considered here. One could also examine a set of variables (Z_j) at a group level; however, for purely didactic reasons and in order to keep the example simple, I will focus here on just one: belonging or not belonging to working groups. At the moment, we are not considering the variable (Z_j), which is measured at group level or which can constitute an aggregate value. In order to predict the response variable (Y_{ij}) on the basis of the explanatory variable (X_{ij}), the VCMs establish a regression equation for each group. The regression equation used in the classic strategies for analyzing grouped data, including ANCOVA, is expressed as follows:

$$Y_{ij} = a_j + b_j x_{ij} + e_{ij} \qquad \text{(equation 5.2)}$$

It is important to note that the fundamental difference of this model in relation to the model expressed by the equation (equation 5.1) lies in the subindex (j) that has been added to the coefficients (*a*) and (*b*). This indicates that for each group (j), we take into account the specific value of the intercept and the specific value of the intensity of the relation between the variables (X) and (Y). In this way, (a_j) represents the values of the intercepts and (b_j) the values that the slopes take on in the different groups. In the same way as the single level regression models, the subindex (*i*) refers to individuals. The term (e_{ij}) represents the error component, with an expected average of zero and a variance that we well call (σ^2). In these VCMs, (Y_{ij}) and (e_{ij}) are the only random variables. However, as we will see shortly, in RCMs, both the (a_j) or the intercepts, as well as the (b_j) or slopes, can also have a random character.

Figures 5.2.a, 5.2.b, and 5.2.c, according to the VCMs, represent three linear models that include an explanatory variable at an individual level (X_{ij}) and a response variable at an individual level (Y_{ij}). In these figures, separate parameters are estimated for four imaginary groups, allowing each group its own regression line. In figure 5.2.a, the four groups have the same slope, but the intercepts differ, indicating a situation that is characteristic of ANCOVA analyses. The parallel lines indicate that the regression slope of (Y), *work satisfaction*, on (X), *perceived self-management*, is the same for all the groups. Nevertheless, the lines start from different points, indicating that once the level of self-management has been considered the average level of work satisfaction is higher for some groups than for others. In contrast, figure 5.2.b represents the situation of groups with the same value in terms of the intercept but with different slopes. For some groups, the intensity of the relation between the variables (X) and (Y) is greater than for others. Finally, figure 5.2.c, in which both the intercepts and the slopes are different for each group, represents a more realistic situation than figures 5.2. a and 5.2.b.

On this point, it is interesting to ask why the groups vary or if there is a variable at the macro level that could explain the differences observed between the groups. These questions define the key objective of multilevel regression analysis—to predict variation in the intercepts and in the slopes, introducing explanatory variables from the macro level.

Having said that, this question could be addressed with both VCMs and RCMs.

VCMs consider the parameters obtained on each regression line (the intercept and the slope) as response variables that can be valued on the basis of regression functions at a macro level. Explanatory variables are introduced into these functions at a macro level (Z_j)—in our example, *belonging or not belonging to working groups*. Such a prediction is reflected in the following equations:

$$a_j = c_0 + c_1 z_j \qquad \text{(equation 5.3)}$$

$$b_j = d_0 + d_1 z_j \qquad \text{(equation 5.4)}$$

where (a_j) and (b_j) are the regression coefficients for the intercept and the slope respectively.

We obtain as many (a_j) and (b_j) values as the groups that we are studying. The macro equations (5.3) and (5.4) include the macro intercepts $(c_0; d_0)$ and the macro slopes $(c_1; d_1)$ for each of the within-group intercepts (a_j) and slopes (b_j). These equations highlight the fact that the group variable (Z_j) is used to explain the variation observed in the intercepts and slopes.

Given that an analysis is needed for each group or context, the VCMs enable the specificity of these contexts to be examined. However, this is not at all practical when trying to analyze many groups. In these cases, a better alternative to these models can be found by extending them to RCMs. These models offer a practical response to the question of why groups vary. Furthermore, the RCMs do not only take into account the idiosyncratic nature of each group, but also any aspects they may have in common. These models do not estimate coefficients for each context separately, but instead offer a single solution by taking into consideration the variability between groups both in terms of their intercepts and of their slopes, or in both of them together. Figures 5.3.a, 5.3.b, and 5.3.c show the estimate of a single model in respect of which the four groups of our example may vary. These figures correspond to figures 5.2.a, 5.2.b, and 5.2.c, respectively, showing the differences arising form the use of VCMs (figures 5.2.a, 5.2b, and 5.2.c) or RCMs (figures 5.3.a, 5.3.b, and 5.3.c) in each case.

Figure 5.3.a shows a model for four groups with equal slopes and different intercepts. In this figure, the thickest line (average line) represents the average intercept, and the two thinner lines indicate the variation of

Figures 5.2a, 5.2b, 5.2c and 5.3a, 5.3b, 5.3c

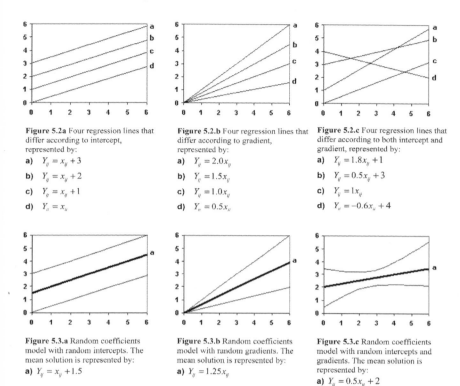

Figure 5.2a Four regression lines that differ according to intercept, represented by:

a) $Y_{ij} = x_{ij} + 3$

b) $Y_{ij} = x_{ij} + 2$

c) $Y_{ij} = x_{ij} + 1$

d) $Y_{ii} = x_{ii}$

Figure 5.2.b Four regression lines that differ according to gradient, represented by:

a) $Y_{ij} = 2.0x_{ij}$

b) $Y_{ij} = 1.5x_{ij}$

c) $Y_{ij} = 1.0x_{ij}$

d) $Y_{ii} = 0.5x_{ii}$

Figure 5.2.c Four regression lines that differ according to both intercept and gradient, represented by:

a) $Y_{ij} = 1.8x_{ij} + 1$

b) $Y_{ij} = 0.5x_{ij} + 3$

c) $Y_{ij} = 1x_{ij}$

d) $Y_{ii} = -0.6x_{ii} + 4$

Figure 5.3.a Random coefficients model with random intercepts. The mean solution is represented by:

a) $Y_{ij} = x_{ij} + 1.5$

Figure 5.3.b Random coefficients model with random gradients. The mean solution is represented by:

a) $Y_{ij} = 1.25x_{ij}$

Figure 5.3.c Random coefficients model with random intercepts and gradients. The mean solution is represented by:

a) $Y_{ij} = 0.5x_{ij} + 2$

the four groups with regards to this intercept. The value of the variance on the thick line is the same for all the values of (X) at any point of the regression function. In figure 5.3.b, a model is shown for four groups with the same intercept and different slopes. In this figure, the distance from the thickest line is not the same for all the values of (X). Therefore, the greater the value of (X), the greater the variation of the average slope will be. Finally, figure 5.3.c represents a solution in which the variability of the intercepts, the variability of the slopes, and the covariation between both are reflected. The total variance on the thickest line constitutes the total of the two variances in addition to the covariance, which means that the variation pattern of the four groups with regards to the average line is irregular.

As can be deduced from the above, in the face of the question of whether grouping variables exist (at a macro, contextual level) that explain the variability (in the intercepts, in the slopes, or in both) observed in the groups, RCMs offer a substantially different solution to that of VCMs. In the case of the former, each coefficient of the regression equation has its own variance, which allows each group to be unique. This is represented in the extent to which each group has its own variability in relation to the average solution. Figures 5.3.a, 5.3.b, and 5.3.c show that the estimated coefficients for each group are represented according to how they vary in relation to the average line. This average solution and the specific variability of each group are expressed through two components in the regression equation: an average value or fixed component and a variance or random component. In order to see what these two components of the regression equation consist of, we need to take up once again the initial regression function formula for data with a nested structure:

$$Y_{ij} = a_j + b_j x_{ij} + e_{ij} \qquad \text{(equation 5.2)}$$

In this case, the meaning of the coefficients (Y_{ij}), (x_{ij}) and (e_{ij}) does not vary in relation to that of the VCMs, but the coefficient (a_j) reflects the random intercept and (b_j) reflects the random slope. The fact that the coefficients of the regression are random means that they may vary according to the units at level 2 or the different groups. Because of this, the fundamental difference compared to VCMs is that, in RCMs, the intercepts and slopes are random, whereas, in the previous case, they were fixed for each group. Each coefficient in RCMs is estimated as a principal effect with a corresponding variation component. This variation shows the deviation among groups (between-group variability) with respect to this principal effect or average solution (the thickest lines in figures 5.3.a, 5.3.b, and 5.3.c). Here we see how the random intercept and the random slope are presented through equations at a macro level.

$$a_j = \gamma_{00} + u_{0j} \qquad \text{(equation 5.5)}$$

$$b_j = \gamma_{10} + u_{1j} \qquad \text{(equation 5.6)}$$

Random coefficients are made up of average population values of a fixed nature for the intercept and the slope $(\gamma_{00}; \gamma_{01})$, in addition to a distortion or error component at group level $(u_{0j}; u_{1j})$. These errors at a macro level show that both the intercept (γ_{00}) and the slope (γ_{10}) vary across the different groups or contexts. The intercept average of all the groups is represented by (γ_{00}), whereas (u_{0j}) indicates the deviation of all the groups in relation to this global average. In the same way, the average slope of the different groups is shown by (γ_{10}), whereas (u_{1j}) represents the deviation of all the groups in relation to this global slope. The random components of the model for estimating (a_j) and (b_j) are (u_{0j}) and (u_{1j}), which, in the same way as the errors at a macro level, have an expected average value of zero and the variances (τ_{00}) and (τ_{11}) respectively, with the covariance between both being expressed by (τ_{01}).

The following model sums up the components of the variance of an RCM with a random intercept and slope.

$$\mathbf{T} = \begin{array}{c} u_{0j} \\ u_{1j} \end{array} \overset{\begin{array}{cc} u_{0i} & u_{1i} \end{array}}{\begin{pmatrix} \tau_{00} & \tau_{01} \\ \tau_{10} & \tau_{11} \end{pmatrix}} \qquad \text{(equation 5.7)}$$

The T elements of the model represent the degree to which the groups differ from the general average estimate of the regression line. In order to show that the equations that have been presented in an isolated way are not actually isolated, but that, in fact, they all contribute to the configuration of an RCM, we need to replace equations 5.5 and 5.6 with equation 5.2 in such a way that we obtain:

$$Y_{ij} = (\gamma_{00} + u_{0j}) + (\gamma_{10} + u_{1j})x_{ij} + e_{ij} \qquad \text{(equation 5.8)}$$

which, by developing and regrouping the terms, can be expressed as follows:

$$Y_{ij} = \gamma_{00} + \gamma_{10}x_{ij} + (u_{0j} + u_{1j}x_{ij} + e_{ij}) \quad \text{(5.9)}$$

whereby:

Y_{ij} = Value of the dependent variable for the i–th subject of level 1 nested within the j-th group of level 2.

γ_{00} = Average population of the intercept.

γ_{10} = Average population of the slope, adjusted according to the predictor variable (x_{ij}).

x_{ij} = Value of the dependent variable for the i–th subject of level 1 nested within the j-th group of level 2.

u_{0j} = Deviation (random effect) of the intercept of the j-th group of level 2 in relation to the average intercept (γ_{00}).

u_{1j} = Deviation (random effect) of the slope of the j-th group of level 2 in relation to the average slope (γ_{10}), after taking into account the effect of the predictor variable (x_{ij}).

e_{ij} = Random error associated with the i-th subject of level 1 within the j-th group of level 2.

In the right-hand side of the equality equation, the fixed effects () are located outside the parenthesis, while the error components ($u;$) are grouped within the parentheses. The variance of the macro error term of the slope depends on the values adopted by the explanatory variable (X). As already indicated, the result of the analysis of random coefficients is a single regression line on which the specificities of each context or group are expressed by the macro error terms (u). The groups fluctuate according to this line. If the macro variances corresponding to the error term of the intercept (), of the slope (), and/or the covariance between both () are significantly different from zero, it can be deduced that contextual effects are present. Basing their study on theoretical suppositions and specific hypotheses, it is task of researchers to analyze which variable or variables may explain such variability at a macro level. RCMs, unlike other regression models, enable such an analysis to be carried out parsimoniously, while also taking into account the patterns of complex variability that exist in structures with nested data.

Multilevel analysis, which has been briefly outlined here, represents a methodological strategy that allows both the specificity of individuals and their meaningful contexts to be taken into account, or, if one prefers, what is specific to groups and their different contexts. The perspective that we adopt should be in line with the theory that we are trying to test and should be carried out at the appropriate level of analysis for our study. This kind of analysis constitutes one of the most effective approaches— both conceptually and methodologically—for examining all the relations that exist at the multiple levels present in an organizational system.

The methodological approach proposed here has attempted to offer a new contribution to the overall consideration of the principles that regulate the functioning of complex systems in organizational analysis. I believe that the theoretical contribution offered and the methodological approach developed represent an operational accomplishment, both for an overall consideration of the variables found at different levels, as well as for an analysis of the principles of systems theory. However, the development of a multilevel, organizational, theoretical, and methodological corpus that is both applicable and generalizable is a complex and exciting challenge that will most probably require many years of further study.

References

Agazarian, Yvonne M. 1989. "Group-as-a-Whole Systems Theory and Practice." *Group* 13, nos. 3–4: 131–54.

———. 1992. "Contemporary Theories of Group Psychotherapy: A Systems Approach to the Group-as-a-Whole." *International Journal of Group Psychotherapy* 42, no. 2: 177–203.

Agazarian Yvonne M., and Sandra J. Yanoff. 1993. "Systems Theory and Small Groups." *Comprehensive Group Psychotherapy*, edited by Harold I. Kaplan and Benjamin J. Sadock. 3rd ed. Baltimore, MD: Williams and Wilkins.

Bion, Wilfred R. 1976. *Experiences in Groups*. New York: Basic Books.

Bryk, Anthony S., and Steven W. Raudenbush. 1992. *Hierarchical Lineal Models: Applications and Data Analysis Methods*. Newbury Park, CA: Sage Publications.

Cameron, Kim S., and Robert E. Quinn. 1999. *Diagnosing and Changing Organizational Culture: Based on the Competing Values Framework*. Reading, MA: Addison-Wesley Publishing Company, Inc.

Chan, David. 1998. "Functional Relations among Constructs in the Same Content Domain at Different Levels of Analysis: A Typology of Composition Models." *Journal of Applied Psychology* 83: 234–46.

Coleman, James S. 1986. "Social Theory, Social Research, and a Theory of Action." *American Journal of Sociology* 91, no. 6: 1309–35.

Dawe, Alan. 1978. "Theories of Social Action." In *A History of Sociological Analysis*, edited by Tom Bottomore and Robert Nisbet. New York: Basic Books.

De Leeuw, Jan and Ita Kreft. 1986. "Random Coefficient Models for Multilevel Analysis." *Journal of Educational Statistics* 11, no. 1: 57–85.

Durkin, James E. 1972. "Group Therapy and General System Theory." In *Progress in Group and Family Therapy*, edited by Clifford J. Sager and Helen Singer Kaplan. New York: Brunner-Mazel.

———. 1981. *Living Group: Group Psychotherapy and General System Theory*. New York: Brunner-Mazel.

Goldstein, Harvey. 1995. *Multilevel Statistical Models*. New York: John Wiley and Sons.

House, Robert J. 1988. "Power and Personality in Complex Organizations." In *Research in Organizational Behavior*, edited by B.M. Staw and L.L. Cummings. Volume 10. Greenwich, CT: JAI Press.

House, Robert, Denise M. Rousseau, and Melissa Thomas-Hunt. 1995. "The Meso Paradigm: A Framework for the Integration of Micro and Macro Organizational Behavior." *Research in Organizational Behavior* 17: 71–114.

James, Lawrence R., Robert G. Demaree, and Gerrit Wolf. 1984. "Estimating Within-group Interrater Reliability with and Without Responses Bias." *Journal of Applied Psychology* 69, no. 1: 85–98.

Katz, Daniel, and Robert L. Kahn. 1966. *The Social Psychology of Organizations*. New York: Wiley.

Kozlowski, Steve W. J., and Keith Hattrup. 1992. "A Disagreement about Within-group Agreement: Disentangling Issues of Consistency versus Consensus." *Journal of Applied Psychology* 77, no. 2: 161–67.

Kozlowski, Steve W.J., and Katherine J. Klein. 2000. "A Multilevel Approach to Theory and Research in Organizations: Contextual, Temporal, and Emergent Processes." In *Multilevel Theory, Research and Methods in Organizations: Foundations, Extensions and New Directions*, edited by Katherine J. Klein and Steve W.J. Kozlowski. San Francisco: Jossey-Bass.

Lewin, Kurt. 1935. *Dynamic Theory of Personality*. New York: McGraw-Hill.

———. 1951. *Field Theory in Social Sciences*. New York: Harper and Row.

Miller, James Grier. 1978. *Living Systems*. New York: McGraw-Hill.

Munich, Richard L. 1993. "Group Dynamics." *Comprehensive Group Psychotherapy*, edited by Harold I. Kaplan and Benjamin J. Sadock. 3rd ed. Baltimore, MD: Williams and Wilkins.

Oliver, Juan C., Jesús Rosel, and Pilar Jara. 2000. "Modelos de regresión multinivel: Aplicación en psicología escolar." *Psicothema* 12: 487–94.

Prosser, Robert, Jon Rasbash, and Harvey Goldstein. 1991. *ML3 Software for Three-level Analysis: User's Guide for V.2*. London: Institute of Education, University of London.

Robinson, W.S. 1950. "Ecological Correlations and the Behavior of Individuals." *American Sociological Review* 15, no. 3: 351–57.

Rousseau, Denise M. 1985. "Issues of Level in Organizational Research: Multi-level and Cross Level Perspectives." *Research in Organizational Behavior* 7: 1–37.

Rousseau, Denise M., and Robert J. House. 1994. "Meso Organizational Behavior: Avoiding Three Fundamental Biases." In *Trends in Organizational Behavior*, edited by Cary L. Cooper and Denise M. Rousseau. Vol. 1. London: Wiley.

Snijders, T.A.B., and Roel Bosker. 1999. *Multilevel Analysis: An Introduction to Basic and Advanced Multilevel Modelling*. London: Sage.

Spronk, W.E.E.C., and T.H.L. Compernolle. 1997. "Systems Theory and Family Therapy: From a Critique on System Theory to a Theory on System Change." *Contemporary Family Therapy,* 19, no. 2: 147–75.

Staw, Barry M., and Robert I. Sutton. 1992. "Macro Organizational Psychology." In *Social Psychology in Organizations: Advances in Theory and Research*, edited by J. Keith Murnighan. Englewood Cliffs, NJ: Prentice-Hall.

Taylor, G.S., and Spencer, B.A. 1989. "Cross-level Research: An Empirical Technique for Multilevel Analysis in Organizational Research." *Behavioral Science, 34*, 61–69.

Von Bertalanffy, Ludwig. 1968. *General System Theory: Formulations, Developments and Applications*. London: Brazilier.

Weick, Karl E. 1976. "Educational Organizations as Loosely Coupled Systems." *Administrative Science Quarterly* 21: 1–19.

———. 1992. "Agenda Settings in Organizational Behavior: A Theory-focused Approach." *Journal of Management Inquiry* 1: 171–83.

Weick, Karl E., and Robert E. Quinn. 1999. "Organizational Change and Development." *Annual Review of Psychology* 50: 361–86.

Whitehead, Alfred North. 1952. *Science and the Modern World*. New York: Macmillan.

6

How Do Cultural Changes Influence the Psychological Contract between Worker and Organization?

José Valencia Gárate

Translated by Jennifer R. Ottman

The context of work is changing: From a mechanized environment, we are moving to jobs based on knowledge creation. Workers are being asked for greater personal involvement: In addition to being asked to do their jobs well, they are being asked to think about client or user needs and try to find new ways of responding to those needs. Innovation consists in finding new responses to society's needs. The demand for innovation modifies the mutual expectations between workers and company management. Workers contribute effort, time, skills, and creativity. The company contributes resources and recognition of workers' autonomy on the job. This change in their relationship takes concrete shape in the form of shared leadership and shared ownership of the company. In a work environment based on knowledge creation, an alliance between the entrepreneur's capital and the worker's knowledge is required in order for a company to grow. By way of an example, in the Basque case groups of entrepreneurs who have met to discuss labor relations in a knowledge society arrived at the idea that, in

* This study was conducted with the support of the Gipuzkoa Provincial Council (Diputación Foral de Gipuzkoa), through the Gipuzkoan Network of Science, Technology, and Innovation Program (Programa Red Guipuzcoana de Ciencia, Tecnología e Innovación/ Zientzia, Teknologia eta Berrikuntzaren Gipuzkoako Sarea Programa).

addition to the legal contract, another kind of contract has to be established, based on workers' commitment to companies' objectives. Without naming it, they were referring to the psychological contract.[1]

This change in the work context is taking us in the direction of more individualized and less collective labor relationships (Guest 2004, 542). Certainly, direct communication between managers and workers favors the individualization of promises and obligations, making the content of the psychological contract more explicit. Moreover, the process of communication implied by these new labor relationships may parallel the process of communicating the psychological contract (Guest and Conway 2002, 23).

The psychological contract has been defined as "an individual's belief in mutual obligations between that person and another party such as an employer" (Rousseau and Tijoriwala 1998, 679). Building on the idea of exchange and of a contract between two parties, David E. Guest gives the following definition of the psychological contract: "The perception of both parties to the employment relationship, organization and individual, of the reciprocal promises and obligations implied in that relationship" (2004, 545). The perception of *promises* and *obligations* varies according to how those promises and obligations are transmitted. In collectivist cultures, whether that collectivism is vertical (stratified and hierarchical) or horizontal (egalitarian), the psychological contract is based on the organization's declared values. The organization's statements of mission, vision, and values *implicitly* define the promises and obligations made and undertaken by the organization and the workers' collective. Awareness of *non-fulfillment of the psychological contract* has its objective basis in the lack of agreement between the *declared values* of and the *values practiced* in a particular organization. The explanatory basis of the psychological contract is to be found in the organization's culture, and specifically in the values declared in its mission statement (Topa 2005, 42).

The development of more individualized and flexible work relationships has resulted in individuals, rather than collectives, becoming the final referent of these promises and obligations and these promises and obligation becoming ever more explicit. The values of horizontal individualism (personal responsibility, initiative, commitment, and competence) together with the values of horizontal collectivism (shared

---

1. Personal experience in the entrepreneurs' groups of Innobasque (the Basque Innovation Agency).

responsibility, synergy, and teamwork) modify the conceptual framework habitually used in investigating the psychological contract (Guest 2004, 544).

This modification of the conceptual framework affects the following three elements. First, it affects the collective versus individualized character of the mutual promises and obligations in the psychological contract. To the extent that work relationships become more individualized and flexible, the psychological contract becomes more individualized, and to the same extent, its promises and obligations become ever more explicit. Then, it also affects the content of the psychological contract: the psychological contract becomes more focused on relational aspects, leaving the more transactional aspects for the legal contract. Transactional content refers to specific monetary aspects such as pay, incentives for meeting objectives, job stability, and so on (Zhao et al. 2007), whereas relational content refers to more personal and prolonged exchanges, such as personal support, the meaningfulness of the work, kind of supervision, career development, training, promotion, and so on. Finally, this modification affects the state of the psychological contract. Hence, following David E. Guest and Neil Conway (2002), Inmaculada Silla, Francisco Javier Gracia, and José María Peiró (2005) introduce three basic elements into the state of the psychological contract: whether promises are kept; trust in the organization; and distributive, procedural, and interactive justice.

Given the importance of the content of the psychological contract, we should pay greater attention to perceptions of justice and trust as explanatory factors for non-fulfillment and, above all, breach of the psychological contract (Silla, Gracia, and Peiró 2005). *Distributive justice* refers to equity between the contributions made by one party and the considerations received in return from the other party. *Procedural justice* refers to equity in procedural matters. *Interactive justice* refers to equity in personal interactions between supervisors and workers.

The Company's Organizational Culture

The organization in which this study was conducted has a strong culture that can be defined as "horizontal collectivism." In this culture, a series of values are stressed. Some of those declared values are:

- Jobs are secure.
- The pay is relatively good.

- The company creates jobs.
- There is little difference in compensation among shareholders of the cooperative, and there is no discrimination based on their performance on the job.
- There is little distance between managers and workers. All are equally shareholders and owners of the firm, even if they exercise different functions in the firm.
- Internal promotion is a possibility.
- Information is transparent.
- Shareholders' children have preference for joining the firm.
- Most workers are shareholders of the cooperative and share ownership of the firm.

In accordance with Triandis's cultural dimensions (Ros and Gouveia 2001, 110), the company's *declared values* correspond to a form of horizontal collectivism. However, the company's development in recent years and the management model implemented have sharpened the differences between its different levels: managers and supervisors, non-production or administrative staff, and production workers. The *values practiced* thus indicate a form of vertical collectivism.

- The company's growth in recent years and the consequent centralization of decision-making has created a great distance between managers and workers.
- The information that workers receive about the company's strategic decisions, which affect them as shareholders, is limited and partial, due to its confidentiality and to the company's need to protect itself against competitors. In addition, this information is highly technical and beyond the ability of a large part of the workers to understand. The result is widespread suspicion that information is being hidden from them.
- Rapid technological development, together with a system of personnel recruitment based on geographical proximity and family ties, has reduced the possibility of internal promotion and forced the company to hire qualified outside personnel.
- The absence of a system for evaluating workers' performance has promoted "social loafing" or "seat-warming" behavior and has given rise to a feeling of injustice.

Method

This chapter is based on the following method:

Structured Group Interviews

Five group interviews were held with managers, and nine group interviews were held with workers from the company's different lines of business.

All interviews were based on same three questions:

- Is there a feeling that the promises made have not been kept, both by the firm in relation to its workers and vice versa?
- If so, to what is this feeling attributed?
- What are the consequences of this feeling?

There were two discrepancies between managers and workers. Managers placed greater stress than workers on non-fulfillment related to "job security," "income," and "job creation." Managers' perceptions centered on the transactional content of the psychological contract, yet workers did not show particular concern about the transactional aspects of the psychological contract during the interviews.

Workers, for their part, placed greater emphasis than managers on non-fulfillment related to "training" and "information." They were especially critical of the training department, which they blamed for workers' lack of the technical qualifications demanded by technological progress and changes in the work environment. This criticism is related to the system by which the firm initially selects workers, to technological progress, and to the difficulty of keeping the promise of internal promotion. The firm had to resort to hiring qualified outside personnel to meet the needs of the RDI (research, development, and innovation) department. With regard to information, they considered it scarce, and above all, excessively technical and difficult for workers to understand.

Both collectives agreed on nonfulfillment related to "distance between the managerial level and that of workers," reduced "internal promotion," and increased "seat-warming behavior." The *distance between workers and managers* is due, in large part, to the company's expansion and centralization of its strategic decision-making. Meanwhile, *reduced internal promotion* is explained by the mismatch between the personnel recruitment system, job security, and the demand for technical qualifications arising from the company's technological development and the need to promote innovation. Finally, *seat-warming behavior* refers to workers' lack of motivation and personal involvement.

Working Hypotheses

Since the items in the questionnaire were formulated in positive terms, in reality the results reflect the degree to which the company's personnel are conscious of the "fulfillment of promises." For this reason, the hypotheses were formulated positively, in terms of the "fulfillment of promises."

Starting from the results obtained in the group interviews, the working hypotheses were the following:

The *general hypothesis* was that the feeling that promises have not been kept is due to a cultural change not shared by the organization's managers and its workers. Among workers, there is a shift underway from horizontal collectivism toward horizontal individualism. Managers, in contrast, are evolving in the direction of vertical collectivism.

More *specific hypotheses* could be formulated as follows:

H1: One expected that the fundamental variable conditioning the consciousness of fulfillment of promises would be "trust in the organization."

H2: One expected that trust in the organization would be conditioned by the following variables:

H2.1 Possibilities for training and internal promotion

H2.2 Proximity between managers/supervisors and workers

H2.3 Autonomy on the job

H2.4 Involvement with the firm's objectives and perceived value of performance

H2.5 Trust in the Governing Council and Shareholders' Council

H2.6 Value assigned to the job

Procedure

The company hands out an annual questionnaire that measures the level of worker satisfaction. I was allowed to add an item referring to the fulfillment of promises. The final questionnaire consisted of sixty-two items and measured the following dimensions:

- Physical conditions of work
- Economic conditions of work
- Professional development: training
- Professional development: suitability of job to person
- Professional development: promotion and professional growth
- Organization of work

- The company's internal communication
- Communication between supervisors and subordinates
- Participation in the job area
- Participation in company management
- Work environment
- Managerial and supervisors' performance
- The company's strategies, objectives, and future
- Corporate values
- Time management

I used the item "I am satisfied with the extent to which the company has fulfilled its promises to me" as my *criterion variable*. This variable, taken from Sandra L. Robinson and Elizabeth Wolfe Morrison (1995, 297), is a global measure of promise fulfillment.

Measures of the following socio-demographic variables were also used: *status* (1 = "member"; 2 = "non-member"); *group* (1 = "managers and supervisors"; 2 = "sales, administrative, and technical staff"; 3 = "production workers"); *education* (1 = "primary education"; 2 = "secondary-level technical degree or qualification"; 3 = "senior high school/secretarial qualification"; 4 = "post-secondary-level technical degree or qualification"; 5 = "higher education"); *index* (1 = "from 1.00 to 1.35"; 2 = "from 1.36 to 1.60"; 3 = "from 1.61 to 2.00"; 4 = "from 2.01 to 2.40"; 5 = "2.41 and higher"); *years at the firm;* and *age.*

Sample
The sample was made up of 1,282 subjects, distributed as follows: managers and supervisors: 113 (8.81 percent); sales, administrative, and technical staff: 273 (21.29 percent); and production workers: 896 (69.89 percent).

Results
The results obtained are listed in the following sections.

Factor Analysis of Principal Components
The goal of factor analysis is to reduce the number of variables, grouping items according to the correlations between them. The method used in this reduction of variables was the following:

First, an exploratory factor analysis was performed with oblimin rotation, and nine factors were obtained. In a second phase, the nine-factor model was subjected to confirmatory factor analysis and was not confirmed. In a third pass, the items with a contribution less than 0.40 were eliminated. On this condition, the exploratory factor analysis extracted seven factors. On the fourth pass, the null model (absence of relation between items) was contrasted with the second model (the seven-factor model). This seven-factor model was found to be a good fit according to all indicators. By convention, a good fit between the data and the model requires an AGFI greater than 0.90, an RMSR less than 0.05, and an X^2/df ratio less than 5.

These are the seven factors extracted by factor analysis, under the condition of eliminating all items with a contribution less than .40. These seven factors, extracted by factor analysis, explain 61.50 percent of the total variability. Seventeen items were eliminated due to a contribution less than .40.

I subsequently performed an analysis of the correlation between the criterion variable and the weighted sums of the seven dimensions of the factor analysis. The criterion variable correlates, first of all, with "trust in the organization" (F2), "possibilities for training and internal promotion" (F4), and "supervisor-worker proximity" (F1). In second place, it correlates with "autonomy on the job" (F3) and with "trust in the governing council and members' council" (F5). Finally, "involvement with the organization's objectives and evaluation of performance" (F6) and "value assigned to the job" (F7) had the lowest correlation.

Hierarchical Regression Analysis

Hierarchical regression analysis enables us to determine which of the factors most influence the criterion variable: "I am satisfied with the extent to which the firm has met the expectations I had when I joined."

The results of the hierarchical regression analysis clearly indicate that the variables "group" and "index" have a strong influence on the criterion variable ("fulfillment of the psychological contract"), but when the variables "supervisor-worker proximity," "trust in the governing council and members' council," "involvement with the organization's objectives and evaluation of performance," and "value assigned to the job" are introduced into the regression, their influence disappears. This means that the effect of socio-demographic variables on the criterion variable occurs by way of the other factors. In addition, when the more important factors are introduced into the regression, the influence of the factors with lower regression significance also disappears or is reduced. In a word, the three variables that most influence fulfillment of the psychological contract are "trust in the organization," "possibilities for training and internal promotion," and "autonomy on the job."

On the other hand, we find that the socio-demographic variables (especially the "index") influence "trust in the organization" by way of the organizational variables: "trust in the governing council and members' council," "involvement with the organization's objectives and evaluation of performance," "autonomy on the job," "supervisor-worker proximity," "possibilities for training and internal promotion," and "value assigned to the job." The organizational variables influence "trust in the organization," and this directly affects the fulfillment of the psychological contract.

Discussion

One of the survey's most significant results involves items 9 and 12. When a cluster analysis was performed with all the questionnaire items, allowing for assignment to three clusters, it was found that these two items (which measure equity of performance) were those that obtained the most support from the personnel: item 9, "I consider it important that differences among workers in terms of their performance on the job be recognized" ($X = 4.08$, $X = 3.68$, $X = 3.27$ for the high, middle, and low clusters respectively), and item 12, "I believe that when incorporating new workers into the company, professional competence should take precedence over other criteria (family relationships and geographical proximity)" ($X = 3.99$, $X = 3.55$, $X = 3.28$ for the high, middle, and low clusters respectively).

These results indicate that workers want to introduce competitiveness within the firm, both in personnel selection and in internal promotion. This entails a significant change in the workers' culture: A shift is under-way from horizontal collectivism to horizontal individualism. Company management, by contrast, is evolving in the direction of vertical collectivism. This is a cultural conflict that must necessarily affect "trust in the organization."

In accordance with our specific hypothesis H1, *trust in the organization* (factor 2) is the variable with the greatest impact on the perception of the fulfillment of the psychological contract. The hierarchical regression analysis leaves no doubt in this regard. Workers' perception of the fulfillment of the psychological contract depends, in the first instance, on their trust in the organization (β = .338).

Specifically, *trust in the organization* depends on the following factors:

- *Trust in the governing council and members' council* (factor 5). In reality, these two councils constitute the link between the organization and its workers, determining the organization's information policy. Workers complain that information is scarce, too technical, and difficult to understand. They feel that information is being controlled. This is one of the essential points for reinforcing trust in the organization. The company's internal information policies need to be analyzed in greater depth. Workers know that there is "restricted information," and they accept that, but it is fundamental that information declared restricted really be treated as such. What undermines trust in the organization is when members find out by word of mouth or in the press about issues that were declared restricted in internal meetings.

- *Involvement with the organization's objectives and evaluation of performance* (factor 6). Our factor analysis combined these two items related to competitiveness within the company (items 9 and 12, see above) into a single factor with item 21, "I consider it important that the company has a system of objectives deployed throughout the organization" (X = 4.00, X = 3.46, X = 2.81 for the high, middle, and low clusters respectively) and item 57, "Everyone's involvement in our daily work, as members, should be our chief competitive weapon" (X = 4.30, X = 3.92, X = 3.46 for the high, middle, and low clusters respectively). The fact that these four items are united in a single factor has a triple significance: that justice, both in personnel selection and in the evaluation of job performance, is a significant variable in creating a culture of trust in the organization; that both selection and the evaluation of job performance have to be aligned with the organization's objectives; and that internal competitiveness should accompany an awareness that all individuals in the organization are at the service of the company's greater competitiveness in the market. This is a good synthesis of what is understood by competitiveness integrated into a relationship of cooperation and is what defines a *horizontal individualist culture.*

- *Autonomy on the job* (factor 3). This is a logical consequence of the preceding paragraphs: A competitive culture integrated into a relationship of cooperation demands as its counterpart autonomy on the job. Workers themselves must pool their knowledge to promote innovation that can favor the organization's competitiveness in the market.

- *Supervisor-worker proximity* (factor 1). This factor explains 37.80 percent of variability, in other words, of all the individual variations with respect to the mean. This means that this factor has a great deal of influence on workers' general level of satisfaction or dissatisfaction. It also has a significant influence on "trust in the organization." The items included in this factor are related to familiarity between the company's supervisors and workers and with the latter's participation in decisions that affect their work environment.

- *Possibilities for training and internal promotion* (factor 4). Training appears linked to internal promotion. This association is implicit in the criteria that have been used in personnel selection. Since selection criteria were not aligned with the organization's objectives, and since competitiveness criteria were not used in the selection process, internal promotion inevitably had to be based on the technical training offered by the organization. If selection and performance-evaluation criteria are modified, technical training could be expected to precede a worker's joining the organization. This notably modifies the content of workers' expectations with regard to training.

- *Value assigned to the job* (factor 7). The two items included in this factor were the following: item 3, "Compared to other positions with similar responsibilities, I think that my position is assigned an appropriate value within the structure of my company" ($X = 3.06$, $X = 2.57$, $X = 1.77$ for the high, middle, and low clusters respectively), and item 10, "Compared to positions at the same or a similar professional level in other, outside companies, I consider my company's level of overall compensation good" ($X = 3.02$, $X = 2.78$, $X = 2.19$ for the high, middle, and low clusters respectively).

The value assigned to a job appears to be economic in nature, since it is related to pay. Along these lines, it is related to the "index" variable. In fact, in the hierarchical regression, the "index" variable had a significant influence on "trust in the organization" on the first pass (β = .242**), but once the organizational factors were introduced into the regression, the influence of the "index" variable disappeared, meaning that the "index" impacts "trust in the organization" by way of the organizational variables, especially factor 7.

Conclusion

The Taylorist model of work is being replaced by work based on knowledge creation and innovation. This change brings with it a new organizational culture, characterized by greater worker participation in company management. Trust between workers and the organization will become the basis of a more individualized psychological contract and one in which promises and obligations are more explicit. In theory, owners and employees agree on this formulation, the real behavior of both groups differs signifcantly from the model of labor relations formulated theoretically. The exercise of shared leadership requires both managers and workers to learn new ways of doing things.

Research on the psychological contract needs to analyze and clarify with greater precision the conditions that favor the development of trust between workers and company management. This study was limited in that it had to accept measurement instruments imposed by the organization.

Business organizations want rapid changes on the behavioral level and are not interested in theoretical research. This is not a situation that encourages accumulating knowledge based on experience (tacit knowledge) and codifying it in scholarly form (explicit knowledge). In short, the current situation with which we are faced does not favor collaboration between business organizations and universities (Bradford and Burke 2005).

References

Bradford, David L., and W. Warner Burke, eds. 2005. *Reinventing Organization Development: New Approaches to Change Organizations.* San Francisco: Pfeiffer.

Guest. David E. 2004. "The Psychology of the Employment Relationship:

An Analysis Based on the Psychological Contract." *Applied Psychology* 53, no. 4: 541–55.

Guest, David E., and Neil Conway. 2002. "Communicating the Psychological Contract: An Employer Perspective." *Human Resource Management Journal* 12, no. 2: 22–38.

Robinson, Sandra L., and Elizabeth Wolfe Morrison. 1995. "Psychological Contracts and OCB: The Effects of Unfulfilled Obligations on Civic Virtue Behavior." *Journal of Organizational Behavior* 16, no. 3: 289–98.

Ros, María, and Valdiney V. Gouveia, eds. 2001. *Psicología social de los valores humanos.* Madrid: Biblioteca Nueva.

Rousseau, Denise M., and Snehal A. Tijoriwala. 1998. "Assessing Psychological Contracts: Issues, Alternatives and Measures." *Journal of Organizational Behavior* 19, no. 7: 679–95.

Silla, Inmaculada, Francisco Javier Gracia, and José María Peiró. 2005. "Diferencias en el contenido del contrato psicológico en función del tipo de contrato y de la gestión empresarial pública o privada." *Revista de Psicología Social* 20, no. 1: 61–72.

Topa, Gabriela. 2005. "Introducción: Perspectivas de futuro para el contrato psicológico." *Revista de Psicología Social* 20, no. 1: 41–43.

Zhao, Hao, Sandy J. Wayne, Brian C. Glibkowski, and Jesus Bravo. 2007. "The Impact of Psychological Contract Breach on Work Related Outcomes: A Meta-Analysis." *Personnel Psychology* 60, no. 3: 647–80.

7

Leadership Conduct and its Consequences for Organizations in the Basque Country

Juan Jose Arrospide, Daniel Hermosilla, Félix Yenes, and Iñigo Calvo

Translated by Julie Waddington

The ability of a leader to inspire, motivate, and foster commitment to common goals is crucial (Bass 1997b; Avolio, Walumbwa, and Weber 2009). These skills are similar to the characteristics of transformational leadership (Bass 1985; Burns 1978). Unlike traditional leadership theories that focus, above all, on rational processes, theories of transformational and charismatic leadership (House 1977) emphasize emotions and values (Yukl 1998) and take for granted that leaders and their subordinates drive each other on to higher levels of morality and motivation (Burns 1978). Transformational leaders widen and heighten the interest of their subordinates, creating awareness and acceptance among followers and motivating them to go beyond personal interest for the good of the group (Bass 1997b). The main components of transformational leadership have been considered to be: charisma/idealized influence and motivational inspiration, providing the basis of a charismatic role model, and articulating a future vision that can be shared. Individualized consideration, which involves the leader paying attention to individual differences, is also important, as is stimulation, which is defined as the ability to question old assumptions and the status quo (Bass and Avolio 1995).

Transformational leadership is, by definition, a form of leadership that motivates subordinates to exceed expectations. More specifically, transformational leaders communicate a clear vision, inspire commitment through this vision, as well as engender confidence and motivation among subordinates. In sum, subordinates tend to perform beyond expectations in ways that boost organizational effectiveness (Bass 1985; Howell and Avolio 1993; Podsakoff, MacKenzie, and Bommer 1996; Yukl 1998). Research has shown that transformational leadership is related to organizational achievement and civil conduct such as commitment, satisfaction, and confidence on the part of subordinates (Judge and Bono 2000; Masi and Cooke 2000; Pillai, Schriesheim, and Williams 1999; Podsakoff, MacKenzie, and Bommer 1996; Podsakoff, MacKenzie, Moorman, and Fetter 1990). In contrast to the inspirational aspects of transformational leadership, transactional leadership is based on a balance of exchanges (Bass 1985; Lowe, Kroeck, and Sivasubramaniam 1996), in which the focus of attention is placed on efficiency by reinforcing negotiated levels of performance. In order to achieve the expected performance, transactional leaders offer suitable rewards for results obtained and manage by exception. In addition to transformational and transactional leadership, research also covers passive leadership or the absence of leadership (Bass 1985; Den Hartog, Van Muijen, and Koopman 1997). In general, passive leaders avoid taking decisions, exercising their duties, and supervisorial responsibilities.

Numerous studies have reported significant correlations between transformational leadership and organizational performance. Transformational leadership has been linked to different kinds of results, such as the commitment of the employee to the organization (Barling, Weber, and Kelloway 1996), commitment and low levels of work-related stress (Podsakoff, Mackenzie, and Bommer 1996), and satisfaction in their work and with their leader (Koh, Steers, and Terborg 1995; Lowe, Kroeck, and Sivasubramaniam 1996). Beyond the individual level, the effectiveness of transformational teams and organizations has also been documented (Bass 1997b; Hofmann and Jones 2005; Tichy and Devanna 1990).

Transformational leadership has been contrasted with transactional conduct in which cooperation is obtained through the exchange of rewards. James MacGregor Burns (1978) argues that while transactional leaders motivate their subordinates to perform as expected, the transformational leader inspires followers to perform better than initial expectations. According to Boas Shamir (1991), leaders must directly address their followers' sense of worth in order to inspire them to be committed to the organization; this is one of the most robust motivating factors that transformational leadership adds to transactional exchange. Researchers of leadership styles treat the attributes of followers as results of the leadership process rather than as initial factors, even though there are numerous calls for the consideration of the role that followers play in the leadership process. Shamir (2007) suggests that the leadership effectiveness is a consequence of both good subordinates as well as of good leaders. Shamir (2007) provides some specific recommendations for future research centered on followers, indicating the inclusion of needs, identities, and the implicit theories of the followers; how their expectations, values, and attitudes determine the leader's conduct; how followers' expectations affect the leader's motivation and results; how followers' acceptance of the leader and their support affect the leader's self-confidence, self-efficacy, and the conduct; and how followers' characteristics determine the nature of relations with the leader.

The theory of transformational leadership clearly indicates the main assumption that transformational conduct can be learned (Bass 1998). However, the components of transformational leadership are conceptually related to personality traits that are assumed to represent stable dispositions. Numerous studies have linked personality to transformational behavior. Using a model with the five most significant factors as a frame of reference, Timothy A. Judge and Joyce E. Bono (2000) find that extraversion and agreeableness are positive indicators, and David A. Hofman and Lisa M. Jones (2005) find that transformational leadership is positively linked collectively to openness, agreeableness, extraversion, and responsibility.

According to Dianne N. Den Hartog, Robert J. House, Paul J. Hanges, and S. Antonio Ruiz-Quintanilla (1999), on the basis of a transcultural study, many attributes associated with transformational leadership are shown to be culturally contingent, including traits such as the assumption of risk, self-efficacy, compassion, sensitivity, and ambition. Attributes such as communication skills, integrity, and the ability to encourage, appear universally as components that are highlighted as leadership skills. The contingency of the attributes may reflect differences in cultural values. For example, in a culture that fosters an authoritarian style, a leader's sensitivity could be interpreted as a weakness, whereas in a culture that encourages a form of protection, the same sensitivity is probably essential for effective leadership. With the widening of global markets, culturally diverse working teams, and foreign work assignments, the leader's awareness of such similarities and differences may be highly beneficial for effective management and direction (Segalla, Fischer, and Sandner 2000). The main aim of this study is to expand on current knowledge of the characteristics and results that are associated with transformational leadership in the Basque Country. Authors have addressed the subject of the superiority of transformational leadership in different cultures, both from a theoretical (Bass 1997b) and an empirical perspective (Den Hartog, House, Hanges, and Ruiz-Quintanilla 1999; Koopman, Den Hartog, and Konrad 1999).

In the first part of the chapter, we examine whether previous studies' empirical findings of the link between transformational leadership and positive results may be replicated in the context of the Basque Country. According to "the augmentation hypothesis" proposed by Bass (1985; et al. 2003), transformational leadership augments transactional leadership's explanatory power to predict the satisfaction and achievement of subordinates. Some studies have carried out research into this particular sense, and the results have confirmed the initial proposal (Hater and Bass 1988), but our intention here is to carry out a replica in the Basque Country.

Evaluations of transformational, transactional, and passive-avoidant leadership, as well as measurements of their results, have been based on the multifactor leadership questionnaire (MLQ) (Bass and Avolio 1995; Molero 1994). Measurements of the results include evaluations of effectiveness, satisfaction with the leader, and motivation in the workplace. Initially, we analyzed the MLQ's main components to examine if its scope could be replicated in the context of the Basque Country. In order to overcome any potential biases due to the fact that the data is from the same source, we have included indices for subordinates and for managers. Furthermore, including these different perspectives allows for a comparison to be drawn between these different perspectives, in terms of subordinates and superiors (Conway, Lombardo, and Sanders 2001).

Hypothesis

The indices of transformational leadership provided by subordinates and managers are related to the variables of the results and go beyond any explanation that transactional or passive-avoidant leadership forms could give.

Sample

The sample was composed of 47 mid-level managers and 107 subordinates. Of the participants, 38 percent were women. The age of the sample ranged between 24 and 64, with the average being 39 (SD=9.6). On average, the participants were 5.36 years (SD=5.58) in this job. A significant majority (76 percent) of the sample participants had university qualifications, while 20 percent had a lower level of education. The sample participants were recruited from three different organizations in the Basque Country: a public service institution and two private service institutions.

Means

The "Multifactor Leadership Questionnaire—Form 5X" (MLQ 5X; Bass and Avolio 1995) was used to obtain an evaluation of leadership conduct and the results. The MLQ is a questionnaire with forty-five items that describe conduct and each question can be answered on a scale of 5 points (0 = rarely, 4 = frequently). Our study uses a version translated and adapted into Spanish by Fernando Molero (1994).

The MLQ outlines the dimensions of transformational, transactional, and passive-avoidant leadership, while the scope of the results includes satisfaction with the leader, effectiveness of the leader, and motivation in the workplace (extra effort).

In order to ensure that the scales constructed to measure aspects of transformational leadership present a high level of correlation, we calculated an overall score by adding the scores of the four scales (Alpha de Cronbach =.93), a procedure suggested in other studies (Carless 1998; Hofmann and Jones 2005; Ross and Offerman 1997; Molero forthcoming). Overall scores were also calculated for the conduct of transactional and passive-avoidant leadership. The overall score of transactional leadership includes contingent rewards and (active) management by exception (Alpha de Cronbach=.78), whereas passive-avoidant leadership (Alpha de Cronbach=.81) includes laissez-faire leadership and (passive) management by exception. In previous studies, (passive) management by exception was included as a subscale of transactional leadership. Subsequent research suggests that the style of (passive) management by exception should be combined with laissez-faire leadership given that these two scales correlate positively between each other and negatively with the others (Avolio, Bass, and Jung 1999; Bass and Avolio 2000; Den Hartog, Van Muijen, and Koopman 1997; Molero forthcoming). The last structure that is applied in this study results from renaming the third dimension— changing the name of laissez-faire for passive-avoidant leadership.

Procedure

As noted, the study focused on three organizations, and the senior management of these organizations recommended participation. The questionnaires were distributed by post, and respondents were asked to fill in the form and then send it directly to the researcher. The aim of this was to attain the highest level of confidentiality possible. Managers as well as subordinates were assured that all the data would be treated confidentially and would not have any effect whatsoever on their professional careers. Finally, the results were returned on an individual basis.

Results

The relative importance of transformational leadership for the outcome variables was analyzed in two parts. First, the Pearson correlation was calculated between the variables of the study, and second, the regression analysis was calculated. The correlation analysis revealed that the variables of the three kinds of leadership conduct correlate significantly with the outcome variables, both in the managers' responses as well as in the case of subordinates.

Factorial Structure of the MLQ in the Basque Country

The factorial analysis of the main components with varimax rotation provides three factors. Bartlett's sphericity test is significant (.000), and the Kaiser-Meyer-Olkin measure was acceptable (.94). In total, the three factors account for 79 percent of the variance. The first factor accounts for 64.04 percent of the variance, and this factor covers all the transformational leadership scales as well as the scale of contingent rewards that, in principle, belongs to the transactional leadership scales. Moreover, and consistent with the high correlations recorded, the outcome variables saturate the first factor in a way that is more significant than the rest. The second factor accounts for 9.49 percent of the variance, and (active) management by exception saturates this factor. The third factor is saturated by laissez-faire leadership and (passive) management by exception, which accounts for 5.53 percent of the variance. Most importantly, the factorial structure found in this study managed to replicate the scope of the transformational, transactional, and passive-avoidant leadership styles detected in other studies with the MLQ. In any event, the high saturation of contingent reward in the first factor is worth mentioning and may suggest problems with discriminant validity for the transformational and transactional leadership scales (Hetland and Sandal 2003).

Leadership and Measurement of the Outcome Scales of Satisfaction, Effectiveness, and Motivation in the Workplace

The regression analysis is calculated with the three outcome results as dependent variables. Separate analyses are calculated for managers and subordinates. Table 7.1 shows the results of the analyses. The total R^2 is shown at the bottom of the table. These analyses indicate a strong and significant association between the leadership indices and the three outcome variables for managers and for subordinates. The variance part attributable to transformational leadership is significant if we compare it to the others in nearly all the results. Transactional leadership is only associated more significantly with high effectiveness by superiors and not by subordinates.

Table 7.1. Summary of regression analysis based on transformational, transactional, and passive-avoidant leadership, with results understood as dependent variables (N = 107 for subordinates, N = 47 for leaders)

	Satisfaction			Effectiveness			Motivation at work		
	Beta	Sig.		Beta	Sig.		Beta	Sig.	
Subordinates									
Passive-avoidant	−.154	.039		−.151	.039		−.062	.415	
Transactional	.024	.822		.107	.309		.029	.795	
Transformational	.716	.000	**	.657	.000**		.762	.000	**
		R^2	.688		R^2	.704		R^2	.674
Leaders									
Passive-avoidant	−.077	.480		−.044	.710		.062	.555	
Transactional	.315	.032	*	.493	.002**		.092	.510	
Transformational	.523	.002	**	.359	.042*		.830	.000	**
		R^2	.702		R^2	.689		R^2	.756

Discussion

The results of this study provide substantial evidence to support the pre-eminence of the practice of transformational leadership in organizations in the Basque Country. Across the three organizations that participated in the study, two private and one public, transformational leadership shows solid and consistent relations with outcome variables such as satisfaction and motivation in the workplace, regardless of whether or not the source of the information comes from managers. Transformational leadership is strongly linked to effectiveness according to the perspective of the subordinates. However, when taken from the perspective of the superiors, it is transactional leadership that shows a strong relation to effectiveness.

Confirming "the augmentation hypothesis" (Bass 1985), which maintains that transformational leadership augments the explanatory power of transactional leadership to be able to predict the satisfaction and achievement of subordinates, the variance is attributable to transformational leadership over and above transactional and passive-avoidant leadership.

Structure of the MLQ

The validity of the MLQ structure has, though, been questioned. One of the questions posed is the extent to which the components of transformational, transactional, and laissez-faire leadership styles constitute separate factors. The result of the analysis of the main components in this study shows that transformation, transactional, and passive-avoidant leadership styles can be extracted as separate factors. In any event, and as in other studies (Hetland and Sandal 2003), the contingent reward factor considerably saturates the transformational leadership factor in a more significant way than that of transactional leadership. This is a fairly common finding that can be explained by the fact that the contingent reward factor is located in the midway point perceived between the transformational and the transactional (Tejeda, Scandura, and Pillai 2001). Transformational leaders also make frequent use of contingent rewards, which could provide another explanation for the high correlation between these variables. Within the theory considered, this result points to the fact that contingent rewards may be a necessary platform for building transformational leadership. But, on the other hand, this transformational leadership adds aspects that go beyond the exchange of rewards. According to Bernard M. Bass et al., transactional leadership can be taken as the basis for transformational leadership:

> It appears that transactional leadership is needed to establish clear standards and expectations of performance. Transactional leadership can build a base level of trust in the leader as he or she reliably executes what has been agreed to over time. When clarity exists around expectations and performance objectives, followers come to learn that their leaders and peers, when asked to execute a task, do so reliably.

Transformational leadership may build on these initial levels of trust by establishing a deeper sense of identification among followers with respect to the unit's values, mission, and vision. (Bass et al. 2003, 216)

Transformational Leadership and Performance Indices

In line with previous studies (Hater and Bass 1988), and confirming the hypothesis presented here, transformational leadership correlates positively with how effective the leader is perceived to be, with the effort that subordinates show they are willing to make for their manager, and with their degree of satisfaction with the leader. What is not so clear is how the transformational leader changes people and organizations. A kind of implied empowering has been suggested as a hypothesis (Yukl 1998), in a way that augments self-efficacy, thereby implying an intrinsic motivation in contrast to mere extrinsic motivation (Bandura 1986). Robert G. Lord and Douglas J. Brown (2001) examine two specific ways that leaders can influence how their followers choose to behave, based on the kind of motivation they use to regulate performance and behavior. The first way is related to values and emphasizes the promotion of certain values among followers and encourages their motivation toward fulfilling or achieving these. The second way is related to followers' self-concept. The leader activates a kind of identity that the follower can share, creating a collective identity that can be assumed by the follower. Both ways, value-based and self-concept-based, are seen as mediators between the leader's conduct and that of the follower.

As in other studies (Alimo-Metcalfe 1998; Scullen, Mount, and Sytsma 1996), moderate correlations were found between the indices provided by superiors and those provided by subordinates. The favorable evaluations provided by the superiors suggest that transformational leaders at middle-management level can facilitate good vertical-upward communication and, in this way, contribute to creating a healthy working environment. These leaders may also potentially increase their chances of being promoted as a consequence of being positively evaluated by their superiors (Judge and Bono 2000). The results of this study corroborate the idea that transformational leadership obtains better satisfaction, more effectiveness, and greater motivation in the workplace than transactional leadership (Bass 1997a). Despite the high correlation between transformational and transactional leadership, it is worth noting that transactional leadership is not significantly related to the outcome evaluations among subordinates. The opposite appears in terms of the satisfaction and effectiveness provided by the superiors. This is a significant result given that transactional conduct includes factors that have been traditionally emphasized as important leadership components, such as contingent rewards and (active) management by exception.

This result also questions the findings of other studies (Den Hartog, Van Muijen, and Koopman 1997; Hater and Bass 1988; Howell and Avolio 1993). The moderate agreement between the indices of the subordinates found in this study substantiates previous studies (London 2001). An explanation for the discrepancies in the indices may lie in the fact that subordinates create different relations with their leaders based on their own dispositions such as their personality and values (Ehrhart and Klein 2001; Klein and House 1995; Lord and Brown 2001; Thomas, Dickson, and Bliese 2001). The potential impact of personality and attribution processes needs further research. The negative impact of passive-avoidant leadership on the motivation of subordinates in their work is consistent with previous findings (Judge and Bono 2000; Hetland and Sandal 2003). In the same way, the results of recent studies indicate that passive leadership can have negative consequences in terms of employees' work, health, and well-being (Corrigan et al. 2000; Hetland 2008).

Conclusions

The study presented here suggests that the superiority of transformational leadership, which has been documented in a significant number of studies, also appears with this sample in the context of the Basque Country. In the context of expanding globalization, it is highly pertinent and important to study cultural similarities and differences with regards to leadership (among other aspects) because organizations in the Basque Country are facing growing demands to join in the day-to-day experience of other organizations throughout the world.

More research is needed to verify many of the theories that transformational leadership processes entail. Focus is now being placed on how the characteristics of subordinates affect the results and how subordinates construct transformational relations with the leader. More research is needed concerning the impact of transformational leadership on the health and well-being of employees, beyond the question of organizational satisfaction and commitment. Transformational leaders are crucial as motivators in organizations. Our study demonstrates the importance of transformational leadership in yet another culture.

References

Alimo-Metcalfe, Beverly. 1998. "360 Degree Feedback and Leadership Development." *International Journal of Selection and Assessment* 6, no. 1: 35–44.

Avolio, Bruce J., Bernard M. Bass, and Dong I. Jung. 1999. "Re-examining the Components of Transformational and Transactional Leadership using the Multifactor Leadership Questionnaire." *Journal of Occupational and Organizational Psychology* 72, no. 4: 441–62.

Avolio, Bruce J., Fred O. Walumbwa, and Todd J. Weber. 2009. "Leadership: Current Theories, Research, and Future Directions." *Annual Review of Psychology* 60: 421–49.

Bandura, Albert. 1986. *Social Foundations of Thoughts and Actions: A Social Cognitive Theory.* Englewood Cliffs, NJ: Prentice-Hall.

Barling, Julian, Tom Weber, and E. Kevin Kelloway. 1996. "Effects of Transformational Leadership Training on Attitudinal and Financial Outcomes: A Field Experiment." *Journal of Applied Psychology* 81, no. 6: 827–32.

Bass, Bernard M. 1985. *Leadership Beyond Expectation.* New York: Free Press.

———. 1997a. *Bass and Stogdill's Handbook of Leadership: Theory, Research and Managerial Applications.* New York: Free Press.

———. 1997b. "Does the Transactional–Transformational Leadership Paradigm Transcend Organizational and National Boundaries?" *American Psychologist* 52 no. 2: 130–139.

———. 1998. *Transformational Leadership: Industrial, Military, and Educational Impact.* Mahwah, NJ: Lawrence Erlbaum Associates, Inc.

Bass, Bernard M., and Bruce J. Avolio. 1995. *Transformational Leadership Development: Manual for the Multifactor Leadership Questionnaire.* Palo Alto, CA: Consulting Psychologists Press.

———. 2000. *Platoon Readiness as a Function of Leadership, Platoon and Company Cultures.* Final Report to the US Army Research Institute for the Behavioral and Social Sciences. Binghamton, New York: Research Foundation of the State University of New York, Office of Research and Sponsored Programs.

Bass, Bernard M., Bruce J. Avolio, Dong I. Jung, and Yair Berson. 2003. "Predicting Unit Performance by Assessing Transformational and Transactional Leadership." *Journal of Applied Psychology* 88, no. 2: 207–18.

Burns, James MacGregor. 1978. *Leadership*. New York: Harper and Row.

Carless, Sally A. 1998. "Short Research Note: Assessing the Discriminant Validity of Transformational Leader Behavior as Measured by MLQ." *Journal of Occupational and Organizational Psychology* 71, no. 4: 353–58.

Conway, James M., Kristie Lombardo, and Kelley C. Sanders. 2001. "A Meta-analysis of Incremental Validity and Nomological Networks for Subordinate and Peer Ratings." *Human Performance* 14, no. 4: 267–303.

Corrigan, Patrick W., Sarah E. Lickey, John Campion, and Fadwa Rashid. 2000. "Mental Health Team Leadership and Consumer's Satisfaction and Quality of Life." *Psychiatric Services* 51, no. 6: 781–85.

Den Hartog, Deanne N., Robert J. House, Paul J. Hanges, and S. Antonio Ruiz-Quintanilla. 1999. "Culture Specific and Crosscultural Generalizable Implicit Leadership Theories: Are Attributes of Charismatic/Transformational Leadership Universally Endorsed?" *Leadership Quarterly* 10, no. 2: 219–56.

Den Hartog, Deanne N., Jaap J. Van Muijen, and Paul L. Koopman. 1997. "Transactional Versus Transformational Leadership: An Analysis of the MLQ." *Journal of Occupational and Organizational Psychology* 70, no. 1: 19–34.

Ehrhart, Mark G. and Katherine J. Klein. 2001. "Predicting Followers' Preference for Charismatic Leadership: The Influence of Follower Values and Personality." *Leadership Quarterly* 12, no. 2: 153–79.

Hater, John J., and Bernard M. Bass. 1988. "Superiors' Evaluations and Subordinates' Perceptions of Transformational and Transactional Leadership." *Journal of Applied Psychology* 73, no.4: 695–702.

Hetland, Hilde. 2008. "Transformational Leadership: Motivation for Change." *Tidsskrift for Norsk Psykologforening* 45, no. 3: 265–71.

Hetland, Hilde, and Gro M. Sandal. 2003. "Transformational Leadership in Norway: Outcomes and Personality Correlates." *European Journal of Work and Organizational Psychology* 12, no. 2: 147–70.

Hofmann, David A., and Lisa M. Jones. 2005. "Leadership, Collective Personality, and Performance." *Journal of Applied Psychology* 90, no.3: 509–22.

House, Robert J. 1977. "A Theory of Charismatic Leadership." In *Leadership: The Cutting Edge*, edited by James G. Hunt and Lars L. Larson. Carbondale, IL: Southern Illinois University Press.

Howell, Jane M., and Bernard J. Avolio. 1993. "Transformational Leadership, Transactional Leadership, Locus of Control, and Support for Innovation: Key Predictors of Consolidated-Business-Unit Performance." *Journal of Applied Psychology* 78, no. 6: 891–902.

Judge, Timothy A., and Joyce E. Bono. 2000. "Five-factor Model of Personality and Transformational Leadership." *Journal of Applied Psychology* 85, no. 5: 751–65.

Klein, Katherine J., and Robert J. House. 1995. "On Fire: Charismatic Leadership and Levels of Analysis." *Leadership Quarterly* 6, no. 2: 183–98.

Koh, William L., Richard M. Steers, and James R. Terborg. 1995. "The Effects of Transformational Leadership on Teacher Attitudes and Student Performance in Singapore." *Journal of Organizational Behavior* 16, no. 4: 319–33.

Koopman, Paul L., Dianne N. Den Hartog, and Edvard Konrad. 1999. "National Culture and Leadership Profiles in Europe: Some Results from the GLOBE Study." *European Journal of Work and Organizational Psychology* 8, no. 4: 503–20.

London, Manuel, ed. 2001. *How People Evaluate Others in Organizations*. Mahwah, NJ: Lawrence Erlbaum Associates, Inc.

Lord, Robert G., and Douglas J. Brown. 2001. "Leadership, Values and Subordinate Self-Concept." *Leadership Quarterly* 12, no. 2: 133–52.

Lowe, Kevin B., K. Galen Kroeck, and Nagaraj Sivasubramaniam. 1996. "Effectiveness Correlates of Transformational and Transactional Leadership: A Meta-analytic Review of the MLQ Literature." *Leadership Quarterly* 7, no. 3: 385–425.

Masi, Ralph J., and Robert A. Cooke. 2000. "Effects of Transformational Leadership on Subordinate Motivation, Empowering Norms, and Organizational Productivity." *The International Journal of Organizational Analysis* 8, no. 1: 16–47.

Molero, Fernando. 1994. "Carisma y liderazgo carismático: Una aproximación empírica desde las perspectivas de Bass y Friedman." Ph.D. Diss. UNED, Madrid.

——. In press. "Transformational and Transactional Leadership: An Analysis of the Factor Structure of the Multifactor Leadership Questionnaire (MLQ) in a Spanish sample. *Psicothema*.

Morales, J. Francisco, and Fernando Molero. 1995. "Leadership in Two Types of Healthcare Organization." In *Work and Organizational Psychology: European Contributions of the Nineties*, edited by José María Peiró, Fernando Prieto, José Luis Meliá, and Oto Luque. East Sussex: Erlbaum.

Pillai, Rajnandini, Chester A. Schriesheim, and Eric S. Williams. 1999. "Fairness Perceptions and Trust as Mediators for Transformational and Transactional Leadership: A Two-Sample Study." *Journal of Management* 25, no. 6: 897–934.

Podsakoff, Philip M., Scott B. Mackenzie, and William H. Bommer. 1996. "Transformational Leadership Behaviors and Substitutes for Leadership as Determinants of Employee Satisfaction, Commitment, Trust, and Organizational Citizenship Behaviors." *Journal of Management* 22, no.2: 259–98.

Podsakoff, Philip M., Scott B. MacKenzie, Robert H. Moorman, and Richard Fetter. 1990. "Transformational Leader Behaviors and their Effects on Followers' Trust in Leader, Satisfaction, and Organizational Citizenship Behavior." *Leadership Quarterly* 1, no. 2: 107–42.

Ross, Shirley M., and Lynn R. Offerman. 1997. "Transformational Leaders: Measurement of Personality Attributes and Work Group Performance." *Personality and Social Psychology Bulletin* 23, no. 10: 1078–86.

Scullen, Steven E., Michael K. Mount, and Marcia R. Sytsma. 1996. "Comparisons of Self, Peer, Direct Report, and Boss Ratings of Managers' Performance." Paper presented at the 11th annual meeting of the Society for Industrial and Organizational Psychology, San Diego, CA.

Segalla, Michael, Lorenz Fischer, and Karl Sandner. 2000. "Making Cross-Cultural Research Relevant to European Corporate Integration: Old Problem-New Approach." *European Management Journal* 18, no. 1: 38–51.

Shamir, Boas. 1991. "Meaning, Self and Motivation in Organizations." *Organizational Studies* 12, no. 3: 405–24.

——. 2007. "From Passive Recipients to Active Coproducers: Followers' Roles in the Leadership Process." In *Follower-Centered Perspectives on Leadership: A Tribute to the Memory of James R. Meindl,* edited by Boas Shamir, Rajnandini Pillai, Michelle G. Bligh, and Mary Uhl-Bien. Greenwich, CT: Inform Age.

Tejeda, Manuel J., Terri A. Scandura, and Rajnandini Pillai. 2001. "The MLQ Revisited: Psychometric Properties and Recommendations." *Leadership Quarterly* 12, no. 1: 31–52.

Thomas, Jeffrey L., Marcus W. Dickson, and Paul D. Bliese. 2001. "Values Predicting Leader Performance in the US Army Reserve Officer Training Corps Assessment Center: Evidence for a Personality-Mediated Model." *Leadership Quarterly* 12, no.2: 181–96.

Tichy, Noel M., and Mary Anne Devanna. 1990. *The Transformational Leader.* 2nd ed. New York: Wiley.

Yukl, Gary A. 1998. *Leadership in Organizations.* 4th ed. Upper Saddle River, NJ: Prentice-Hall.

8

Emotional Intelligence and Innovation: An Exploratory Study in Organizational Settings

AITOR ARITZETA

Translated by Jennifer Martin

Ever since Freud's "primary-process thinking" (Russ 2000) and Jung's "fantasy thinking" concepts (Chodrow 2006), emotional and creative processes have been inextricably intertwined. Recent research suggests that emotions are related to the organizational innovation process as both positive and negative affect contributes to real changes in individual creativity (Amabile, Barsade, Mueller, and Staw 2005).

Current organizational models underline the importance of emotional processes on the job (Barsade and Gibson; Brief and Weiss 2002; Kelly and Barsade 2001). Globalization processes, trends toward a service economy, technological advances, and the development of a knowledge society have made the individualized consideration of a person in the workplace key to ensuring the competitive capacity of businesses (Ashkanasy, Härtel, and Daus 2002; Rousseau and Schalk 2000). Consequently, the fundamental organizational values are now oriented toward more emotional dimensions and the affective consideration of the individual has become an indispensable axiom for organizational performance (Barsade, Brief, and Spataro 2003; De Dreu, West, Fischer, and MacCurtain 2001; Fisher and Ashkanasy 2000).

Today, there is a widely held belief that European organizations need to continuously innovate in order to hold on to their competitive potential. In addition to innovation, efficiency, and productivity, the learning capacity of the organization itself is essential, as theories and research on managerial processes suggest (Finger and Woolis 1994).

In effect, organizations look for strategies that connect their strategy and their organizational methods with their socioeconomic environment, and in the case of the Basque Country, just as in the rest of Europe, the environment prioritizes internationalization and innovation strategies. An innovation strategy requires a people-based organization. There are clear examples in the Basque context that aim to strengthen such innovation strategies. One example is the Provincial Council of Gipuzkoa, which, through its Department of Innovation and the Knowledge Society, has been working since 2005 on the development of programs and projects regarding social and emotional competencies and the promotion of social innovation and lifelong learning, deployed in educational, familial, social community, and organizational areas (Aritzeta, Ramos, and Gartzia 2008). Another example is Innobasque, the Basque Innovation Agency (www.innobasque.com), whose vision is to convert the Basque Country into a benchmark for European innovation, and which contains an Emotional Intelligence Consortium. Similarly, many other activities promoting innovation are being developed in the Basque Country (see www.euskadinnova.net); one need only mention, for example, the "Innovation Forums," the "Innovation Agenda," the "Lider21," "Directiv@21," and the "Red Innova" initiatives. The strategic objective of all these initiatives is "to develop an innovation culture, training people in new competencies and abilities and new values such as creativity, risk tolerance, curiosity, or the entrepreneurial spirit."

Organizational change processes that seek to establish innovative cultures are more effective when emotionally intelligent professionals who participate in decision-making promote them (Scott-Ladd and Chan 2004). This is because emotionally intelligent workers not only demonstrate a greater capacity to adapt to change, but also know when they should use behavior associated with such change. Furthermore, the intellectual use of emotions influences cognitive processes, making these workers more insightful and innovative. Such workers know their limitations and their strengths well; they are optimistic, creative, and more adaptable to new ideas (Bellack 1999; Goleman 1995). Although much of the research done in this area has focused on people's emotional response to organizational change, these emotional reactions are strongly linked to the cognitive processes that impact decision-making as well as attitudes.

In fact, Neal M. Ashkanas and Barry Tse (2000) defend the idea that emotional intelligence (EI), which involves the ability to use emotions to facilitate thought, favors cognitive processes associated with flexibility in task planning and creative thinking.

Taking all this into account, it seems clear that EI can influence both innovation processes and change through, for example, emotion regulation processes. Therefore, the goal of this chapter is to determine if there is actually any relationship between EI and innovative/creative cognitive styles in a sample of workers from twenty-five Basque companies. I will, then, first explain the concepts of EI and cognitive styles. Then I will demonstrate empirical evidence from the relevant literature that links both variables. Finally, I will establish a working hypothesis.

Emotional Intelligence

The notion of EI emerged in the 1990s in response to the focus on purely cognitive intelligences and was clearly critical of those who championed traditional intelligence tests. This focus quickly became popular in the non-academic press because, among other reasons, it issued a novel and attractive message: namely, that It was possible to achieve success in life without possessing great academic skills. Daniel Goleman's informative book (1995) quickly turned into a bestseller, although the corresponding research was still in its early stages.

Despite the numerous definitions of EI that exist, I will return to the one that, in my view, is the best substantiated both theoretically and empirically. Thus, according to John D. Mayer and Peter Salovey (1997, 10): "Emotional intelligence involves the ability to perceive accurately, appraise, and express emotion; the ability to access and/or generate feelings when they facilitate thought; the ability to understand emotion and emotional knowledge; and the ability to regulate emotions to promote emotional and intellectual growth."

Therefore, EI involves the intelligent use of emotions in such a way that it is possible to intentionally make emotions work for self-benefit; in other words, that help in making appropriate decisions in different areas of life. EI is not a directly observable construct, but rather a group of meta-abilities that can be learned.

There are two key approaches to EI. Normally, they are identified as mixed models and ability models. This chapter focuses on the ability models, while briefly defining the mixed models.

Mixed Models

The mixed models are the most used models in applied contexts such as organizational psychology, despite the fact that the competencies they develop cannot be directly linked to intelligence; they are really a skill and differ substantially from other personality dimensions. These models assume situational consistency in behavior, manifested above all, in empathy, assertiveness, and optimism. They utilize measurement instruments very similar to those used to evaluate personality: standardized self-reports that measure typical behavior. Variables such as empathy, optimism, and impulsiveness, and even other more eclectic variables such as motivation, self-awareness, and happiness are included in these EI measurement instruments. Among many specific examples of such models, the Goleman models (1995) and Reuven Bar-On's multi-factorial model (1997) stand out.

Ability Models

In ability models, EI is conceived (from an information processing perspective) as a set of abilities that involves the processing of relevant emotional information and is related to intelligence. These skills must be evaluated through ability tests, of maximum, non-typical behavior—in other words, through objective tests, similar to intelligence tests that examine correct and incorrect performance.

One of the fundamental models here is Salovey and Mayer's "Four Branch Model." In their approach to EI (in terms of sets of abilities, such as perceiving, assimilating, understanding, and managing emotions), emotional abilities are viewed as elements of intelligence that can be developed.

This model points out the fact that employees face daily situations in the workplace in which they must turn to the use of emotional abilities in order to adapt appropriately to their environment. This functionalist view regards EI as a skill that is focused on emotional information processing that unifies emotions and reasoning, allowing the use of our emotions to facilitate more effective reasoning and to think more intelligently about our emotional life (Mayer and Salovey 1997). Additionally, it is thought that EI is related to other traditional and well-established intelligences, especially verbal intelligence, because of its link with expression and understanding of feelings (Mayer, Caruso, and Salovey 1999). Unlike mixed models, such authors contend that EI, understood as the ability to process relevant information from our emotions, is independent of stable personality traits (Salovey and Grewal 2005).

Specifically, there are four areas or branches of abilities that distinguish this model and that are organized from the most basic (for example, attention and perception) to the highest psychological or the most psychologically integrated processes (for example, regulation). Furthermore, each branch includes different stages of ability that are mastered sequentially.

1. Emotional perception and expression: This includes the ability to identify emotions in oneself, with their corresponding physical and cognitive correlates, and also (identify emotions) in others, along with the capacity to express emotions in the appropriate place and manner.

2. Emotional facilitation of thought: This includes four other abilities: comparing emotions with other emotions; using emotions to direct attention to important information; encouraging the consideration of different points of view; and facilitating reasoning through emotional states. These are basic abilities in the use of selective attention, self-control, and self-motivation.

3. Emotional understanding: Understanding and analyzing emotions includes four new abilities: that of labeling emotions and recognizing the relations among words that have emotional aspects; the ability to interpret the meanings of emotions and their relationships; the ability to understand complex feelings, or combinations of feelings; and finally, the ability to recognize the transition between different emotions.

4. Emotional management: The fourth branch evolved from the ability to keep oneself open to feelings, whether pleasant or unpleasant, and up to the ability to manage emotions in oneself or others. This process includes two intermediate abilities: that of thoughtfully engaging in or detaching oneself from an emotion according to what is considered convenient or not; and that of controlling emotions in relation to other people, which includes recognizing their clarity, type, and influence. This facet enables social adaptation and problem-solving.

These authors explain that branches one, three, and four include reasoning about emotions, whereas branch number two only includes the use of emotions to enhance reasoning.

These abilities are linked in such a way that without the suitable development of, for example, the identification of one's own emotions, it is impossible to regulate them. This is one of the most popular theoretical approaches. It has also been one of the most consistent and thorough theoretical models on EI for over a decade, because it provides a secure framework for action due to the rigorous way in which its theoretical premises have been tested. In turn, it has been accompanied by the development of measurement instruments, both in self-reporting as well as performance, allowing for its empirical contrast and favoring the development of measurable intervention programs.

In Natalio Extremera and Pablo Fernández-Berrocal's opinion (2001), mixed models have been more widespread because of of Goleman's bestseller. The ability models—and specifically that of Mayer and Salovey—are less well known but enjoy strong empirical support in specialized journals, since they focus exclusively on the emotional processing of information and on the study of capacities related to this processing.

The concept of mixed models has been strongly criticized. This criticism is based on the relationships obtained between EI and other constructs, as well as on the way in which this has been measured: namely, self-report questionnaires. To the critics (Pertrides and Furnham 2000, for example), the correlations between these EI measurements and other constructs demonstrates that EI still does not present a consistent conceptual domination: the data show a high interrelation between them, but it is not clear to what extent a construct that is grouped together with already existing ones is more valid than the sum of these individually. In the end, from this perspective, EI seems more like a conglomerate of constructs with a long scholarly tradition. Meanwhile, from a measurement perspective, the use of self-reports to evaluate EI has been strongly criticized by, for example, Marc A. Brackett and John D. Mayer (2003) on the grounds that a person's use of descriptive expressions about themselves as a way of measuring intelligence abilities depends on the respondent's self-image. If this was very precise, the measurements would be accurate, but the existing data indicate that there is a low correlation between intelligence and self-reports, with values between .00 and .35. In addition, the EI factors incorporate a high degree of social desirability. Therefore, it seems unlikely that EI can be measured correctly through questions that refer to intrapersonal and interpersonal competency levels.

Cognitive Styles

Cognitive styles refer to certain characterization modes, of perceiving, remembering, and thinking, or to different ways of discovering, storing, transforming, and using information. Therefore, they reflect regularities in information processing and are developed in tune with significant personality trends, because they deduce the way people organize and process information and the experience itself from the individual differences (Aranburu 2004). Cognitive styles are associated with individual differences in the performance of cognitive processes. The "cognitive style" concept is often mistakenly used as a personality characteristic instead of being addressed as human information processing.

Cognitive styles are clearly distinguishable from cognitive abilities. Cognitive abilities are unipolar traits, and the styles are bipolar or multidimensional. The abilities are much more restricted in their objectives and are measured in terms of performance levels. These styles exert control over mental functioning.

In general terms, approaches involving the theory and measuring of cognitive styles can be grouped into two models: bipolar models and multidimensional models. Bipolar models were the first to place real emphasis on researching cognitive styles. One example of this approach is Herman A. Witkin's field dependence-independence model (1964). Theoretical approaches and measurements related to hemispheric lateralization can also be found within bipolar models. The hemispheric lateralization concept asserts that the brain is clearly divided into two zones, each of which is allocated control over a type of activity or specific reasoning. This way, for example, the left hemisphere has control over the right hand, and vice versa.

Multidimensional models consider the existence of several dimensions in people's mental performance. One of the best known examples of this approach is that of Katharine Cook Briggs and her daughter Isabel Briggs Myers, established in 1944 (see the Myers-Briggs Type Indicator—MBTI in Myers, McCaulley, Quenk, and Hammer 1998). This considers personality types to be similar to the characteristics people possess, such as right-handedness or left-handedness—in other words, individuals are born with or develop certain ways of thinking and acting. MBTI sorts these psychological differences into four sets of opposite pairs (extrovert/introvert, sensing/intuition, thinking/feeling, and judgment/perception) or "dichotomies" whose combinations give rise to sixteen psychological types. None of these types is "better" or "worse"; however, Briggs and Myers believe that individuals would naturally have a preference toward a specific combination.

One of the more widespread proposed measures of cognitive styles is that of Michael J. Kirton (1976, 1989). He explains how individuals solve problems and make decisions (whether individually or in teams) by referring to their cognitive or creative thinking styles. In addition, rather than defining a set number of styles, Kirton proposes a single bipolar continuum of cognitive styles. At one end of the continuum individuals are classified as extreme adaptors, while at the other end they are classified as extreme innovators. Although previous studies and categorizations reflect similar notions of managerial cognitive styles—such as the theory of managers that do better or different (Drucker 1969) or the conformity or deviant theory of innovators (Legge 1978)—Kirton theoretically develops more fully the differences existing between adaptor and Innovator styles as well as detailing a validation process for the KAI inventory.

Adaptation-innovation is a preferred model for tackling problems at all stages—in other words, a view of the problem, relevant data for its solution, designing an appropriate solution, and implementation. Kirton (1989, 3) argues that the level of structure of problem-solving situations affects how comfortable a person feels depending on his or her adaptor-innovator style. The less the structure, the more comfortable an innovator feels; the greater the structure and the need to consensually agree with decisions, the more comfortable an adaptor feels. Adaption-innovation theory clearly distinguishes between cognitive styles and actual capacity or level of cognition.

Ever since its appearance, and throughout the 1980s and 1990s, adaptation-innovation theory and measurement generated considerable research (Bagozzi and Foxall 1995; Fisher, Macrosson, and Wong 1998; Foxall and Hackett 1994; Kirton 1989; Mudd 1990) and were the object of multiple studies of convergent validities (Carne and Kirton 1982; Kirton 1978 and 1985; Goldsmith 1984).

Factor analysis (Kirton 1989, 17) and subsequent analysis (Bagozzi and Foxall 1995) support the view that the adaptor-innovator styles reflect three orthogonal factors. In terms of the theory, a typical adaptor generates fewer and typically "inside paradigm" solutions to a problem. A typical innovator, meanwhile, suggests many ideas and sometimes unpractical solutions. Adaptors approach efficiency based on conventional rules, whereas innovators seek efficiency by proposing "out-of-paradigm" change. Moreover, while innovators are defined as being more able to resist group pressures by valuing their own initiatives, adaptors easily conform to the group.

A high innovator is described as an undisciplined thinker, tangentially approaching tasks from unanticipated angles, who seeks alternative avenues in the hunt for a solution (Kirton 1989). A high innovator manipulates problems and is able to catalyze and settle groups, although sometimes irreverent about his or her consensual views. In pursuing goals, innovators treat accepted norms with little regard, tend to work for only short bursts, and are able to take control in unstructured situations. They often challenge rules showing little respect for past customs and appear to have little self-doubt when generating ideas, not needing consensus to maintain confidence in face of opposition. In the organization, they are ideal in a crisis. A typical innovator can be defined as abrasive, creating dissonance, unsound, and shocking his or her opposites.

In contrast, a typical adaptor is characterized by precision, reliability, efficiency, prudence, discipline, and conformity. Generally, the adaptor is concerned with resolving problems presented by the current paradigm, reducing problems with a maximum of continuity and stability, and seeking solutions in tried and understood ways. While performing the job, a high adaptor is impervious to boredom and is able to maintain a high degree of accuracy in long spells of detailed work. He or she is an authority within given structures and only challenges rules cautiously, and when assured of strong support. He or she is seen as sound, conforming, safe, and dependable, but tends to have great self-doubt. Adaptors tend to react to criticism by closer outward conformity and are vulnerable to social pressure and authority. Descriptors such as introvert, humble, conscientious, controlled, subdued, emotionally tender, preferring fewer risks, and having a greater need for clarity represent the habitual adaptor.

Kirton states that the innovative style is obviously needed in any organization that aims to to survive, but as an organization grows, it became more bureaucratic, making the adaptive styles more relevant to guard it against unacceptable changes. Bureaucracies are said to aim for precision, reliability, and efficiency, and to exert pressure on individuals to be methodical, prudent, and disciplined. Thus, Kirton explicitly connects organizational bureaucracy theories (Parsons 1951; Merton 1957) with the reinforcement of adaptive style and innovative management theories with innovative cognitive style (Aritzeta, Senior, and Swalies 2005).

Emotional Intelligence and Cognitive Styles

Creativity is found on the border between cognition and emotion (in this study, creativity is regarded as an innovative/creative cognitive style, and not as a performance behavior). Cognitive and emotional behaviors do not substantially differ in their underlying mechanisms. In other words, the same mechanisms (for example, perception, memory, association, judgment, reasoning, and so on) that help to measure cognition also helped to measure emotion, although, maybe in different process combinations and in degree, depending on the circumstances.

Most discussion on emotion and creativity focuses on the influence of emotional states in non-emotional creativity or, put another way, on rational-cognitive type creativity (Shaw and Runco 1994). Much of the research to date has examined the influence of positive and negative moods on creativity without paying much attention to specific emotions. Little is known on the possible effects of emotions such as love, fear, and anger (among others) on the creative process. In spite of that, most experimental studies on affect and creativity demonstrate that a positive affect leads to higher levels of creativity. Most of this research indicates that a positive affect not only facilitates intrinsic motivation (for example, Isen and Reeve 2005), but also flexible thinking and problem-solving, even in particularly complex tasks (Aspinwall 1998). For example, Alice M. Isen (1993) demonstrates that inducing a mildly positive mood (for example, watching a comedy) can facilitate creative solutions to problems in the laboratory and in applied contexts, provided that the task is interesting or important to the individual. When people are in a positive mood, they enjoy exploring new ideas, are more flexible in their thinking, and are more thoughtful in their relationships with others. Thus, it has been observed that people who suffer from bipolar affective disorders are more likely to be creative in a manic phase than when they are depressed (Jamieson 1994).

Research into organizational contexts (for example, Madjar, Oldham, and Pratt 2002), reveals that a positive affect has a positive effect on work results. In this particular study, a positive mood brought about the existing positive relationship between the support to be creative that employees received and the actual creative performance that they demonstrated at their job. Teresa M. Amabile, Sigal G. Barsade, Jennifer S. Mueller, and Barry M. Staw (2005) received multiple measurements on a daily basis of 222 employees in seven different companies over the course of several weeks, and recorded multiple creativity measurements. Their findings demonstrated a positive linear relationship among positive affect as an antecedent of creativity. In another study, workers demonstrated increased creativity when the positive mood was elevated and the negative mood was also high, and work supervision was carried out in a supportive leadership style (George and Zhou 2007).

However, other studies question this association between emotion and creativity. Geir Kaufmann (2003) refutes the general argument that a positive mood reliably facilitates creativity. Some studies show that a positive mood can facilitate productivity, but not the quality of ideas (for example, Vosburg 1998). Other researchers find that, despite the fact that experimental manipulations can positively affect an improved mood and reduce anxiety, these do not necessarily increase divergent thinking (for example, Clapham 2001).

If we focus on EI, we observe how high levels of this ability involve the use of emotions in order to facilitate/help thought. Creative thinking can be driven by this ability through the generation of emotions that allow us to understand each other and express ourselves better, by means of the consideration of multiple perspectives obtained from diverse emotions, and by the capacity to concentrate on activities that are stimulated by certain emotions.

In this respect, Susan D. Batastini (2001) finds a high correlation between self-perceived EI and creativity. Uwe Wolfradt, Jörg Felfe, and Torsten Köster (2002) demonstrate that the people with high scores in self-perceived EI produce more creative responses than people with low scores. On the other hand, Stephen J. Guastello, Denise D. Guastello, and Casey A. Hanson (2004) observe that the relation between EI and creative production persisted once the effects of clinical disorders in university students were controlled. The fluidity of ideas and EI are positively related. These results lead to the conclusion that EI serves as a positive moderating factor of mood alterations and as a promoting element of creative production.

Therefore, one can assume that EI will be displayed as positive and significantly related to innovative/creative cognitive style and negatively correlated with the adaptive cognitive style.

Method

Participants

There were 292 workers belonging to twenty-five industrial and service companies in the Basque Country who participated in this study. The average age was 39.28 years (RD 8.07) and the average number of years with the company was 12.65 (RD 8.9). Men made up 67.1 percent of the sample. A questionnaire was given to the participants, who responded voluntarily as part of a social and emotional competency-training program.

Tools

The Mayer-Salovey-Caruso Emotional Intelligence Test (MSCEIT) was used to measure EI ability (Mayer et al. 2002). The test contained 8 tasks and 141 items that asked a respondent to solve emotional problems pertaining to four abilities (branches): (1) perception of emotions, (2) using emotions to facilitate thinking, (3) understanding emotions, and (4) regulation of emotion. The test publisher provided normative scores—one for each branch and a total score. As reported in the technical manual, the split-half reliabilities for branch scores are between .76 and .90, and .93 for the total EI.

The Kirton Adaptor-Innovator Inventory (KAI) was used to examine the degree of innovative/adaptive cognitive styles of participants (Kirton 1976 and 1977). The inventory consisted of thirty-two items in which responses were recorded on a five-point scale anchored "very hard" to "very easy." Some studies report positive psychometric properties of the KAI. For a detailed review of internal consistency and validity studies, see Richard P. Bagozzi and Gordon R. Foxall (1995) and Kirton (1989, 14–19).

Results

With the purpose of testing whether EI could be shown as positive and significantly related to innovative/creative cognitive style and negatively correlated with the adaptive cognitive style, a correlation analysis was carried out. Table 8.1 displays the results of this analysis, along with the basic descriptive results.

The correlations between total EI and cognitive styles are of a very low magnitude (Cohen 1988). Despite the fact that they show consistency with the established hypothesis, I could not verify that a sufficient correlation existed between both variables. Regarding the branches of the Mayer and Salovey (1997) model, only emotional understanding and regulation display significant statistical correlations. Although both branches are positively related to the innovative cognitive style and negatively related with the adaptive style, the sizes of both correlations were of low magnitude (.21 and -.17 respectively).

Table 8.1. Averages, typical deviations, Cronbach's reliabilities, and Pearson's correlations, among other variables

Dimensions	Av.	Dev.	Reliability	1	2	3	4	5	6
1.Total emotional intelligence	87.81	14.44	.87	-					
2. Emotional Perception	92.56	15.48	.76	.74**	-				
3. Emotional facilitation	92.96	13.89	.79	.65**	.42**	-			
4. Emotional understanding	89.01	14.04	.85	.67**	.23**	.34**	-		
5. Emotional regulation	91.94	15.04	.86	.62**	.26**	.46**	.43**	-	
6. Innovative/creative cognitive style	24.15	3.96	.82	.18*	-.08	.03	.24**	.19**	-
7. Adaptative cognitive style	19.93	2.92	.75	-.17**	.05	-08	-.16*	-.21**	-.39**

Note: The values of cognitive styles are based on direct scores.
* p<.05; ** p<.01

Discussion and Conclusions

This chapter has explored examined the existing relationship between EI measured as ability (Mayer and Salovey 1997) and creativity examined by means of Kirton's innovative cognitive style (1977). Even though I establish that creative thinking can be driven by EI through generating emotions that allow us to understand each other and express ourselves better, through considering multiple perspectives obtained from diverse emotions, and by the capacity to concentrate on activities that are stimulated by certain emotions, this association is not proven in this research. A number of the previously referenced studies that demonstrate positive correlations between EI and creativity use self-perception measurements to determine the degree of EI (Batastini 2001; Wolfradt, Felfe, and Köster 2002). It is possible that the correlations found with self-perception measurements and with those of ability are not the same, not only because they encompass distinct processes (self-perceptions versus performance), but also because in the first case, there are common method variance biases (Brackett and Mayer 2003).

Therefore, the results of this research lead me to harbor serious doubts concerning the existing relationship between EI and the innovative/creative cognitive style. Such doubts have been corroborated in a recent study (Ivcevic, Brackett, and Mayer 2007), in which the relation between EI, emotional creativity, and the capacity of each one of these constructs to predict creative behavior is examined. Zorana Ivcevic, Marc A. Brackett, and John D. Mayer find correlation values between -.11 and .19 among total EI, creative cognitive styles, and creative behaviors (indicating effect sizes similar to my research). They conclude that emotional creativity, more than EI, predicts creative behavior. Emotional creativity is understood as an ability to experience and express combinations of original, appropriate, and real emotions, and thus generate ideas and thought that are distinct from those expected as a rule or the norm. In other words, emotional creativity requires analyzing the extent to which an individual's response distances itself from a standard or expected response (Averill 1999). While EI requires analytical ability and the convergence of a correct response to an emotional problem, emotional creativity refers to the ability to be different from the ordinary (standard) and to generate novel emotional reactions, and with these, novel ideas. In this respect, in order to predict innovative cognitive styles and creative behaviors in organizational contexts that lead to higher levels of innovation, we must examine, in addition to EI levels, the predictive capacity of emotional creativity.

It is the same in group therapeutic processes, in which individual change factors require both intense emotional experiences as well as the patient's cognitive ability to elaborate these experiences (Yalom 1970). Most likely, when creativity—or an individual's capacity to generate responses different from the norm—is analyzed, there is not enough cognitive ability included in the EI. In addition to such ability, it is necessary for a person to incorporate into his or her repertoire of responses, those emotional experiences that will allow him or her, before a given event, to have an emotional experience different from the expected. Such differentiated and subjective emotional experience, a unit of one's cognitive ability, is that offering creative solutions that are most likely to be implemented (the most innovative solutions).

We know now that innovation in organizational contexts is not one-dimensional; it is a complex concept with multiple application areas, such as strategic innovation, marketing, processing, and organizational. All of these are necessary to achieve a culture of innovation or, put another way, the systematic management of innovation in all areas of the company; nevertheless, none of these innovations is sufficient by itself. We need to observe what predictive capacity EI and emotional creativity hold over the different types of organizational innovation.

If it is not organizations but people that perform, then people are the innovators. If people are those who innovate, it is essential to examine how they innovate; to analyze what psychological processes and what rational behaviors and emotions are decisive in innovative behavior. Studying the mechanisms related to innovative or creative behaviors in depth is, without a doubt, a stimulating challenge that will help us to clarify the strategies that boost organizational innovation, and simultaneously, our ability to be competitive by the value added from our ideas.

References

Amabile, Teresa M., Sigal G. Barsade, Jennifer S. Mueller, and Barry M. Staw. 2005. "Affect and Creativity at Work." *Administrative Science Quarterly* 50, no. 3: 367–403.

Aritzeta, Aitor, Elsa Ramos, and Leire Gartzia. 2008. *Emociones y trabajo: la inteligencia emocional en contextos organizacionales.* San Sebastián: Erein.

Aritzeta, Aitor, Barbara Senior, and Stephen Swalies. 2005. "Team Role Preference and Cognitive Styles: A Convergent Validity Study." *Small Group Research* 36, no. 4: 404–36.

Ashkanasy, Neal M., Charmine E.J. Härtel, and Catherine S. Daus. 2002. "Diversity and Emotion: The New Frontiers in Organizational Behavior Research." *Journal of Management* 28, no. 3: 307–38.

Ashkanasy, Neal M., and Barry Tse. 2000. "Transformational Leadership as Management of Emotions: A Conceptual Review." In *Emotions in the Workplace: Research, Theory and Practice*, edited by Neal M., Ashkanasy, Charmine E. J. Härtel, and Wilfred J. Zerbe. London: Quorum.

Averill, James R. 1999. "Individual Differences in Emotional Creativity: Structure and Correlates." *Journal of Personality* 67, no. 2: 331–71.

Aspinwall Lisa G. 1998. "Rethinking the Role of Positive Affect in Self-regulation." *Motivation and Emotion* 22, no. 1: 1–32.

Bagozzi, Richard P., and Gordon R. Foxall. 1995. "Construct Validity and Generalizability of the Kirton Adaption-Innovation Inventory." *European Journal of Personality* 9, no. 3: 185–206.

Bar-On, Reuven. 1997. *Bar-On Emotional Quotient Inventory (EQ-i): Technical Manual.* Toronto: Multi-Health Systems.

Barsade, Sigal G., and Donald E. Gibson. 2007. "Why does Affect Matter in Organizations?" *Academy of Management Perspectives* (February): 36–59.

Barsade, Sigal G., Arthur P. Brief, and Sandra E. Spataro. 2003. "The Affective Revolution in Organizational Behavior: The Emergence of a Paradigm." In *Organizational Behavior: The State of the Science,* edited by Jerald Greenberg. Mahwah, NJ: Lawrence Erlbaum and Associates.

Batastini, Susan D. 2001. "The Relationship Among Students' Emotional Intelligence, Creativity and Leadership." Ph.D. Diss. Drexel University.

Bellack, Janis P. 1999. "Emotional Intelligence: A Missing Ingredient?" *Journal of Nursing Education* 38, no. 1: 3–4.

Brackett, Marc A., and John D. Mayer. 2003. "Convergent, Discriminate and Incremental Validity of Competing Measures of Emotional Intelligence." *Personality and Social Psychology Bulletin* 29: 1147–58.

Brief, Arthur P., and Howard M. Weiss. 2002. "Organizational Behavior: Affect in the Workplace." *Annual Review of Psychology* 53, no. 1: 279–307.

Carne, J.C., and Michael J. Kirton. 1982. "Styles of Creativity: Test Score Correlations between the Kirton Adaption-Innovation Inventory and the Myers-Briggs Type Indicator." *Psychological Reports* 50: 31–36.

Chodrow, Joan. 2006. "Active Imagination." In *The Handbook of Jungian Psychology*, edited by Renos K. Papadopoulous. London: Routledge.

Cohen, Jacob. 1988. *Statistical Power Analysis for the Behavioral Sciences.* 2nd ed. Hillsdale, NJ: Lawrence Erlbaum Associates.

Clapham, Maria M. 2001. "The Effects of Affect Manipulation and Information Exposure on Divergent Thinking." *Creativity Research Journal* 13, nos. 3–4: 335–50.

De Dreu, Carsten K.W., Michael A. West, Agneta H. Fischer, and Sarah MacCurtain. 2001. "Origins and Consequences of Emotions in Organizational Teams." In *Emotions at Work: Theory Research and Applications in Management*, edited by Roy L. Payne and Cary L. Cooper. Chichester: John Wiley and Sons.

Drucker, Peter F. 1969. "Management's New Role." *Harvard Business Review* 47, no. 6: 49–54.

Extremera, Natalio, and Pablo Fernández-Berrocal. 2001. "El modelo de Inteligencia Emocional de Mayer y Salovey: Implicaciones educativas para padres y profesores." In *III Jornadas de Innovación Pedagógica: Inteligencia Emocional; una brújula para el siglo XXI*, 132–45. Granada: Universidad de Granada.

Finger, Matthias, and Diana Woolis. 1994. "Organizational Learning, the

Learning Organization, and Adult Education." In *Proceedings from the 35th Annual Adult Education Research Conference*, edited by M. Hyams, J. Armstrong, and E. Anderson. Knoxville, TN: University of Tennessee.

Fisher, Cynthia D. and Neal M. Ashkanasy. 2000. "The Emerging Role of Emotions in Work Life: An Introduction." *Journal of Organizational Behavior* 21, no. 2: 123–29.

Fisher, Stephen G., W.D. Keith Macrosson, and John Wong. 1998. "Cognitive Style and Team Role Preference." *Journal of Managerial Psychology* 13, no. 8: 544–57.

Foxall, Gordon R., and Paul M.W. Hackett. 1994. "Styles of Managerial Creativity: A Comparison of Adaption-Innovation in the United Kingdom, Australia and the United States." *British Journal of Management* 5, no. 3: 85–100.

George, Jennifer M., and Jing Zhou. 2007. "Dual Tuning in a Supportive Context: Joint Contributions of Positive Mood, Negative Mood, and Supervisory Behaviors to Employee Creativity." *Academy of Management Journal* 50, no. 3: 605–22.

Goldsmith, Ronald E. 1984. "Personality Characteristics Associated with Adaption-Innovation." *Journal of Psychology* 117, no. 2: 159–65.

Goleman, Daniel. 1995. *Emotional Intelligence: Why it Can Matter More Than IQ*. New York: Bantam Books.

Guastello, Stephen J., Denise D. Guastello, and Casey A. Hanson. 2004. "Creativity, Mood Disorders, and Emotional Intelligence." *The Journal of Creative Behavior* 38, no. 4: 260–81.

Isen, Alice M. 1993. "Positive Affect and Decision Making." In *Handbook of Emotions*, edited by Michael Lewis and Jeanette M. Haviland. New York: Guilford.

Isen, Alice M. and J. Reeve. 2005. "The Influence of Positive." *Motivation and Emotion* 29: 297–325.

Ivcevic, Zorana, Marc A. Brackett, and John D. Mayer. 2007. "Emotional Intelligence and Emotional Creativity." *Journal of Personality* 75, no. 2: 199–235.

Jamison, Kay Redfield. 1994. *Touched with Fire: Manic-depressive Illness and the Artistic Temperament*. New York: Free Press.

Kaufmann Geir. 2003. "Expanding the Mood-creativity Equation." *Creativity Research Journal* 15, nos. 2–3: 131–35.

Kelly, Janice R., and Sigal G. Barsade. 2001. "Mood and Emotions in Small Groups and Work Teams." *Organizational Behavior and Human Decision Processes* 86, no. 1: 99–130.

Kirton, Michael J. 1976. "Adaptors and Innovators: A Description and Measure." *Journal of Applied Psychology* 5, no. 61: 622–29.

——. 1977. *Manual of the Kirton Adaption-Innovation Inventory.* London: National Foundation for Educational Research.

——. 1978. "Adaptors and Innovators in Culture Clash." *Current Anthropology* 19, no. 3: 611–12.

——. 1985. "Adaptors, Innovators and Paradigm Consistency." *Psychological Reports* 57, no. 2: 487–90.

——. 1989. *Adaptors and Innovators: Styles of Creativity and Problem Solving.* London: Routledge.

Legge, Karen. 1978. *Power, Innovation and Problem-solving in Personnel Management.* London: McGraw-Hill.

Madjar, Nora, Greg R. Oldham, and Michael G. Pratt. 2002. "There's No Place Like Home? The Contributions of Work and Nonwork Creativity Support to Employees' Creative Performance." *Academy of Management* 45, no. 4: 757–67.

Mayer, John D., David R. Caruso, and Peter Salovey. 1999. "Emotional Intelligence Meets Traditional Standards for an Intelligence." *Intelligence* 27: 267–98.

Mayer, John D., and Peter Salovey. 1997. "What is Emotional Intelligence?" In *Emotional Development and Emotional Intelligence: Implications for Educators*, edited by Peter Salovey and David J. Sluyter. New York: Basic Books.

Mayer, John D., Peter Salovey, and David R. Caruso. 2002. *MSCEIT Item Booklet Version2.0.* Toronto, ON: Multi-Health Systems.

Merton, Robert K. 1957. *Bureaucratic Structure and Personality in Social Theory and Social Structure.* New York: Free Press of Glencoe.

Mudd, Samuel. 1990. "The Place of Innovativeness in Models of the Adoption Process: An Integrative Review." *Technovation* 10, no. 2: 119–38.

Myers, Isabel Briggs, Mary H. McCaulley, Naomi L. Quenk, and Allen L. Hammer. 1998. *MBTI Manual (A Guide to the Development and Use of the Myers Briggs Type Indicator).* 3rd ed. Palo Alto, CA: Consulting Psychologists Press.

Parsons, Talcott. 1951. *The Social System*. New York: Free Press of Glencoe.

Petrides, K.V. and Adrian Furnham. 2000. "On the Dimensional Structure of Emotional Intelligence." *Personality and Individual Differences* 29, no. 2: 313–20.

Rousseau, Denise, and M.J.D. René Schalk, eds. 2000. *Psychological Contract in Employment: Crossnational Perspectives*. Newbury Park: Sage.

Russ, Sandra W. 2000. "'Primary Process Thinking' and Creativity: Affect and Cognition." *Creativity Research Journal* 13, no. 1: 27–35.

Salovey, Peter, and D. Grewal. 2005. "The Science of Emotional Intelligence." *Current Directions in Psychological Science* 14, no. 6: 281–87.

Scott-Ladd, Brenda, and Christopher C.A. Chan 2004. "Emotional Intelligence and Participation in Decision Making: Strategies for Promoting Organizational Learning and Change." *Strategic Change* 13: 95–105.

Shaw, Melvin P. and Mark A. Runco, eds. 1994. *Creativity and Affect*. Norwood, NJ: Ablex.

Vosburg, Suzanne K. 1998. "Mood and the Quantity and Quality of Ideas." *Creativity Research Journal* 11, no. 4: 315–31.

Witkin, Herman A. 1964. "Origins of Cognitive Style." In *Cognition: Theory, Research, Promise,* edited by Constance Scheerer. New York: Harper & Row.

Wolfradt, Uwe, Jörg Felfe, and Torsten Köster. 2002. "Self-perceived Emotional Intelligence and Creative Personality." *Imagination, Cognition and Personality* 21, no. 4: 293–309.

Yalom, Irvin D. 1970. *The Theory and Practice of Group Psychotherapy*. New York: Basic Books.

Index

A

adaptation-innovation theory, 190
advanced management:
    companies, 36, 36n6; practices,
    26. *See also* management
additive model, 134, 136
agency theory, 11, 82–83, 85–87,
    90–93
Allianz, 59
appliances. *See* home appliances
    industry
Araba (Álava), 109
Austria, 57, 59, 64, 72
auxiliary automotive industry,
    36–37, 109, 112

B

BASF, 59
Basque Country: economic
    crisis, 110; economic growth,
    106–11, 114, 116; education,
    109; emotional intelligence,
    19; human resources, 25–43;
    industrial clusters, 12,
    99–116; GDP, 101, 110–11;
    industrialization, 101–2, 106–8,
    110, 116; innovation in, 25–43,
    184; knowledge cluster, 36,
    36n5; leadership, 18, 170–77;
    organization, 184; R&D, 110;

value-added base, 101, 111. *See
    also* Comunidad Autónoma del
    País Vasco/Euskal Autonomia
    Erkidegoa (CAPV/EAE,
    Autonomous Community of the
    Basque Country)
Basque government, 36, 110, 111
behavior, 18, 130, 164, 175, 184;
    cognitive, 192; creative, 19,
    195–96; emotional, 192; ethical,
    14; group, 124; human, 8, 13;
    individual, 130; innovative, 196;
    non-typical, 186; of economic
    agents, 113, 116; organizational,
    7–8, 133; personal, 20; rational,
    196; "seat-warming," 156–57;
    transformational, 169; typical,
    186
Belgium, 57, 70, 106n11
best practices, 33, 49–50, 55, 71, 72
Bilbao, 107, 111
Bizkaia (Vizcaya), 107, 109
Buber, Martin, 127–28
business climate, 47, 51, 52, 56, 61

C

Catalonia, 106
CIE Automotive, 37n8
climate change, 48, 51

clusters: industrial, 12–13, 99–116; knowledge, 36

cognitive styles, 19, 185, 189–96; emotional intelligence and, 192–95

collectivism, 17–18, 136, 154–56, 158, 161

commercialization process innovation, 38*t*,

company law, 56–60, 65, 73

competitiveness, 7–10, 84, 99–103, 129, 183–84, 197; Basque, 25–26, 110–12, 114–16; EU strategy for, 25, 47–53, 65, 68–69, 71–72; in companies, 161–63; innovation and, 25–27, 32, 36; regional, 103–4, 105n10, 116

Comunidad Autónoma del País Vasco/Euskal Autonomia Erkidegoa (CAPV/EAE, Autonomous Community of the Basque Country), 8, 112. *See also* Basque Country

concept generation, 33, 37n9, 38*t*, 39

cooperation, 30, 163, 168: among companies, 58, 59, 115; among cooperatives, 82; between firms and institutions, 100n2, 115; between individuals and organizations, 105n10; between workers and managers, 7; group, 134, 139

cooperativism, 81–83, 156

corporate citizenship theory, 80, 86–91

corporate governance, 9, 79–94

corporate social responsibility (CSR), 11, 68, 81–89

Cotec, 36n4, 39n11

creative behavior, 19, 195–96. *See also* behavior

CSR. *See* corporate social responsibility

culture of innovation, 20, 37n9, 196

customer orientation, 29, 32, 38*t*, 83*f*, 84

D

decision-making, 9, 30, 32, 184; business, 92; centralization of, 156, 157; corporate, 80

Denmark, 57, 64, 65

direct consensus model, 134–35, 136, 139

dispersion model, 134, 135

E

economic crisis, 49, 67–69, 72, 108, 111; 1970s and 1980s, 12, 101, 110, 114

economic sustainability, 8–9, 25, 48, 51, 67, 69

EI. *See* emotional intelligence

Eibar region, 107–8

electrical equipment industry, 37, 108–9, 111–12

Elcoteq, 59

"emerging intermediaries," 15–16

emotional creativity, 19–20, 195–96; non-, 192

emotional intelligence (EI), 19–20, 185–88, 193–94, 196; ability models, 186–88, 194–95; cognitive styles and, 185, 192–95; creativity and, 193, 195–96; definition of, 185, 186–87; innovation and, 185, 195, 195*t*; mixed models, 186

Emotional Intelligence
Consortium, 184
employee participation, 11–12, 14,
61, 64–65, 79–94, 163–64
energy efficiency, 48, 51, 111
EU. *See* European Union
*Europe 2020: A Strategy for
Smart, Sustainable and Inclusive
Growth*, 9, 47, 51–52, 67–71
European Commission, 25, 47–71
European Company (*Societas
Europaea*), 56–58
European Cooperative Society,
56–60
European Council, 25, 47–53, 70,
73
European Economic Community,
110
European Economic Interests
Grouping, 56–58, 60
European Parliament, 50, 64, 65,
73
European Private Company
(*Societas Privata Europaea*, SPE),
10, 54–65
*European Strategy for Growth and
Jobs*, 47, 66
European Union (EU), 9, 10,
25, 101, 106; company law, 10,
47–73; employment strategy, 9,
25, 47–51, 57, 65–72; foreign
policy, 69–70; governance,
10–11, 71–72; innovation, 25,
184; member states and, 48–50,
54–57, 59–60, 70, 72–73; R&D,
37, 49; SMEs, 10, 52–55, 61;
"Think Small First" principle,
47, 51, 52–54, 72; types of
company in, 57–59, 61–62. *See
also* European Private Company;
"flexicurity"; Lisbon Strategy;
"Small Business Act"
Eurozone, 49, 50

F

Fagor Appliances, 37n8
Finland, 57, 64
Firearms industry, 107, 108
flexicurity, 9–10, 47, 50–51, 65–72
food and beverage industry, 107,
109, 111
France, 59, 61, 62
Freeman, R. Edward, 81, 84, 90–91
Friedman, Milton, 81, 84
Fresenius, 59

G

Gamesa, 37n8, 115
general systems theory, 13, 124–25
Germany, 59, 61, 62, 64, 71, 110
Gipuzkoa, 107, 108, 109, 184
globalization, 52, 70, 103, 169, 176,
183. *See also* globalized economy
globalized economy, 26, 36n5,
48–53, 70–72, 114–15. *See also*
globalization
governance, 7, 10, 48–54, 65,
67–73; corporate, 9, 79–94
Great Britain, 61, 124
growth, economic, 48–52, 65–66,
70, 114, 116; exponential, 49; in
Basque Country, 106–11, 114,
116; inclusive, 51, 67, 69; smart,
51, 67, 69; sustainable, 9, 25,
48, 51, 67, 69. *See also* Lisbon
Strategy
growth, professional, 7, 18, 158,
185

H

hierarchization, 124–33

home appliances industry, 37, 109–12

horizontal collectivism, 17, 18, 154–56, 158, 161

horizontal individualism, 17, 154, 158, 161, 163

HR. *See* human resources

human resource management, 8, 26, 30, 34–35, 40, 81. *See also* management

human resources (HR), 8–9, 26, 102; components of, 40*f*; innovation and 8, 25–43; innovation management and, 9, 34–42; management practices, 34–35; participatory, 92; policies, 26, 35, 40–43; science and technology, 102

I

ICA. *See* International Co-operative Alliance

Iceland, 57

ICTs. *See* information and communication technologies

IESE Business School, University of Navarre, 27, 33

ILO. *See* International Labour Organisation

IM. *See* innovation management

IMTs. *See* innovation management methodologies and tools

individualism, 17, 136, 139, 154, 158, 161–63

information and communication technologies (ICTs), 29, 31, 37n9, 38*t*, 39–42, 113

Innobasque (Basque Innovation Agency), 13–14, 36n5, 154n1, 184

innovation, 7–9, 14–20, 48–53, 101–5, 115, 153; adaption-, 190, 194; behavior, 196; capacity, 14, 25, 28, 39, 41, 42; clusters, 36, 101n5; culture of, 20, 30, 37n9, 38*t*, 41, 184; definition of, 35; emotional intelligence and, 185, 195, 195*t*; financial resources (funding), 29, 31, 32, 38*t*, 39, 42; human resources and, 25–43; in Basque Country, 25–43, 184; in European Union, 25, 184; knowledge and, 27–35, 51, 108, 113, 163–64, 184; monitoring, 30, 32; organizational, 19–20, 127, 183, 196–97; process, 29, 29n3, 31–35, 37n9, 38*t*, 185; production process, 33, 37n9, 38*t*, 39; strategy, 30, 31, 35, 68, 115, 184; sustainable, 8–9; technology and, 27, 28, 31, 113, 114, 157

innovation management (IM), 9, 20, 26–29, 31, 191, 196; importance of elements in, 38*t*; in Basque Country, 35–43; models, 29, 33. *See also* management; technology management

innovation management methodologies and tools (IMTs), 31, 39

innovative cognitive style, 19, 191, 194–96

International Co-operative Alliance (ICA), 82–83

International Labour Organisation (ILO), 70–71
Iron and steel industry, 107–8
isomorphism, 13, 124–32, 137
ITP Group (Industria de Turbo Propulsores), 37n8, 115

K

Kirton Adaptor-Innovator Inventory (KAI), 190, 194
Kirton's cognitive style of innovation, 19, 190–91, 194–95
knowledge, 12, 25–30, 40*f*, 99, 102–9, 129; applied, 34; based economy, 9, 48, 52; collective, 132; creation, 17, 25n1, 34, 153, 164; emotional, 185; exchange, 19, 34–35, 114, 132, 163–64; external, 114–16; individual, 132; innovation and, 27–35, 51, 108, 113, 163–64, 184; society, 153, 183–84. *See also* knowledge management
knowledge management, 29, 31, 37n9, 38*t*, 39, 39n11

L

labor market, 9, 10, 48, 50, 65–71
labor relations, 51, 68, 71, 72, 153–54, 164
leadership; ethical; external, 19; passive-avoidant, 173*t*; shared, 19; transactional, 18–19, 173*t*; transformational, 18–19, 173*t*
learning, 38*t*, 39, 103, 108, 113, 183; continual (lifelong), 29, 67–68, 184; group, 14, 49; organizational, 32, 37n9, 100n1
Lisbon Strategy. 9, 25, 47–53, 66–73

Lisbon Summit (2000). *See* Lisbon Strategy
London Business School, 33

M

machine tools industry, 37, 107–12
MACTOR methodology, 92
Man (company), 59
management, 17–18, 25–43, 80, 84–94, 131, 161; active, 171–72, 176; effective, 169–70; emotional, 19, 187; human resource, 8, 26, 30, 34–35, 40, 81; in European Union, 58, 60, 62–65; innovation, 9, 20, 26–29, 31, 196; knowledge, 29, 31, 37n9, 38*t*, 39, 39n11; labor processes, 7; participatory, 92, 159, 164; passive, 171–72; self-, 139, 142–43; technology, 27, 31, 37n9, 38*t*, 39, 39n11. *See also* advanced management; human resource management; innovation management; knowledge management
maritime transportation industry, 107
marketing, 28, 33–35, 37n9, 85, 91, 196; innovation in, 20, 33–34, 37n9, 39
Mayer-Salovey-Caruso Emotional Intelligence Test (MSCEIT), 194
micro- and macro-level adjustments, 140*f*
multifiduciary theory, 80, 86–88, 90–93
multilevel organizational theory, 13, 124, 129–36

N
Netherlands, 64, 65, 70
network society, 36n5
networking, 29, 32, 37n9, 38*t*
networks: companies as, 34, 79, 80,
  86; regional, 102–3, 108; social,
  105n10

O
Organisation for Economic Cooperation and Development
  (OECD), 35
organizational analysis, 131, 134,
  141, 148
organizational behavior, 7–8, 133.
  See also behavior
organizational change, 128, 184;
  studies on, 100n1; vectors of,
  8–10, 12, 13, 47, 51, 56
organizational climate, 136
organizational development,
  15–16, 28, 29
organizational innovation, 19–20,
  127, 183, 196–97
organizational learning, 32, 37n9,
  100n1
Oslo Manual, 35
ownership, 11–12, 79–83, 88, 92,
  153, 156

P
País Vasco (Basque Country). *See*
  Basque Country; Comunidad
  Autónoma del País Vasco/Euskal
  Autonomia Erkidegoa (CAPV/
  EAE, Autonomous Community
  of the Basque Country)
paper industry, 101n4, 107, 109,
  111–15
past-dependency, 104, 116

path-dependency, 13, 99–106, 111,
  116
personnel, 41, 84, 158, 161;
  development policies, 39–41;
  involvement, 43; initiative, 43;
  motivation, 18, 43; outside,
  156, 157; recruitment, 156,
  157; retention policies, 40;
  reward policies, 35, 40; selection
  policies, 39–40, 161–63
place-dependency, 99, 102, 104
Plan de Estrategia Tecnológica
  (PET, Technology Startegy Plan),
  110–11
Porsche, 59
Porter Diamond, 101
Porter, Michael E., 84, 111
positioning approach, 83*f*
process model, 134, 136
product development, 28, 33–34,
  37n9, 38*t*
production process innovation, 33,
  37n9, 38*t*, 39
productivity, 26, 100n2, 184, 193;
  European Union, 10, 25, 48,
  52–53, 69
psychological climate, 135, 139
psychological contract, 16–18,
  154–57, 160–64

R
R&D. *See* research & development
RDI. *See* research, development,
  and innovation
referent-shift model, 134, 135
regression analysis, 137, 143,
  160–61, 172, 173, 173*t*
relative autonomy, 13, 124–33, 136
research, development, and
  innovation (RDI), 157

research & development (R&D), 28, 36n6, 37, 49–50, 101–3, 114–15
resources approach, 83*f*
Rhur (Germany), 110

S
SCOR, 59
Scotland, 110
shareholder theory, 81–92
small and medium enterprises (SMEs), 10, 37n7, 39n12, 48, 50–61, 72
small business, 9–10, 53–56
"Small Business Act," 10, 53, 54–56
SMEs. *See* small and medium enterprises
social capital, 99, 102–5, 108, 113–16
social cohesion, 9, 25, 48, 52, 67, 70
social economy, 80, 82–83, 91
social responsibility. *See* corporate social responsibility
Societas Europaea. See European Company
Societas Privata Europaea. See European Private Company
Spain: customs borders, 107; economy, 12, 110–12; EU Presidency, 65, 70; European Company in, 58; industry, 106, 106n12, 107–9, 112, 112n14; labor-market reform, 71–72; per capita GDP, 101, 106, 111; political regime, 110; Sociedad de Responsabilidad Limitada (SL), 61; tax system, 108
SPE. *See* European Private Company

SPRI (Basque Development Agency), 36, 112n14
stakeholder theory, 11, 80–81, 83*f*, 84–94
Stanford Research Institute, 110
Strabag, 59
strategic approaches in companies, 83*f*
Sweden, 57, 64, 65
systems, definition, 124
systems theory, 13, 123–48

T
Tavistock Institute (London), 15, 124
Taylorism, 18–19, 164
teamwork, 16, 18, 30, 40*f*, 41, 80, 155
technology management, 27, 31, 37n9, 38*t*, 39, 39n11. *See also* management; innovation management
Tecno-Lógica, 33
textiles industry, 107, 108
"Think Small First" principle, 47, 51, 52–54, 72. *See also* European Union
training, 18, 66, 155–63, 184, 194; business management, 36n5; cooperative, 82; for innovative success, 31; in Basque Country, 108, 109, 114
transactional leadership, 18–19, 173*t*
transformational leadership, 18–19, 173*t*

U
United States: organizational development, 15; small and

medium enterprises (SMEs),
52–53
Universidad de la País Vasco/
Euskal Herriko Unibertsitatea
(UPV/EHU, University of the
Basque Country), 13
Urola region, 108

W
Wales, 110

World Trade Organization
(WTO), 10–11, 69
working environment, 17, 19, 175
working relations, 17–18
working team, 14–15, 169
WTO. *See* World Trade
Organization

List of Contributors

For full biographical information about the contributors, links to their projects, and more, visit www.basque.unr.edu/currentresearch/contributors.

Igone Altzelai
Andrés Araujo de la Mata
Aitor Aritzeta
Sabino Ayestarán
Nekane Balluerka
Jon Barrutia Guenaga
Iñigo Calvo
Aitziber Elola
Daniel Hermosilla
Maria Jose Aranguren
Juan Jose Arrospide
Santiago López
Jose Luis Retolaza
Jesús Maria Valdaliso
Juan Pablo Landa
Leire San-Jose
José Valencia Gárate
Eva Velasco Balmaseda
Félix Yenes
Ibon Zamanillo Elguezabal